PAYOFF

The Role of Organized Crime
In American Politics

Other Books by Michael Dorman

We Shall Overcome
The Secret Service Story
The Second Man: The Changing Role of the Vice Presidency
King of the Courtroom: Percy Foreman for the Defense
Under 21: A Young People's Guide to Legal Rights

PAYOFF

The Role of Organized Crime
In American Politics

by

Michael Dorman

AVID McKAY COMPANY, INC.
w York

PAYOFF

The Role of Organized Crime In American Politics

COPYRIGHT © 1972 BY MICHAEL DORMAN

LIBRARY OF CONGRESS CATALOG CARD NUMBER: 73–186559

MANUFACTURED IN THE UNITED STATES OF AMERICA

For Alan Hathway,
who knows where
the bodies are buried
and helped teach me
how to find them.

Introduction

On February 8, 1972, as a result of conducting the research for this book, I was called to testify as a more or less "expert witness" before a special grand jury assigned to investigate organized crime in Texas. Although grand jury testimony normally is secret, I was granted permission to describe portions of my own testimony for readers of this book.

The most relevant question asked me was: "Mr. Dorman, in your research, you have interviewed many of the leaders of organized crime and others with knowledge of the subject. From your broad experience, do we have organized crime within the jurisdiction of this grand jury?"

I answered: "It depends on your definition of organized crime. To me, the answer is yes. You definitely have Mafia characters operating here, but it's broader than that. To me, organized crime also involves the government officials, political figures, and supposedly 'legitimate' businessmen who deal with the racketeers." I then proceeded to name as persons in those categories a former President, a current Cabinet official, a current leader of the American diplomatic community, past and present governors, senators, congressmen, state legislators, and others. "To me, they are part of organized crime."

The foreman and several members of the grand jury exchanged what I took to be knowing smiles, as if to say: Suspicions confirmed. The local district attorney, who is himself a creature of the very political system I was discussing, quickly changed the line of questioning. I was not surprised. I have no reason to believe the DA is anything but an honest man. His allegiance to the political forces that elected him, however, creates a dilemma for him: How to "fight organized crime" without committing political suicide?

It is a dilemma that confronts many other public officials. Knowledge of that problem and those allied with it are central to any understanding of the subject matter of this book. It is true, as indicated by my testimony, that I have traveled across this country and others—interviewing the leading racketeers in what we have come to call the Mafia. Many of them have talked candidly—perhaps too candidly for their own good—with me. In some cases, they were willing to be quoted by name; in others they provided me with the information I needed on the promise that they would not be identified. Do I have some sort of secret "alliance" with the underworld? No. The promises of confidentiality I made were identical to those I have made to Presidents and former Presidents of the United States. To a writer, protection of sources is essential. I would no more "sell out" a Mafia family boss by breaking my word to him than I would "sell out" an official of the government or a political party.

I am often asked, by those in the publishing world and in politics, why purported Mafia bosses would tell me *anything*. I can respond to that question only with the answers they have given me. In substance, they contend that so much hogwash has been published about the Mob that they feel the record should be made clear. For the past fifteen years, first as a newspaper reporter and later as a full-time freelancer, I have cultivated sources of information inside organized crime. For whatever reason, these men (and some of their women) have come to feel comfortable with me. I have never broken my word to any of them. Nor, may I add, has any one of them broken his or her word to me.

That brings up a related question or two. For example, is there a Mafia? The answer given me by the alleged leaders of the organization may be fairly summarized as follows: "Look, we don't deny we've been in the rackets. Some of us are still in the rackets. But, by this time, we're millionaires. We're in 'legitimate' business. We own banks, hotels, restaurants—hell, you know what we own. Don't we have the same right to be in those businesses as anyone else? Are we supposed to suffer because we're Sicilian or Italian—because our names end in vowels? As for the Mafia, that's a lot of horseshit. Yes, we are organized but we don't call ourselves Mafia or Cosa Nostra or anything like that. We talk about a guy as being one of our 'friends.' Or we call it the 'organization' or the 'company' or the 'outfit.' But we never call it the Mafia."

Nonetheless, the reader will find the word Mafia sprinkled liberally through this book. I have chosen to use it because, until recently, it was the accepted term for the major organized crime syndicate in this country. It should be made clear that there are many racketeers who are not Mafia members or even Mafia associates. But those who have been publicly identified as leaders of the Mafia (Cosa Nostra, to me, has always been a myth) are so identified in this book. To my acquaintances who are so identified— and who deny being Mafiosi—let me say that I understand your position but I don't think the reader will find it credible.

A final word should be said about the much-misused Sicilian word *omerta*. Hack writers have made much of the word and its relation to the underworld code of silence. Yes, *omerta* means silence but, as any underworld "button man" knows, it also implies honor. A man who keeps silent—who refuses to betray his friends—is considered honorable by underworld standards. He is also considered honorable by my standards. For I, too, must live by a code of honor that many find curious. I, too, must remain silent at times when my voice might be used to "fight organized crime." The moment I succumbed to the temptation to speak, however, I would be breaking my word to my sources of information. And I would immediately lose those sources. I want to "fight organized crime," but my best tool for doing so is my typewriter—not my mouth.

To my friends on both sides of the law and on all sides of the political fence, I say only this: I have a rule. I never intentionally sit down to break bread with anyone I consider a hypocrite. Those of you with whom I have broken bread know who you are. You are welcome at my table anytime. I wish I could say the same for many of our "leading citizens."

My rule is based on the old bromide that if you sit down to eat with the hogs, you're going to rise from the table with slop on your face. I may sit down once with a hog by accident, but I'll never do it deliberately a second time.

I think I have written an honest book—one that will destroy some of the myths about organized crime and provide a sensible guide to future action to eliminate political corruption. To any honest person who disagrees, I offer the opportunity to discuss the subject with me. No hypocrites need apply.

MICHAEL DORMAN
DIX HILLS, NEW YORK
March 1st, 1972

Contents

"Organized crime will put a man in the White House someday and he won't know it until they hand him the bill."

—Ralph Salerno, former Mafia expert for the New York City Police Department.

PAYOFF

*The Role of Organized Crime
In American Politics*

[1]

The Mob Behind
the Scenes

The iron-fisted rulers who control the Mafia have locked a strangle hold on American politics. Using such tactics as bribes, campaign contributions, threats, blackmail, ballot-box manipulation and delivery of large voting blocs, they have spread their tentacles of power through every level of government. From city halls to state capitols and from the halls of Congress even to the White House, no public official is regarded by the Mob as exempt from possible corruption. Except for its political connections, the Mafia could be driven out of business virtually in the twinkling of an eye. It survives and prospers only because influential politicians and law-enforcement officers find secret alliances with mobsters both expedient and profitable.

Generally, the public is aware of the Mafia's pervasive role in dominating the narcotics traffic, bookmaking, the numbers game, loansharking and other rackets. But the average citizen is only dimly aware—if he is aware at all—of the Mob's behind-the-scenes political clout.

Yet, the most significant of all Mob operations are those carried out in the political sphere. They provide the very lifeblood of organized crime. And, even more than narcotics, gambling, or gangland violence, they tear at the fabric of American society. Today, the Mafia's corruption of political life is greater than ever before in our history. As the President's Commission on Law Enforcement put it:

> All available data indicate that organized crime flourishes only where it has corrupted officials. As the scope and variety of organized crime's activities have expanded, its need to involve officials at every level of government has grown. And as government regulation expands into more and more areas of private and business activity, the power to corrupt likewise affords the corrupter more control over matters affecting the everyday life of each citizen. . . . The potential harm of corruption is greater today if only because the governmental activity is greater. In different places at different times, organized crime has corrupted police officials, prosecutors, legislators, judges, regulatory agency officials, mayors, councilmen, and other public officials, whose legitimate exercise of duties would block organized crime and whose illegal exercise of duties helps it.

If anything, the commission understated the case. The corruption of politics and law enforcement is no mere sporadic, hit-or-miss proposition. It is systematic, tenacious, and ubiquitous—grasping day in and day out for greater power over the machinery of government and the life of the average citizen. A few examples should be illustrative.

Item: A congressman from Illinois hires as his aide the son-in-law of Chicago's top Mafia boss. While on the congressional payroll, the son-in-law serves as legal adviser to the Mafioso in a court fight aimed at halting FBI surveillance of the mobster. The son-in-law later pleads the Fifth Amendment in three appearances before a grand jury investigating organized crime.

Item: J. Edgar Hoover's right-hand man retires from the

FBI and takes a $100,000-a-year job as executive vice president of a huge liquor company with alleged ties to syndicate racketeers. With the help of high-powered lobbying activities, the liquor company obtains Federal legislation giving the firm a multimillion-dollar tax windfall. The former FBI official later becomes an adviser on law enforcement to Richard M. Nixon. And the liquor company's founder, who has been linked to top mobsters, contributes more than $1 million to create a tax-free entity called the J. Edgar Hoover Foundation.

Item: The mobsters who control the numbers racket in New York's ghetto neighborhoods decide they need a particularly heavy voter turnout in support of their chosen candidate slate. They offer a free play on the numbers to any citizen who registers and votes. They even provide Mob-employed chauffeurs to haul voters to the polls and babysitters to care for children while their mothers are voting. A record voter turnout results, and the candidates backed by the racketeers are elected.

Item: The Mafia boss of New England offers a $100,000 "campaign contribution" to a candidate for governor of Massachusetts. In return, the Mafioso wants protection from official harassment if the candidate is elected. When the candidate rejects the contribution, the Mafia boss retaliates by spreading word that the money has been accepted. The false rumor, given wide distribution, helps lead to the candidate's defeat.

Item: A Mafia-controlled labor union in St. Louis, Missouri, arranges to provide the workers required to convert a mothballed steel foundry into an Army munitions factory that is urgently needed to produce artillery shells for the Vietnam war. The union pads the payroll with fictitious names and the names of racketeers who do little or no work. Union leaders connive to have workers paid for phony overtime claims, in return for kickbacks on the employees' salaries. Work slowdowns and other union shenanigans further inflate the costs. By the time the plant conversion is completed, it has cost the government $22 million—nearly triple the $8 million originally anticipated.

The corruption of politics and law-enforcement is made possible by the enormous amounts of money at the Mafia's command. President Nixon, in a message to Congress seeking new legislation to combat organized crime, estimated the Mob's take in the United States from gambling alone at $20 billion to $50 billion a year. His estimate, which many experts consider conservative, would mean that the gambling take equals two to five percent of the Gross National Product. With the addition of the take from other rackets—such as narcotics, loansharking and extortion—the figure becomes even more astronomical.

Simultaneously with its corruption of public officials, the Mafia has stepped up enormously its covert campaign to seize control of legitimate businesses. The two activities often dovetail. For example, Mob-owned construction companies can make millions of dollars by bribing government officials to give them public works contracts. The firms fulfill the contracts at inflated prices, enriching both the racketeers and the corrupt officials. In some cases, Mafia-controlled companies can even obtain financing from the government. Early in 1970 the U.S. Small Business Administration conceded with great embarrassment that it had made hundreds of thousands of dollars' worth of loans to a trucking company in New York, a motel in New Orleans, and a suburban transit firm in Chicago—all dominated by Mob figures.

Infiltration of legitimate business provides mobsters with numerous benefits. Since they cannot pay taxes on their illegal income without exposing their criminal activities to official scrutiny, they need some means to explain their sources of wealth to the Internal Revenue Service. By entering legitimate business they establish sources of income that appear legal and often pay just enough taxes to avoid prosecution. The legitimate businesses give them opportunities to reinvest money made in the rackets. Such businesses themselves can be extremely profitable, especially when the Mob succeeds through terror tactics in gaining a local or regional monopoly in providing a certain product or service. In addition, operation of legitimate businesses sometimes gives racketeers a cloak of respectability and social standing that, among other things, makes it more practical for politicians to deal with them. A politician caught taking a campaign contribution from a Mafioso, for example, can claim he considered the mobster merely a respectable businessman.

Syndicate racketeers are known to be involved in at least ninety types of legitimate business—including enterprises in such fields as banking, hotels and motels, real estate, garbage removal, vending machines, automobile agencies, trucking, construction, garment manufacture, insurance, restaurants, nightclubs, linen-supply, laundries, stocks and bonds, resorts, and funeral homes. Federal authorities say one Mafia family alone owns real-estate interests with an estimated value of $300 million. Other Mafia interests include control of a nationwide hotel chain, domination of a bank with assets of $90 million and ownership of a commercial laundry that grosses more than $20 million a year.

In the past, most books dealing with the Mafia have been preoccupied with such sensational matters as gangland killings and other violence—neglecting the significance of the Mob's corruption of political figures and its infiltration of legitimate business. Thus, many of the most important questions about organized crime have been left unanswered. Just how serious is the threat posed by the Mafia's penetration of politics and government? How does the Mob go about corrupting politicians? Precisely what does it get from them? What does it give them? How imminent is the threat, described by Mafia expert Ralph Salerno, that "organized crime will put a man in the White House someday and he won't know it until they hand him the bill"? What can be done to wipe out corrupt alliances between mobsters and political figures?

This book seeks to rip aside the shroud of camouflage that has too long masked the answers to such questions. The American people have it within their power to turn back the tide of corruption—purging crooked politicians from their temples of power and obliterating the scourge of organized crime. But first they must recognize and understand the enemy.

[2]

Any Big City
in the U.S.A.

If an organized crime syndicate somehow managed to put a man in the White House and to corrupt key members of the Senate and House, it still could not function effectively unless it also controlled important state and local officials. It is an underworld axiom that any large-scale rackets operation must seek the help of corrupt allies at all levels of government. As one Mob corrupter told this writer: "We can't depend on just buying the local guys or just the state guys or just the Feds. We've got to try to buy someone with power at each level—or else anyone along the line can put us out of business."

It is at the local level that mobsters establish their foothold—the base on which they seek to build a pyramid of corrupt alliances. Unless they can gain supremacy at the local level, the money they spend on state and Federal protection will be wasted. How the Mob goes about seizing local power was graphically illustrated in a report on a notorious case of political corruption prepared for the President's Commission on Law Enforcement. The report described how a crime syndicate dominated the affairs of a moderately sized city by corrupting virtually every important city official. The evidence disclosed a classic case of the politics of corruption at the local level. For that reason, the report is worth examining in detail.

7

It was prepared by two consultants to the presidential commission, John A. Gardiner and David J. Olson, both political science teachers at the University of Wisconsin. To avoid stigmatizing the community and individuals involved, they used fictitious names in the report while emphasizing that all the events described were true. They called the city Wincanton, U.S.A. When the report was released by the commission, however, it became immediately apparent that Wincanton was actually the city of Reading, Pennsylvania. Officials, citizens, and newsmen in Reading made clear that the report described in extremely accurate detail events that had occurred in their community. As a news article in *The Reading Times* put it:

> Bone by bone, the skeleton past of Reading and Berks County tumbles from between the blue covers of the latest report from the President's Commission on Law Enforcement. And, although the report lists the name of the city as Wincanton and the county as Alsace, it is not a case of mistaken identity. Anyone familiar with the recent history of the area will recognize Reading and Berks County.

Founded in 1748, Reading is a textile-mill city on the banks of the Schuylkill River about sixty miles northwest of Philadelphia. Most of its 90,000 residents are members of blue-collar families. Its homes are chiefly two-story redbrick affairs built on small lots. Although the homes are old they are well maintained. The sidewalks are swept clean. The city abounds in churches—210 of them. All in all, it would seem, there is nothing on the surface that would make Reading a likely choice as a hotbed of corruption. How, then, did it become so corrupt that the presidential commission deemed it worthy of study under the name of Wincanton?

The answers are varied and complex. "In general, Wincanton represents a city that has toyed with the problem of corruption for many years," the commission report said. (For simplicity's sake, this account will use the fictitious names employed in the report—although the actual names are known.) "Probably more than most cities in the United States, Wincanton has known a high degree of gambling, vice (sexual immorality, including prostitution), and corruption," the report continued. "With the exception of two reform administrations, Wincanton has been wide open since the 1920s."

Bookmakers handled bets on horse races totaling several million dollars a year. A numbers racket—taking bets at most newsstands, cigar counters, and corner grocery stores—did an annual business of $1.3 million. More than 200 illegal pinball machines, equipped to pay off like slot machines, were spread throughout the city. A high-stakes dice game attracted professional gamblers from more than 100 miles away; during one Federal raid on the game, $25,000 was found on the table. A moonshine still, capable of producing $4 million worth of illegal alcohol a year, operated in the city. In addition, prostitution was rampant; there were five large bawdy houses and countless smaller houses catering to men from a large portion of the state.

"As in all cities in which gambling and vice had flourished openly, these illegal activities were protected by local officials," the report said. "Mayors, police chiefs, and many lesser officials were on the payroll of the gambling syndicate while others received periodic 'gifts' or aid during political campaigns. A number of Wincanton officials added to their revenue from the syndicate by extorting kickbacks on the sale or purchase of city equipment or by selling licenses, permits, zoning variances, etc. As the city officials made possible the operations of the racketeers, so frequently the racketeers facilitated the corrupt endeavors of officials by providing liaison men to arrange the deals or 'enforcers' to insure that the deals were carried out."

The makeup of Wincanton's citizenry undoubtedly played a role in allowing the city to be dominated by corrupt forces. Ever since 1930, Wincanton has been slowly dropping in population. Those residents who have remained—resisting the move to the suburbs or to other parts of the country—have chiefly been poorly educated members of the lower middle class. Only eleven percent of the families had annual incomes higher than $10,000 at the time the study was made; the median family income was $5,453. Only twenty-seven percent of the adults had finished high school.

The various ethnic groups in the city tended to retain their separate identities. Poles, Germans, Italians, and Negroes have their own neighborhoods, clubs, shopping places, and favorite politicians. Italian and Polish politicians, in particular, cater openly to Old World loyalties. The ethnic clubs, during election campaigns, are centers of political activity. Wincanton Democrats outnumber Republicans by two to one, but frequent Democratic party fights have prevented any single group of politicians from maintaining long-time control of the city.

Amid this political ferment, the one constant factor has been the prevalence of corruption. And the central figure in the corruption has been the head of Wincanton's organized-crime syndicate, a man identified in the commission report as Irving Stern. A European immigrant, Stern settled in Wincanton at the turn of the century. He worked first as a fruit peddler, but during the Prohibition era became a bootlegger for the state's beer baron, Heinz Glickman. Toward the end of Prohibition, Glickman was murdered and Stern took over his business. He continued selling untaxed liquor even after the Prohibition laws were repealed in 1933. Stern was convicted of several liquor violations during the 1930s and spent more than a year in Federal prison.

About 1940, the commission report said, Stern announced that he had reformed and went into his family's wholesale produce business. But the reform was only partial; in leaving the bootlegging business, Stern was entering the gambling rackets. Even in those days Wincanton was wide open for gambling, but operations were only loosely organized. Stern set about organizing them on a much more systematic and profitable basis. With help from some of his bootlegging friends, he started a numbers-racket bank and soon added horse-race betting, a dice game, and slot machines to his operations.

To keep his syndicate flourishing, Stern made payoffs to numerous public officials and law-enforcement officers. Throughout the 1940s he controlled the majority of gambling in the area, although he was forced to share the slot-machine trade with a Wincanton native named Klaus Braun. It was estimated at the time that gambling was a $5 million-a-year business in Wincanton. Stern's take from bookmaking alone was about $40,000 a week, and Braun's take from slot machines was $75,000 to $100,000 a year.

In the early 1950s, however, the Stern syndicate suffered a temporary setback when a state legislative investigation of Wincanton corruption resulted in the election of a reform Republican administration. The new mayor, Hal Craig, decided to follow a policy aimed at bringing about what he called "pearl-gray purity." The policy would permit isolated bookmakers, prostitutes, and numbers writers,

but seek to eliminate all forms of organized crime sufficiently lucrative to make it worth anyone's while to offer
bribes to officials or policemen.

Within six weeks after taking office, Mayor Craig and a
reform district attorney conducted a series of raids on
Stern's gambling parlors and Braun's slot-machine locations. Stern and Braun decided to close operations, at least
temporarily. U.S. Internal Revenue agents, investigating
past gambling activities in Wincanton, obtained tax-evasion convictions against Braun, and Stern's nephew and
business associate, Dave Feinman; both were imprisoned.
During a three-year period following the election of the reform administration, there was scattered gambling and
prostitution—but nothing like the organized operations of
previous years.

By 1955, however, it became clear that the citizenry was
unhappy with the reform movement and that an administration favoring a more liberal attitude toward gambling
and vice would soon be swept into office. Stern met with
leaders of two East Coast Mafia families to begin planning
to rebuild his organization. (The commission report did
not identify the Mafia leaders, but Pennsylvania law-enforcement officials say they were top men in the late Joseph Profaci's New York family and Angelo Bruno's Philadelphia family.) The Mafia leaders agreed to provide
Stern with money, technical help, and, when necessary,
strong-arm men. In return, Stern agreed to cut the Mob
bosses in for a share of the profits.

Stern decided to make several changes from his old system of operation when he reopened. For one thing, he was
determined to centralize all Wincanton gambling and vice
under his control. Previously, besides allowing Braun to
maintain a slot-machine business, Stern had refrained
from playing any role in the prostitution rackets. Now,

while broadening his power to include all gambling and vice, he simultaneously contrived to keep his own activities better hidden from public view than in the past—turning over the more visible aspects of rackets management to subordinates.

When a new Democratic city administration headed by Mayor Gene Donnelly succeeded the reform administration, Stern quickly put his plans into successful operation. One of his first steps was to reorganize the numbers racket. During the reform period, some numbers writers had continued operating on a small-time, unorganized basis. Because of the lack of organization and financial backing, these writers frequently were forced to renege on paying winning bettors if an unusually popular number were "hit." Stern's subordinates notified the independent writers that they were now working for Stern—or else. "Those who objected were 'persuaded' by Stern's men or else arrested by the police, as were any of the others who were suspected of holding out on their receipts," the commission report said. "Few objected for very long."

Under the reorganized system, eleven numbers-racket subbanks reported to Stern's central accounting office. Each subbank employed from five to thirty numbers writers. Thirty-five percent of the gross receipts went to the writers. The net profits, after deductions for paying winning bettors and other expenses, were divided equally between Stern and the operators of the subbanks. Stern arranged for protection from public officials and police, and handled "layoff" bets for the subbanks—underwriting them against the threat of catastrophic losses.

With the help of his out-of-state Mafia associates, Stern established a new big-money dice game. Upward of fifty men were employed in running the game—drivers to haul players into Wincanton from points sometimes more than

100 miles away; croupiers; guards; bartenders; waiters; doormen to check players' credentials; even loansharks to offer instant credit to losers. The payroll for these employees in 1960 was more than $350,000. Some idea of the game's take can be gauged by the fact that one businessman reported he had lost $75,000 there in one night. Stern, in addition to receiving a cut of the game's profits, got a $1,000 weekly fee from his associates for providing protection. When a competing dice game was set up in the Wincanton area, Stern asked his Mafia pals for help in disrupting the rival operation. The Mafia sent six out-of-state gunmen to crash the competing game; robbing, and terrifying the customers. The competitors got the message and closed up shop.

Stern and his Mafia associates also were partners in the operation of a huge moonshine still erected in a riverfront warehouse in Wincanton. For a fee and a share of the profits, Stern arranged for protection of the still by city officials and policemen. He even managed to get permission for the still to be tied in to city water and sewage lines. His Mafia partners helped provide the $200,000 worth of equipment and expert consultants needed to construct the still. The operation, capable of producing $4 million worth of alcohol a year, provided moonshine to major wholesalers in a five-state area. When it was finally raided and destroyed by U.S. Treasury agents, it was described as the largest still discovered in this country since Prohibition.

In addition to running his own rackets, Stern also controlled prostitution and several kinds of gambling on a "franchise" basis. Although he took no active part in operating these enterprises and got no cut of the profits, he was paid regular fees for providing them with protection. His "clients" for such services included a number of bookmakers, some paying him as much as $600 a week. When necessary, Stern used a combination of political manipulation and strong-arm muscle to demonstrate the value of his "franchises" to prospective customers. For example, at Stern's instigation, Mayor Gene Donnelly announced immediately after taking office that all pinball machines were illegal and would be seized by the police. Distributors of the pinballs, who had been operating on an unorganized basis during the previous administration, were uncertain what to do next. A Stern subordinate then notified the distributors that they would face no interference from the police if they employed Stern's nephew, Dave Feinman (by then free from prison), as a "public relations consultant." Some of the distributors rebelled and formed an Alsace County Amusement Operators Association in an attempt to protect their interests. But their rebellion evaporated when Feinman showed up at an association meeting with two Mafia enforcers from New York, who roughed up the group's president. The distributors quickly agreed to pay Feinman $2,000 a week to promote their "public relations."

Stern's system for corrupting public officials and law-enforcement officers rested on two basic principles—to pay the top people as much as necessary and to pay lesser amounts to as many others as possible in order to implicate them and prevent them from blowing the whistle. Some officials got regular weekly payoffs while relatively unimportant patrolmen on the beat were bought with nothing more than a Christmas turkey.

A payoff list found in Stern's central-numbers bank listed payments totaling $2,400 a week for protection of the numbers operation alone. Among the recipients on the list were local officials, state legislators, the police chief, a captain in charge of detectives, and persons mysteriously de-

scribed only as "state" and "county." For protecting
Stern's dice game, one official got $750 a week, the police
chief got $100, and other officials and policemen got lesser
amounts. The commission report noted that some men
were silenced without charge. Low-ranking policemen, for
example, learned to keep quiet when men who reported
gambling or prostitution to their superiors were ignored or
transferred to the midnight shift.

The commission report said:

> Stern was a major [if undisclosed] contributor dur-
> ing political campaigns—sometimes giving money to
> all candidates, not caring who won, sometimes sup-
> porting a "regular" to defeat a possible reformer,
> sometimes paying a candidate not to oppose a pre-
> ferred man.
>
> Since there were few legitimate sources of large
> contributions for candidates, Stern's money was fre-
> quently regarded as essential for victory, for the costs
> of buying radio and television time and paying poll-
> watchers were high. When popular sentiment was
> running strongly in favor of reform, however, even
> Stern's contributions could not guarantee victory.
> Bob Walasek, later to be as corrupt as any Wincanton
> mayor, ran as a reform candidate in the Democratic
> primary and defeated Stern-financed incumbent Gene
> Donnelly. Never a man to bear grudges, Stern
> financed Walasek in the general election that year
> and put him on the "payroll" when he took office.

Such arrangements are typical of organized crime's
machinations in the political arena. The Mob cares little, if
at all, about political philosophies; it probably would support even a candidate of the Vegetarian Party if he stood a
chance of winning and could be corrupted. In Irv Stern's

case, besides putting officials on his regular payoff list, he found other ways to place them in his debt. Some received mortgage loans from him when they had trouble obtaining them from banks. Others were treated to expenses-paid vacations. The commission report described a telephone conversation disclosed by County Court Judge Ralph Vaughan in which such a vacation was offered. Shortly after his election (with Stern's support), Judge Vaughan said, he got a call from Stern's nephew, Dave Feinman.

"Congratulations, Judge," Feinman said. "When do you think you and your wife would like a vacation in Florida?"

"Florida? Why on earth would I want to go there?"

"But all the other judges and the guys in City Hall—Irv [Stern] takes them all to Florida whenever they want to get away."

"Thanks anyway, but I'm not interested."

"Well, how about a mink coat instead? What size does your wife wear?"

Stern helped keep public officials in line by setting up lucrative deals for them at no cost to himself. He served as a broker in bringing the politicians into contact with salesmen, merchants, and lawyers willing to offer bribes to get city business. He also provided middlemen, able to handle the bribe money without endangering the officials' reputations, and strong-arm men who discouraged potential troublemakers from rocking the boat.

Although he did not profit financially from most of these deals, they served several useful purposes to Stern. For one thing, they kept down the size of the payoffs demanded directly from him by the officials. As the commission report noted, "If a councilman was able to pick up $1,000 on the purchase of city equipment, he would demand a lower payment for the protection of gambling."

For another thing, Stern's intimate knowledge of the details of all the corrupt deals could be used as a threat against any official who tried to double cross him. For still another thing, Stern found it prudent to supervise the corruption in order to protect the officials against their own greed and heavy handedness.

A typical example of the need for such protection arose in the case of Mayor Walasek, who became so avaricious that he tried to cut himself in for a profit on virtually every contract signed by the city. Stern soon found it necessary to oversee many of Walasek's crooked deals to prevent the mayor from bungling his way into a public scandal. Walasek tried to double the size of the fix on a city parking meter purchase—prompting Stern to intercede, set the contract price, supply an untraceable middleman, and smooth over any feathers that got ruffled. Police Chief Dave Phillips, who took part in the corruption for a time but eventually blew the whistle on some of his former allies, gave this account of the parking-meter affair: "I told Irv [Stern] that Walasek wanted $12 on each meter instead of the $6 we got on the last meter deal. He became furious. He said, 'Walasek is going to fool around and wind up in jail. You come and see me. I'll tell Walasek what he is going to buy.'" And that's the way the matter was handled—with the organized crime boss dictating to the mayor the terms of the bribe.

Many of the bribes and kickbacks paid to Wincanton officials were given in the guise of "campaign contributions." Even if the money had found its way into political party coffers, the transactions would have been illegal—but in numerous cases the "campaign contributions" went nowhere but the officials' pockets. During Mayor Donnelly's administration, all City Hall employees were notified that they were expected to contribute two percent of their salaries "voluntarily" to the Democratic Party. Donnelly never turned the money over to the party. He also informed salesmen doing business with the city that companies supporting the party would get preferential treatment. In one case, he solicited a $2,000 "political contribution" from a salesman whose company wanted an $81,000 contract to provide the city with three fire engines. Donnelly got the money and the company got the contract.

State laws requiring the city to take competitive bids contained numerous loopholes that allowed the corrupt officials to ignore or throw out bids by companies that refused to play ball. "Professional services," for example, were exempt from competitive bidding. Thus, when an internationally renowned engineering firm refused to pay a kickback on a contract to design a huge sewage-disposal plant, its proposal was rejected. A local company got the job, and paid $10,700 of its $225,000 fee to an associate of Stern and Donnelly as a "finder's fee."

Mayor Walasek, in the parking-meter deal negotiated by Stern, received kickbacks of $10,500 plus an $880 clock for his home. Other officials divided $20,000 for approving the city's sale of a piece of property for $22,000 that was immediately resold for $75,000. When Walasek took office, he placed the city bureaus of building and plumbing inspection under his direct control. He then held up approval of building permits until the petitioners paid him bribes or threatened to sue. In some cases, building designs were not approved until an architect with political connections was retained as a "consultant." In other cases, developers were forced to make payoffs for zoning variances allowing them to build supermarkets and apartment houses.

Wincanton officials, who were allowed to engage in private business while holding office, found multifarious ways to enrich themselves. Police Chief Phillips, before turning informer, owned a construction company that was hired to remodel the largest bawdy house in the city. A city councilman with an accounting practice handled the books of Irv Stern and other gambling and vice figures. Another councilman received a contract to erect all service stations built in the area by a major oil company—reportedly in return for his vote to give the company the exclusive right to sell gasoline to the city.

Commenting on the broad scale of corruption, the commission report noted:

> With the exception of the local congressman and the city treasurer, it seems that . . . personnel at each level [city, county, and state] and in most offices in City Hall can be identified either with Stern or with some form of freelance corruption. A number of local judges received campaign financing from Stern. . . . Several state legislators were on Stern's payroll, and one Republican councilman charged that a highranking state Democratic official promised Stern first choice of all Alsace County patronage.

In the face of all this blatant corruption, state officials generally took a hands-off attitude—some because they were on Stern's payroll, others apparently because they feared stirring up a hornet's nest. State police, some of whom reportedly were taking payoffs from Stern, moved into Wincanton only on invitation from local officials. On the few occasions when the state police did accept invitations to act against Wincanton gambling and vice, the results were usually negligible. Once, for example, Chief Assistant District Attorney Phil Roper decided to take advantage of the corrupt district attorney's vacation ab-

sence to launch a brief anti-crime crusade. He called in the
state police and raided several bawdy houses. Then, en-
countering a major gambler on the street, Roper made a
citizen's arrest and drove him to police headquarters for
detention and questioning. The local desk sergeant told
him: "I'm sorry, Mr. Roper. We're under orders not to arrest any persons brought in by you." Roper called the state
police back to take custody of the gambler. But, when the
district attorney returned home, he fired Roper for "introducing politics into the district attorney's office." Nothing
substantial came of the raids or arrests.

Ultimately, however, the cozy arrangement between the
Mob and the politicians in Wincanton was broken up because Irv Stern had ignored the axiom that racketeering
needs protection at all levels of government. Although he
had corrupted a majority of local officials and some important state officials, Stern had failed to bring Federal authorities under his control. Thus, he was caught by surprise when Federal agents launched a series of major
investigations in Wincanton. FBI men raided the high-
stakes dice game, seizing $25,000 found on the table and
another $25,000 in the safe. They arrested more than 100
of the gamblers. Agents of the Treasury Department's Alcohol and Tobacco Tax Unit raided and destroyed the
moonshine still. Bookmakers and other gamblers were
rounded up for failure to pay Federal gambling taxes. The
numbers banks were raided by Internal Revenue agents,
who arrested numerous employees and seized valuable
records. Internal Revenue men also began intensive investigations of the tax records of Irv Stern and his corrupt political allies.

The prospective defendants counterattacked. When a
Federal grand jury began looking into the Wincanton cor-

ruption, one of the cooperative witnesses was a garage owner with a city franchise to tow away cars illegally parked or involved in accidents. For each car towed, he had been obliged to pay a kickback to city officials. After he testified, Mayor Walasek promptly canceled his franchise—claiming there were supposed "health violations" at his garage. In addition, the garage owner's equipment was hit with a rash of "accidents." Steering cables on his tow trucks were cut, wheels fell off his trucks out on the highways, and other damages were sustained. Under pressure from local newspapers, which ridiculed the "health violations," the franchise was restored and the "accidents" ceased. But other attempts were made to intimidate witnesses. After former Police Chief Phillips testified before the grand jury, his construction company submitted the lowest bid on a contract to renovate a school athletic field. The bid was thrown out on the ground that there was "a question as to his [Phillips's] moral responsibility."

In the end, Irv Stern was convicted of income-tax evasion, gambling-tax evasion, and extortion on a city parking meter contract. He was sentenced to four years in Federal prison. Mayor Walasek was convicted of extortion in the meter case and given a short jail term. Various other figures in the city's long history of corruption were also jailed.

The scandals, at least briefly, put Wincanton in the publicity spotlight. National news media coverage caused great embarrassment to many local citizens who previously had been willing to tolerate the corruption. One textile manufacturer was quoted in the commission report as saying: "I'd go to a convention on the West Coast and everyone I'd meet would say, 'You're from Wincanton? Boy, have I heard stories about that place!' I would try to talk about textiles or opportunities for industrial development, but they'd keep asking about the girls and the gambling." Members of the armed forces told of being ridiculed by their service buddies because they were from Wincanton. A local judge who had long taken a liberal view of corruption was finally persuaded to act against it when he learned that his daughter was being laughed at by her college friends for being related to a Wincanton official.

With such attitudes prevailing, the voters reacted by electing a genuine reform administration. The new mayor, identified in the commission report as Ed Whitton, led a major cleanup drive. Organized gambling, prostitution, and corruption were crushed. As the commission report put it: "The only gamblers and prostitutes still operating in Wincanton are those whom the police have been unable to catch for reasons of limited manpower, lack of evidence, etc. The police acknowledge that there are still a few gamblers and prostitutes in town, but they have been driven underground."

But this does not necessarily mean that the cleanup will be permanent. In a city with a long history of corruption, there is always the possibility that reform fervor will fade. After the commission report was issued, officials and civic leaders in Reading, Pennsylvania, expressed fears that new attempts might soon be made to throw the city wide open. Reform Mayor Eugene Shirk—the man called "Ed Whitton" in the report—said racketeers were "just waiting in the wings" to resume operations.

Gary, Indiana

While the corruption in Reading may have been more deeply rooted and more broad-scale than that encountered in many other American cities, it is nonetheless true that

the Mob plays a dominant role in the politics and government of numerous municipalities throughout the country.
In Gary, Indiana, for example, there has been a persistent
record of corruption by organized-crime figures. Richard
Hatcher, the city's first Negro mayor, was elected on a reform platform. Hatcher has said that the Mob offered him
$100,000 to withdraw from his initial primary campaign
against the entrenched Democratic machine. When he refused and won the Democratic nomination, he said, he
was offered an identical amount for an "understanding" to
permit gambling and other rackets if elected. He again rejected the offer, won the election, and launched his promised cleanup campaign. But he warned repeatedly that
efforts were being made to return control of the city government to "those who plundered it for so many years."
Hatcher's predecessor as mayor, George Chacharis, was
jailed on charges of avoiding income taxes on kickbacks
from city contracts. Among Chacharis's chief political
lieutenants was a convicted bootlegger known as Doc
James. Hatcher has charged that Chacharis, now out of
jail, and James have been manipulating other politicians
behind the scenes in an attempt to undermine the reform
program. He has pleaded with Gary's citizens to reject the
machinations of "a machine which bought votes wholesale
and stole the rest; a machine which exploited blacks and
Latins and ignored their just demands; a machine greased
with the millions which float from rackets, gambling, and
prostitution."

Seattle, Washington

In Seattle, Washington, collusion among racketeers,
public officials, and policemen resulted in systematic flout-
ing of the law for at least a half-century. Using the excuse
that Seattle's origin as a frontier town gave it a natural his-

tory of tolerance toward gambling and vice, officials sanctioned wide-open conditions as late as 1969. Although state law prohibited all forms of gambling except parimutuel betting on horse races, the Seattle city government actually issued licenses for almost twenty years to operators of gambling houses, and pinball machines were used openly for gambling. The city collected about $165,000 a year in license fees for such illegal operations.

At the same time, officials and policemen regularly collected payoffs from racketeers for permitting them to conduct their licensed businesses. In spite of their licenses, they were in potential danger of arrest for violation of the state laws—but the payoffs protected them from that. Ultimately, a Federal grand jury began investigating organized crime in the area. Former Acting Police Chief M. E. Cook was convicted of perjury in 1970 for denying before the grand jury that he knew anything about the payoffs. Cook appealed the conviction, and his appeal is pending at this writing.

Testimony at Cook's trial disclosed that policemen working in the vice squad and the downtown precinct collected $12,000 a month in payoffs from gamblers, bawdy house operators, and other rackets figures. Policemen with other assignments also got payoffs. The system of corruption was so entrenched that it developed its own bureaucracy, with certain jobs designated for bigger payoffs than others. When one policeman was transferred to a new assignment, he demanded and got a sort of severance settlement in two payments of $150 and $250. Almost 100 members of the 1000-man police department were identified at the trial as payoff recipients.

The Federal grand jury also indicated former King County (Seattle) Sheriff Tim McCullough on perjury charges for his denial that he collected bribes from gamblers. He was convicted in a trial at which underworld figures and law-enforcement officers testified that gambling laws were ignored as a result of payoffs. McCullough, who has repeatedly denied the charges against him, is appealing his conviction at this writing.

Following the Federal investigation, a county grand jury launched its own hearings and indicted forty persons —most of them public officials and law-enforcement officers—on bribery and conspiracy charges. The major indictment accused nineteen persons of conspiring to allow gambling and prostitution to flourish in return for payoffs. Among those indicted in the case were Charles O. Carroll, prosecuting attorney of King County for twenty-two years; Frank Ramon, former Seattle police chief; Charles M. Carroll, president of the Seattle City Council; and Jack Porter, former King County sheriff. The defendants have pleaded not guilty and are awaiting trial at this writing.

The county grand jury charged in its conspiracy indictment that various public officials had shared in bribery proceeds, "sometimes in the form of covert campaign contributions." The indictment said: "Members of the conspiracy gave financial contributions to candidates for the positions of mayor and members of the city council of the city of Seattle and prosecuting attorney and sheriff of the county of King who would support the policy of tolerating the operation of gambling and other illegal activities."

While the corruption investigations were under way, a city election took place and a reform administration headed by Mayor West Uhlman was swept into office. Uhlman launched a cleanup campaign. He temporarily borrowed the highly respected police chief of Oakland, California, Charles R. Gain, to reorganize Seattle's police department, and then appointed as permanent police chief the former chief of Garden Grove, California, George Tielsch. In addition, he hired a retired Oakland police chief, Edward Toothman, to head a departmental investigation of police corruption. As in Reading, Pennsylvania, however, the corruption in Seattle has been of such long duration that it is unclear whether the reform program will achieve lasting results. The racketeers are still present, though driven underground, and are clearly searching for weak links in the new administration.

Honolulu

The idyllic reputation of Honolulu does not usually conjure up images of gangland domination—but the fact is that the Mob has a tight hold on the Hawaiian capital. Syndicate mobsters operate a flourishing gambling racket that is known to take in more than $250,000 a week. They also control sizable prostitution and protection rackets, narcotics rings, and a large trade in the fencing of stolen property. Numerous political campaigns have featured charges of official links with the Mob, but thus far there have been no meaningful steps to eliminate such corrupt alliances.

One indication of racketeers' ties to public officials came to light with the gangland-style murder of State Senator Larry N. Kuriyama on October 23, 1970. The murder investigation disclosed that Kuriyama, who was shot to death outside his Honolulu home, was closely connected with Mob gambling figures involved in an underworld power struggle. Only two days before Kuriyama's death, this power struggle had taken the life of a crime syndicate lieutenant, Francis A. Burke, who was riddled with bullets on a downtown street. All told, since 1962, there have been at least seventeen confirmed gangland murders in Honolulu and seven other cases in which the suspected victims are missing and presumed dead. In some cases the killers avoided using such traditional Mob weapons as the gun, the knife, and the bomb. One victim was burned to death in a city incinerator; two others were hacked with axes in a burned-out building; another was killed with a blowtorch; still another was hurled into a tank full of sharks. All the cases are unsolved. It would thus appear that the Mob can not only operate various rackets in Honolulu, but commit murder as well, with impunity.

Hot Springs, Arkansas

If Honolulu seems an unlikely place for Mob domination, Arkansas seems even less likely. A generally rural state where the Baptist Church has long exerted strong influence, Arkansas would appear on the surface to be one of the last places in the United States where organized crime would gain a foothold. Yet, for more than a century, the resort city of Hot Springs has been a gambling center and hangout for gangsters from all sections of the country. All this has been true despite the fact that Capitol Hill's chief claimant to the title of Mob "scourge" has long been Arkansas Senator John McClellan.

Despite the fact that gambling is illegal in Arkansas, numerous gambling houses built on the order of Las Vegas casinos have operated openly in Hot Springs with the consent of local officials. In addition, the city has served as a major layoff betting center for syndicate bookmaking operations in other states and as a focal point for horse-race wire services. From time to time, under pressure from state officials, these gambling operations have shut down or have at least been forced into semi-underground existence. But eventually, after the heat has faded, they have resumed full-blast activities.

Until his recent death, the most notorious figure in the

Hot Springs racket was Owney "the Killer" Madden, who had shifted his base to Arkansas after a Prohibition era career as a New York mobster. Madden frequently played host in Hot Springs to New York gambler Frank Costello, who long owned a piece of the Arkansas rackets. Numerous meetings of top Mob leaders from other states have taken place in Hot Springs. Even as long ago as Al Capone's heyday, the Chicago mobster often met his associates from other cities at Hot Springs' Arlington Hotel.

Madden and his associates were so confident they could operate without serious interference that they even went so far as to string some of the cables for their racing-wire service across Federal property—a section of the Hot Springs National Forest. Federal agents found the cables and had them dismantled, but the syndicate merely strung new wires at other points outside the Federal property. Local officials in Hot Springs, clearly in league with the racketeers, rarely bothered to deny that they permitted wide-open gambling. They argued, instead, that the city needed gambling to keep alive its resort business.

On one of the rare occasions when state police raided a Hot Springs casino, seizing numerous slot machines and illegal stocks of liquor, they were ordered by a local judge to return the contraband. Another time, a group of clergymen asked a judge on a Saturday to issue a search warrant enabling them to obtain evidence of illegal gambling. The judge told the ministers he was too busy—eating a steak dinner his wife had cooked—to bother with the warrant then. He asked them to return the following Monday. When they did, he claimed he had been ordered by a higher court judge not to issue any search warrants in gambling cases.

St. Louis, Missouri

The blatant sort of wide-open conditions that have existed in Hot Springs, with the obvious cooperation of public officials, have also prevailed in some other American cities. Far more prevalent, however, have been cases in which the dealings between mobsters and officials have been carried out with such secrecy and subtlety that the public has generally been unaware of them. One case involving questionable dealings between a public official and men with criminal reputations has arisen in St. Louis, Missouri. *Life* magazine has accused St. Louis Mayor A. J. Cervantes of having close business, political, and personal ties to leading racketeers.

Mayor Cervantes claims there is no organized crime in St. Louis, but the evidence shows otherwise. In fact, the U.S. government has established a special strike force—composed of men from a half-dozen Federal law-enforcement agencies—to combat organized crime in the area. Among the subjects being investigated by the Federal agents is the connection between racketeering and politics.

Cervantes, currently serving his second term as mayor, previously served ten years as a city alderman and four years as president of the board of aldermen. His closest associate—as political campaign manager, business partner, friend, and unofficial City Hall adviser—is a wealthy insurance and real-estate man named Tony Sansone. Among other things, *Life* charged, Sansone acts as Cervantes's chief liaison man with questionable characters. The St. Louis underworld is dominated by two ethnic mobs that have a cooperative working agreement. One is an old-line Mafia family headed by a veteran racketeer named Anthony Giardino; the other is the so-called Syrian Mob bossed by a former gunman named Jimmy Michaels who has survived numerous bloody gang wars. Michaels is the father-in-law of Tony Sansone and is considered the mobster with the best political connections in St. Louis.

Over the years, *Life* charged, Mayor Cervantes used Sansone as a go-between to arrange various meetings with Michaels and other reputed Mob figures to discuss political problems. For example, shortly after announcing his candidacy for the Democratic mayoralty nomination in late 1964, Cervantes reportedly met with Sansone and Michaels to plot campaign strategy. The discussion was said to have taken place in the office of a vending-machine company controlled by the Mob. Three months later, after Cervantes had won the Democratic primary, Sansone reportedly met at the same office with Michaels and Mafia boss Giardino to get their advice on Cervantes's general election campaign.

Before becoming mayor, Cervantes had operated successful businesses in such fields as insurance, banking, real estate and public transportation. These businesses have continued to function, under the guidance of trustees, during his tenure as mayor. Among them is an insurance firm, Cervantes and Associates, whose licensed brokers include Tony Sansone and his brother, Joseph. (Joseph Sansone has also been appointed city assessor by Cervantes.) As late as 1962, when Cervantes was president of the board of aldermen, Mob boss Michaels wrote insurance through Cervantes and Associates. In that year, however, Missouri passed a new law authorizing state authorities to deny a brokerage license to anyone ever convicted of a felony. Michaels was denied a license and thus forced to give up a lucrative affiliation with Cervantes's firm.

Even without the services of Michaels, Cervantes and Associates has continued to prosper—sometimes with the help of Mob-affiliated companies and City Hall. One such example was provided when Mayor Cervantes voted to approve a city lease giving a company called Premier Service Corporation the exclusive right to provide limousine serv-

ice between the St. Louis airport and local hotels. Premier
Service Corporation is owned by Tony Sansone. Under
the lease granted by the city, Premier was obliged to obtain liability and property-damage insurance on its limou-
sines. The insurance was provided through Cervantes and
Associates. Mayor Cervantes's lawyer, Jack Murphy, who
serves as a trustee of the mayor's businesses, is on the
board of directors of both Premier and Cervantes and Associates. Among the others serving on Premier's board is
Tony Sansone's wife, Mary Ann, the daughter of Jimmy
Michaels. Various rackets figures have turned up on Premier's payroll.

Cervantes has been a partner of Tony Sansone in other
business ventures. In still another venture, in which Sansone was not involved, Cervantes was vice president of a
company doing business with the Mob. The company,
Mound City Tobacco, is a wholesale supplier of cigarettes
and other tobacco products. It was formed as the successor to a firm operated by a St. Louis politician named
Robert Brown—a succession made necessary by the fact
that Brown had been murdered. Shortly after Brown's
death, the business manager of his firm, James Holland,
borrowed $60,000 from Cervantes and Cervantes's lawyer,
Jack Murphy, to buy the company's remaining inventory.
Holland then formed Mound City Tobacco, with Cervantes as part owner and vice president, to take over the business previously handled by Brown's firm. Cervantes was
an alderman at the time. During his tenure as vice president, a major portion of Mound City's business consisted
of supplying cigarettes to Mob-controlled vending machine companies run by such racketeers as Anthony
Giardino and Frank "Buster" Wortman.

Moreover, James Holland and a bank in which Cervantes was a director once helped bail Mafia boss Giardino

out of financial difficulties. Giardino needed money to pay delinquent Federal income taxes in a case in which he had previously been imprisoned. Lindell Trust Company, the bank where Cervantes served on the board of directors, loaned Giardino the money to pay the taxes. The collateral put up on the loan was a savings account passbook belonging to Holland.

Life reported that although Cervantes maintains a steady liaison with the underworld through Sansone, "he has been fairly discreet" about being seen personally with questionable characters. One case where he was seen with such men, the magazine said, was at a gathering at Sansone's home following the funeral of Jimmy Michaels's wife in 1967. The article said Cervantes helped tend bar for the guests, who included Anthony Giardino; his Mafia underboss, John Vitale; a Mafia lieutenant, Shorty Caleca; and Buster Wortman.

Although Cervantes denies that organized crime exists in St. Louis, he concedes the city is plagued by other types of crime. "Muggers, thugs, and troublemakers make citizens afraid to walk our streets," he says. To combat that sort of crime, the mayor created a Commission on Crime and Law Enforcement in 1970. And, to head the commission, Cervantes appointed a St. Louis attorney named Morris Shenker.

The choice of Shenker was considered by some as curious, for Shenker has long been one of the country's leading defense lawyers for the Mob. During the late Senator Estes Kefauver's investigation of organized crime, Shenker represented more racketeers than any other attorney. His list of clients has included such mobsters and labor racketeers as Anthony Giardino, Buster Wortman, John Vitale, Shorty Caleca, Teamster Union President Jimmy Hoffa, and convicted Steamfitters Union official Lawrence Calla-

nan. Of course, Shenker has the right—even the duty—to
represent the most heinous of criminals. But his background does not seem to make him a logical choice as
head of the Commission on Crime and Law Enforcement.
Yet, in appointing him, Mayor Cervantes said: "I can
think of no individual more qualified to head the crime
[drive] than Morris Shenker."

Cervantes has denied the allegations made against him
by *Life*. He has said the magazine's charges were based on
"innuendo, half-truths, untruths, careful omissions, and
old photographs." And he has continued to insist that organized crime does not exist in his city. Thus, the chief
hope for a cleanup of the St. Louis rackets appears to lie
with the Federal strike force against organized crime. Precisely how effective the strike force will be is not yet clear
at this writing, but its mere presence in St. Louis serves as
a constant warning to mobsters that they cannot operate
with impunity.

In New York City where local citizens have long accepted the fact that they live in the organized-crime capital
of the United States, there was nonetheless considerable
furor in 1971 over an investigation that revealed corrupt
alliances between policemen and the underworld. The investigation was conducted by a commission appointed by
Mayor John V. Lindsay and headed by a Wall Street lawyer named Whitman Knapp. Public televised hearings
produced sensational testimony by present and former policemen who admitted taking numerous payoffs from underworld figures and claimed such payoffs were common
throughout the police department. The Knapp Commission was severely criticized by some policemen and also
others who complained that little or no evidence was presented to substantiate these broad-scale charges. There
was little evidence presented tying the corrupt officers to

important Mob leaders. Still, taken for what it seemed worth, the Knapp Commission testimony did disclose alliances between at least some policemen and crime figures.

The law-enforcement problems posed by organized crime are by no means limited to such cities as St. Louis, Reading, Gary, Seattle, Honolulu, Hot Springs, and New York.

The Biggest Network in the U.S.A.

As the President's Commission on Law Enforcement put it: "Organized criminal groups are known to operate in all sections of the country." A commission survey disclosed that local police departments conceded the Mob was functioning in at least eighty percent of American cities with populations of more than a million, in more than half the cities with populations between 100,000 and 250,000, and in at least twenty percent of the cities with populations between 250,000 and a million. In some cases, the commission said, Federal agencies reported the presence of organized crime where local police departments denied it. And, from every indication, the racketeers are moving into previously untapped cities all the time. No citizen or public official in a community of appreciable size can afford to assume that his city will be immune to Mob infiltration and political corruption. Only through "more vigilance against such corruption," said the President's commission, can the sweeping tide of organized crime be reversed.

[3]

The Corrupters

The voice was soft, reasonable, persuasive. It could have belonged to a skilled labor-management negotiator or, with some improvement in syntax, a polished diplomat. But it did not; it was the voice of a Mob corrupter—trying to persuade a high-ranking West Coast police official to protect syndicate bookmaking operations.

"Betting's legal at the track, isn't it?" the mobster asked. "So why isn't it legal here? It's because of those crooks at the State Capitol. They're gettin' plenty—all drivin' Cads. Look at my customers—some of the biggest guys in town —they don't want you to close me down. If you do, they'll just transfer you like that last jerk. And even the judge, what did he do? Fined me a hundred and suspended fifty. Hell, he knows Joe Citizen wants me here, so get smart, be one of the boys, be part of the system. It's a way of life in this town and you're not gonna change it. Tell you what I'll do. I won't give you a nickel; just call in a free bet in the first race every day and you can win or lose. How about it?"

The police official, an honest man, rejected the offer. But he knew that the corrupter would keep probing for a weak spot—approaching one official after another until finding someone willing to play ball. "These people really work on you," the official says. "They make it seem too logical—like you're the one who is out of step."

The approach he described was typical of the tactics used by Mob corrupters. Every Mafia family has at least one top member designated as a corrupter. In many cases, the job is given to the *consiglieri* (counselor to the family boss). Sometimes, however, the boss himself handles this responsibility—as was the case, for example, when Frank Costello headed a New York family. It is the corrupter's job to bribe, intimidate, negotiate, or otherwise maneuver himself into a position of control over public officials and law-enforcement officers.

How does the corrupter go about trying to put a local official or policeman "in his pocket"? A graphic description of the Mafia technique was provided in a secretly made tape recording of a racketeer's purported attempt to bribe an officer to join forces with the Mob. The alleged corrupter in this case was a Mafia boss—Joseph "Joey" Aiuppa, mastermind of the rackets in Cicero, Illinois. One of Aiuppa's underlings, Casper Ciapetti (alias John Carr), had previously been accused of offering a $500 bribe to Detective Donald Shaw of the Cook County Sheriff's Vice Squad in an attempt to fix a case resulting from a Cicero slot-machine raid. Shaw, after informing his superiors of Ciapetti's offer, had accepted the $500 while other officers watched from hiding places. Ciapetti was then arrested and indicted on bribery charges. While Ciapetti was awaiting trial, Aiuppa was accused of making his own attempt to corrupt Shaw—offering him money to weaken his testimony in the bribery case and to provide the Mob with warnings of future raids against gambling rackets.

Aiuppa made his approach to Shaw through an intermediary, Jacob "Dutch" Bergbreiter, a former commanding officer of the sheriff's vice squad. Bergbreiter, who had left the sheriff's office and opened a real-estate business, asked Shaw to meet him and Aiuppa. Shaw agreed, notified his superiors and went to the meeting equipped with a tiny radio transmitter strapped under his jacket. The conversation was secretly transmitted to other officers stationed in a nearby parked car, who tape-recorded it. Part of the conversation went this way:

Aiuppa. Would you have any objection to helping John Carr [Ciapetti] get off the hook in court for a consideration and, if in doing so, it wouldn't hurt your position as a police officer?

Shaw. I wouldn't mind helping if I didn't hurt myself as a police officer and I didn't perjure myself in court.

Aiuppa. You won't hurt yourself and you won't have to be in court. Just give the lawyer a loophole in our prosecution. Now, you wouldn't want to see them put him [Carr] in the pen for ten years.

Shaw. I don't know him. I heard rumors that the guy has been an assassin.

Aiuppa. What?

Shaw. An assassin.

Aiuppa. Never.

Bergbreiter. Don't believe all the stuff you hear. Who told you he was an assassin?

Shaw. I don't know. I just heard.

Aiuppa. Excuse me, do you think there's such a crime as playing a slot machine or a pinball machine?

Shaw. By the law, there is.

Aiuppa. Wait a minute. The laws are flexible, they are made to bend, just like a big tree standing there. It's made to flex. I agree with this. I am a servant of the law and a citizen. . . . Let's put it cold. This is your home town. These are your people. Do you want to let an out-of-town guy like O'Mara [Michael O'Mara, commander of the sheriff's vice squad] come in and wrap you around his finger? Like all these Negroes and these demonstrators. Is that any goal to you? To me, to our friends? To our kids? It's the law. It's not right, but it's the law.

Shaw.   Like I say, it's the law. I get paid to do it.

Aiuppa.   All right, all right. Fine. We understand each other. There are several ways to do things. Take this man like O'Mara. . . . He's going to try to break the syndicate. He's going to try to get with the state's attorney. He's building up his stature, you understand, on your work. He's brainwashing all you young guys. Then [after the next sheriff's election] he dumps you. [Aiuppa then assured Shaw he would take care of his interests if a new sheriff were elected.] You just can't hurt people. . . . You have to use good common sense. You really do, reasoning. Our machines aren't taking money away from children, their milk money or the money they go to school with. When you find out about me, you will see I am a pretty nice guy. All I am interested in is the gambling and night spots in Cicero. It would be different if I sold broads, if I sold junk, if I sold counterfeit money. But I can go into a bar or a drug store and someone might even sit down and have a cup of coffee with me. We have nice people here. You will find out as you travel in Cicero that it is really a nice town. I'll guarantee you that my mother, sister, my daughter, could walk down the residential streets with no problem. I've been here for forty years.

Bergbreiter. And he will still be there when others are gone. I know that he will stand up. What he says, he will do.

Aiuppa. I expect you to stand up, too. If you can't stand up, I don't want to talk to you. We're men, we're friends, we try to help each other. Do you want to go along?

Shaw. Tell me what you want me to do.

[Aiuppa then explained that Shaw could change his testimony in court to indicate that the $500 given him by Carr might have been intended for use in posting bond for a man arrested in the slot-machine raid, Edward Doyle. "Isn't it possible it could have been that way?" Aiuppa asked. But Shaw pointed out that his vice squad partner had also witnessed the payment and would testify at the trial. He said he feared a conflict between his testimony and his partner's.]

Aiuppa. Forget about Jim [the partner]. I know what you said before the grand jury and I know what Jimmy said. I know more about it than you think I do. This is yours—two big ones. [Aiuppa purportedly held up two fingers at that point, indicating he would give Shaw $2,000.] For yourself. Don't tell anybody.

Bergbreiter. Don't even tell your wife. Believe me.

Aiuppa. If you tell anybody, I want no part of it. . . . Every month I will see that there is a C-note [$100] or some worldly goods in your mailbox. You'll be on the [pay] roll.

Shaw. What do you want from me to be on the roll?

Aiuppa. All I want from you is the information [on impending gambling raids], so that they will not be kicking me with the point of the shoe but the side of the shoe. If you find something out, see something you think I should know about, I'll give you a [phone] number. You follow me?

Shaw. The thing of it is, I would suddenly be out of a job if I stopped making pinches. We can do it like you say and kick you with the side of the shoe and not the toe.

Aiuppa. You will never stop making pinches. If you haven't got an out, go ahead. I paid for these pigeons [set-up raids in which Mafia subordinates, but never Aiuppa or his high-ranking associates, were arrested].

Bergbreiter. He will give you some good ones.

Aiuppa. Do you follow me? All I'm interested in is the gambling and the night spots in Cicero. I am not interested in the residential areas. You could go anywhere outside the business district and you will find nothing but a nice area.

Bergbreiter. Shaw, can I give you a little advice, being a boss like I was out there?

Shaw. In vice and gambling?

Bergbreiter. That's right. I used to be the [sheriff's] captain in charge of vice and gambling . . . and the Outfit [the Mob] always took care of me after I got smart and got on their payroll. Do this on your own. This is between the three of us. Don't trust your partner, nobody.

[Aiuppa then explained that if Shaw ever got in trouble and faced a trial, the Mob's money would be available to help him.]

Shaw. Say the [Chicago Police Department] Intelligence Unit had a game under surveillance for a while and then gave it [information on the game] to us and suddenly it wasn't there any more. They would get wise. They would know someone blew the whistle.

Aiuppa. Fine. The tables would be there. The game would be there, but the money wouldn't be on the table [so it couldn't be seized]. Do you follow me? I'll never embarrass you, never hurt you. I can be nice to you. I can help you. I can decorate the mahogany a bit. You know what I mean? I can help with the payments on the new car. I can see that you are taken care of every month. I can see that every month there is a little worldly goods for you. . . . If you walked into a place and saw me there and your superior said, "Pinch him," I never even met you. Go ahead and pinch me. I go along with the show.

Shaw. I kick you with the side of the shoe.

Aiuppa. Now you're catching on. Are you with me now?

Shaw. I guess.

Aiuppa then said he would obtain from inside sources a transcript of Shaw's secret grand jury testimony in the John Carr bribery case, so that Shaw could study it and avoid offering contradictory testimony at the upcoming trial. Aiuppa also made arrangements for Shaw to telephone him to warn of impending gambling raids. A short time after the meeting ended, Bergbreiter appeared at Shaw's home and gave him a $500 down payment on the $2,000 bribe offered by Aiuppa. During the next few weeks, Shaw talked several more times to Bergbreiter and each time the conversation was recorded. But, about a month after Shaw's meeting with Aiuppa and Bergbreiter, it became apparent that information about the potential bribery case against Aiuppa was being leaked to him by someone on the vice squad.

Late one night, as Shaw arrived home, he was confronted by Bergbreiter. "Listen, I hear you were wired for sound when you met Joey," Bergbreiter snapped.

"You crazy?" Shaw replied. "Not me."

"Joey [Aiuppa] learned that there was a guy under your crawlspace."

"You're kidding."

"And Joey learned that a helicopter was used for surveillance on him when he met with you."

"Well, they must be watching me. They wouldn't be watching you."

"Joey don't want to see you again until he gets a chance to test you."

In view of the evident leak of information from the vice squad, Shaw's superiors instructed him to break off his dealings with Aiuppa and Bergbreiter. Meanwhile, they launched an investigation to find the source of the leak. Sheriff Richard B. Ogilvie ordered all members of the vice squad to take lie-detector tests on whether they had given information to Aiuppa. Two officers refused to submit to the tests. They were at first suspended for thirty days and later fired.

Aiuppa and Bergbreiter were indicted on charges of offering bribes to Detective Shaw. Bergbreiter was convicted and sentenced to two years in prison. But Aiuppa, whose defense relied heavily on the fact that he was not present when Bergbreiter paid Shaw the $500, was acquitted by the judge on grounds of insufficient evidence. John Carr also beat his bribery case, using strategy outlined by Aiuppa in his recorded conversation with Shaw. Carr testified that the $500 he had given Shaw was intended as bond money for Edward Doyle. This version was supported by Doyle. The trial judge, commenting that perhaps Doyle's testimony "could be counted on," found Carr not guilty.

The Suburb of Cicero

It was hardly surprising that Aiuppa's bailiwick, Cicero, should be a center of Mafia activity and attempted corruption. For Cicero is a suburb of Chicago—which, ever since the free-wheeling days of Al Capone, has been notorious for its ties between the Mob and crooked politicians. Over the years, most incipient investigations of alliances between racketeers and Chicago political figures have been squelched.

There is an abundance of evidence in the files of Federal law-enforcement agencies documenting such corrupt alliances. Two FBI men questioned the alderman, who denied knowing why his name should be on such a list. But he did admit that he and a mobster named Giancana had been friends for many years.

Agents learned that many of the strip-tease joints on South Wabash and South State Streets in Chicago turned over twenty percent of their profits to the Mob. Over and above those amounts, the agents found, each strip joint paid between $2,000 and $3,000 to the alderman through one of his aides.

Agents compiled evidence that a second alderman was an associate of such mobsters as Giancana, Humphreys, and Alex. They also found that a third alderman was a partner in a finance company with a key Mob loanshark, Sam Lewis.

Other evidence compiled by the Federal men disclosed that an alderman named Benjamin F. Lewis was sharing in the gambling profits of a syndicate racketeer, Leonard "Lenny" Patrick. The secret government file reported that "Ben Lewis . . . is Lenny Patrick's boy and does not do anything without Patrick's okay. Anyone who operates a book [bookmaking enterprise] in the Twenty-fourth Ward

[Lewis's district] is required to give Patrick fifty percent of the proceeds from all operations. . . ." For example, a secret government file contains, among other things, the following items:

Federal agents learned that about forty bookmakers were operating in Chicago's Loop area and that, before a bookie could open shop there, he first had to make proper connections with Gus Alex or a certain alderman. Alex, the Mob boss of the Loop area and a leading political fixer, formerly was an underworld gunman and protégé of the late mobster Jake "Greasy Thumb" Guzik. The alderman is a power in the local Democratic machine.

A confidential informant later told agents that the alderman was the politician most frequently used by such racketeers as Alex, Murray "the Camel" Humphreys, and Frank Ferraro to serve as intermediary in reaching other public officials and judges. The alderman "assumes a subservient attitude when in the company of the above-mentioned hoodlums and there is no doubt that he considers their orders to be mandates to him," the secret government file said.

When top Chicago Mafia boss Sam "Momo" Giancana returned from a trip to Mexico, FBI agents discovered he was carrying a sheet of paper listing the names of fifteen of the city's major racketeers plus those of the alderman and of a local Democratic Party official. Alderman Lewis later reportedly had a falling out with the Mob. In the end, he was found murdered in gangland fashion at his political headquarters—with his wrists handcuffed above his head and three bullet holes in the back of his skull. Despite a $10,000 reward offered by Chicago Mayor Richard Daley, who described Lewis as a "superior alderman," the murder has gone unsolved.

Why, with all the evidence of gangland-political alliances in the hands of its agents, has the Federal government been unable to move effectively against Chicago corruption? The answer rests with the Chicago Democratic machine's national political clout. The machine has consistently been able to apply sufficient pressure in Washington to head off potentially embarrassing investigations.

A former assistant U.S. attorney general, who headed the Justice Department Organized Crime Section, told this writer about a typical example of such obstructionism. He said he once spent a special team of racket-busting Federal agents to Chicago to investigate links between the Mafia and public officials. "We had a great deal of evidence of payoffs to protect syndicate gambling and other rackets," he said. "The Mob had connections all the way to the top—at the Chicago City Hall, the Illinois State House, and in Congress." He said his investigators were impeded at every turn by Chicago officials, members of the local U.S. Attorney's staff (who were on the Justice Department payroll) and even Federal judges—all of whom owed allegiance to the political machine. Finally, he said, a leader of the machine telephoned the White House and got the investigation called off. The racket-busters were recalled to Washington under direct orders from the White House. A short time later, this writer's source said, he resigned from the Justice Department in protest of the political interference with his work.

Making It in New Jersey

While hamstrung in Chicago, Federal investigators have kept busy exposing racketeers' corruption of public officials on other fronts. In New Jersey, for example, Federal agents uncovered perhaps the most widespread Mob domination of local government in recent years. In case after case in city after city across the state, the Federal men revealed the Mob's blatant control over scores of politicians and law-enforcement officers. As the chief Federal prosecutor in the state, U.S. Attorney Frederick B. Lacey, put it: "Organized crime is, in the vernacular, taking us over."

First indications of the Mob's broad-scale corruption of New Jersey politicians were provided by electronic "bugs" secretly planted by FBI agents in the headquarters of several of the state's leading racketeers—including Simone "Sam the Plumber" De Cavalcante, boss of a Mafia family and member of the Mafia's ruling national commission, and Angelo "Ray" De Carlo, a family *caporegime* (captain). Thousands of pages of mobsters' conversations, monitored by the "bugs," were compiled by the FBI and eventually made public on orders from a Federal judge. They disclosed an almost incredible pattern of Mob control of local government in various parts of the state. The Mafia bosses picked the candidates for public office, put up much of the campaign money, dictated government policy, and approved appointments of subordinate officials. Mayors, councilmen, commissioners, judges, sheriffs, police chiefs, and other officials all owed allegiance to the Mob. Together, they looted the public treasuries, extorted money from companies seeking government contracts, and promoted virtually every form of racketeering operation.

The best-known official implicated in the recorded conversations was Hugh J. Addonizio, mayor of Newark, the largest city in New Jersey and the thirteenth largest city in the United States. Before his election as mayor, Addonizio had served fourteen years in Congress. The bugged conversations at De Carlo's headquarters revealed that the Mafia was deeply involved in Addonizio's capture of the mayor's office. Not only did De Carlo and his associates contribute money to Addonizio's campaign; they also campaigned secretly on his behalf and drove rival candidates out of the race through bribes and threats.

One monitored conversation about the Addonizio campaign, for example, involved De Carlo and three of his subordinates—Joseph "Little Joe" De Benedictis, Carl "Leash" Silesia and Joseph "Joe the Indian" Polverino. An FBI summary of part of the discussion disclosed that De Benedictis showed De Carlo a sample poster prepared for use in the campaign. De Benedictis said he planned to have 25,000 of them printed. "The poster will read 'Addonizio for Mayor' and they intend to 'plaster the city' with them," the FBI summary said. "Joe [De Benedictis] asked Ray [De Carlo] if he would share the expense of printing and De Carlo said he would—taking it out of the money he intended to give Addonizio anyway. Joe said they would put two guys in each ward who would put up the signs at night."

The transcript of the bugged conversation described how the Mob went about driving rival candidates out of the race against Addonizio. De Benedictis told of paying a $5,000 bribe to one such rival, Michael "Mickey" Bontempo, to withdraw from the campaign. But then another potential candidate arrived on the scene. The transcript contained the following exchange:

> *De Benedictis.* Now, I got another job for you—and this is a real one. Nick Caputo's gonna file [as a candidate against Addonizio]. . . . I heard about it, so I called him up yesterday. I said, "Nick, is it true you're gonna file?" He said, "Yeah, I'm gonna file." I said, "Why, you jerk, do you know what you're doing?" He said, "Well, I can't win but I can force a runoff. Let

them spend another hundred thousand." I said, "Well, whose money do you think you're spending? You're spending all your friends' money! Are you out of your mind?" So I talked him into a meeting with Hughie [Addonizio]. So we talk it over. I let them go into a room together to iron it out. Now, we need this guy out! We gotta get him out! I talked to him again this morning. What he's asking for is out of this world! This is just between the four of us—he wants to be the administrator of Newark [a major appointive job in the city government]. So, anyhow, I talked to Hughie this morning again. He said, "Joe, this guy's out of his mind. He wants to ruin the campaign." I had told Nick [Caputo], "You S.O.B., you're gonna pull this?" He said, "Well, I'm only looking out for myself." So I said, "I'll tell you what I'm gonna do with you—I'm gonna break your two legs. Don't blame . . . any [other] tough guys. *I'm* gonna break your legs for you if you file. I'm warning you now. I'll be the guy to break your legs."

De Carlo.   If he does, we'll go and break his legs.

[De Carlo then suggested that those who behaved the way Caputo or Bontempo did should be promised anything merely to get rid of them. After the election, he said, they could be forced to keep quiet and the promises wouldn't have to be kept. Such means could have been used with Bontempo, De Carlo said, and the Mob could have been spared paying the $5,000 bribe.]

De Benedictis.   I haven't heard from him [Bontempo] since the day he came over to the house and I gave him that money.

De Carlo.   Well, one thing, he came out for Hughie, at least.

De Benedictis.   He says he's neutral.

De Carlo.   Oh, I thought he came out for Hughie.

De Benedictis.   No.

De Carlo.   Why don't you make him come out for Hughie?

De Benedictis.   We don't want him to come out for Hughie because he's made enemies. Let him go; this way he's out.

[The FBI summary said participants in the meeting went on to describe how they had lined up support for Addonizio from various influential politicians. "The group stressed the importance of insisting that all Italians vote for Addonizio," the summary said.]

After Addonizio's election, there were numerous references in the recorded conversations to his cooperation with the Mob. At one point, De Carlo was overheard telling De Benedictis: "Hughie [Addonizio] helped us along. He give us the city." At other times, De Carlo was heard receiving requests from men who wanted him to intercede with Addonizio on their behalf. Once, for example, a Newark police official, Fred Guidera, complained to De Carlo that he was extremely bitter because Addonizio had not appointed him the city's police director. "He claimed to have played an essential part in Addonizio's election and that he should not have been spurned," said an FBI summary of the conversation. "He said Addonizio had told him in front of his friends that the man who produces would get the job and on that basis he deserves it more than Spina [Addonizio's appointee as police director, Dominick Spina]. De Carlo reminded him that he was promised nothing and that he is upset over nothing. De Carlo ridiculed the claim that Guidera played a major part in the campaign. . . . De Carlo pointed out that Spina worked hard for Addonizio and brought him lots of money. De Carlo attempted to mollify Guidera—saying that, if he'd just keep his mouth shut, he'll make more money than before."

Later, there were various references made by these questionable characters in the recorded conversations to their claims that Police Director Spina, among others, had been taking payoffs. On one occasion, the electronic "bug" recorded a discussion involving De Carlo and two of his associates, Irving Berlin, and Pete Landusco. De Carlo berated Berlin for attending a meeting with Mayor Addonizio without first notifying De Carlo. This exchange followed:

De Carlo.   How come you knew Hughie was going over there and you didn't call me up, Irv?

Berlin.   You told me he [Addonizio] shouldn't make any appointments down there [the New Jersey shore area]—that you wouldn't go down there.

[Berlin claimed he had tried to reach De Carlo to tell him about the meeting, but had failed. The conversation then turned to the claim that Spina, whose nickname is Dick, had apparently been taking payoffs directly from other racketeers—instead of working through middlemen. De Carlo mentioned that a mobster, Anthony "Tony Bananas" Caponigro, was planning to open a dice game in Newark.]

Berlin.   He [apparently Caponigro] brought up the fact about Dick's [Spina] the one who's been taking money direct. He said he's waiting for his own party to rectify everything within thirty days. I went in the other room, the bedroom, with Hughie, to talk about something else.

De Carlo.   Who gave Bananas [Caponigro] all the authority to talk to Dick?

Berlin.   What do you mean authority? He just had a date to come over, so he came over.

De Carlo.   He had to give somebody a call if he said he had a date.

Berlin.   He did call!

De Carlo.   He's [obscene]!

Berlin.   Well, I don't want to get in the middle.

De Carlo.   He [Caponigro] can straighten out his own. We'll straighten out our own.

How well anybody straightened out his own payoff problems is not made clear in the FBI's tapes of the monitored conversations. When transcripts of the tapes were made public, Spina denied taking payoffs. Eventually, however, Spina was indicted on charges of malfeasance. The grand jury accused him of allowing the Mob to operate gambling rackets without police interference. But, when the case came to trial, a judge ordered a directed verdict of acquittal on grounds of insufficient evidence. Mayor Addonizio, though, did not get off so easily as Spina.

On December 17, 1969, a Federal grand jury indicted Addonizio and fourteen other men—including ten public officials and a Mafia leader—on charges of sharing in $1.5 million worth of kickbacks extorted from contractors doing business with the city. The Mafia leader was Anthony "Tony Boy" Boiardo, son of an old-line Mafioso, Ruggerio "Richie the Boot" Boiardo. The other defendants included three Newark city councilmen, four former councilmen, the city's director of public works, his predecessor and the former city corporation counsel. The indictment charged Addonizio, Boiardo, and their codefendants with conspiring "with each other and with other persons to affect interstate commerce by extortion." It said the conspiracy involved thwarting "construction undertaken on behalf of the city of Newark in order to obtain the property of contractors, engineers, and others working on certain municipal construction by [instilling] fear of financial injury." Stripped of its legal verbiage, the indictment accused the defendants of shaking down the contractors for payoffs by threatening to withhold city contracts from them. In a separate indictment, Addonizio, Boiardo, and ten others were accused of income-tax evasion.

The charges against Addonizio and the other officials would have been regarded as sensational even if there had been no Mafia connection with the case. But the affair was made still more volatile by Boiardo's role. For not only was Boiardo a Mafia leader; he was a self-described Mob killer. In one of the conversations at Angelo De Carlo's headquarters that had been monitored by the FBI, Boiardo had been overheard boasting about a murder he and his father had committed. "How about the time we hit [murdered] the little Jew," Boiardo told De Carlo. (The victim was not further identified.) "The Boot [Boiardo's father] hit him with a hammer," Boiardo said. "The guy goes down and he comes up. So I got a crowbar this big. Eight shots in the head."

In the period following the indictment of Boiardo, Addonizio, and their codefendants, suspicion arose that renewed Mob violence might affect the outcome of the case. A key prosecution witness was placed under twenty-four-hour guard after reporting that Boiardo had threatened him. A defendant was killed in a mysterious automobile crash hours after meeting with U.S. Attorney Frederick Lacey and offering to cooperate with the prosecution. Another auto crash took the life of a cooperative government witness. One of the indicted former city councilmen died of what was officially described as a heart attack and various other figures in the case claimed to be suffering from newly acquired ailments of one sort or another. Although the sheer number of such incidents seemed to indicate that something more than mere coincidence might be involved, the authorities were unable to prove foul play.

By the time Addonizio went to trial in mid-1970, only seven of the original fourteen codefendants were in court with him to face the charges. The remainder either were dead or their cases had been severed from Addonizio's because of claims of illness or other reasons. And during the course of the trial two other defendants, including Tony Boy Boiardo, had their cases severed because of what were described as heart ailments. Those whose cases were severed were scheduled to be tried separately at later dates.

When the trial began, prosecutor Lacey told the jurors in his opening summary that the government would prove a dummy bank account had been used to funnel extorted funds to Addonizio and his codefendants. He said a group headed by Boiardo had been responsible for setting up the dummy account. The Boiardo group, Lacey said, was also responsible for arranging the terms of kickbacks from contractors to city officials—so that the officials would "not have to meet the [extortion] victims except under extraordinary circumstances."

Mayor Addonizio, who had refused to relinquish his office after being indicted and was running for re-election even while standing trial, immediately issued a press release calling Lacey's opening statement "the most fantastic story I have ever heard." The release claimed: "There is not a single iota of evidence linking me with such an incredible scheme in any way and there never will be be-

cause I have never been involved with Mr. Boiardo or anybody else in any illegal manner whatsoever."

But Lacey and his chief assistant prosecutor, Herbert J.
Stern, promptly set about proving otherwise. Among their
first witnesses was a Newark businessman, Irving Kantor,
who testified that Boiardo's group had induced him to
open the dummy bank account under the name of the
Kantor Supply Company. Following instructions from
Boiardo and his associates, Kantor said, he then sent false
bills on the supply company's stationery to contractors
doing business with the city. The bills, which referred to
nonexistent supplies ostensibly sold to the contractors,
were made out in the exact amounts of kickbacks being
made by the contractors to city officials. The contractors
sent checks in the required amounts to Kantor, who testified he then deposited them in the dummy account and
converted them into cash. After deducting a small percentage for his services, Kantor said, he turned the cash over
to a Boiardo subordinate, Joseph Biancone, who was a defendant in the trial, or to some other agent designated by
Boiardo. The cash was then divided among members of
the Boiardo group and the city officials taking the kickbacks. All told, Kantor said, he funneled more than $1
million from the contractors to the politicians and racketeers.

Kantor was followed to the stand by the prosecution's
chief witness, Paul Rigo, an engineering contractor who
had been identified as one of the main victims of the extortion scheme. Rigo had been kept under guard by Federal
marshals and agents after reporting that his life had been
threatened by Boiardo. Rigo testified that he had first met
Addonizio when another contractor asked him to give the
mayor his expert advice in a controversy over what kind of
pipe should be used on a city sewer project. The dispute

concerned the relative merits of steel and rubber-jointed pipe versus concrete and rubber-jointed pipe. Rigo said he explained to Addonizio why the steel and rubber pipe was better, but that the mayor replied that "his people thought they could get away with rubber and concrete." He said Addonizio added: "You know, I have an interest in Mario Gallo; he makes rubber and concrete pipe, and that's what we're going to use." (Gallo, a member of Tony Boy Boiardo's group, was the defendant killed in an automobile crash shortly after agreeing to cooperate with the prosecution.)

A few months later, Rigo testified, he again met with the mayor at the Newark City Hall. Also present were two other defendants in the case, City Public Works Director Anthony La Morte, who later became executive director of the Newark Municipal Utilities Authority, and Norman Schiff, then city corporation counsel. La Morte told the mayor at the meeting that he had discussed a projected emergency extension of the Newark water-main system with Boiardo and that Boiardo had "approved" the project, Rigo testified. The idea of city officials having to get the approval of a Mafia leader to undertake a municipal construction project seemed astonishing to some, but Rigo mentioned it as matter-of-factly as if it were standard procedure in Newark.

Rigo said Addonizio was "upset" because pipe manufactured by Mario Gallo was not going to be used on the new project. Steel and rubber-jointed pipe provided by a company called Lockjoint would be required. Rigo quoted the mayor as saying: "Tony [Boiardo] had better figure out a way to get something [a kickback] out of Lockjoint." Corporation Counsel Schiff complained that Boiardo couldn't get "enough." But Rigo said Addonizio replied: "Tony will figure out a way to get enough."

Later, Rigo testified, he began personal dealings with Boiardo. He said Public Works Director La Morte took him to meet Boiardo after emphasizing: "This is the most important meeting you'll ever have. This is the man who really runs Newark!" Again, while the notion of a Mafia leader being described by an important city official as "the man who really runs Newark" might have seemed extraordinary, Rigo took it in stride. By the time of his first meeting with Boiardo, Rigo had obtained a city contract for work on a sewer project known as the Southside Interceptor. He said Boiardo told him at the meeting that he would have to kick back ten percent of his gross earnings on the job. He testified the following exchange then occurred:

Rigo. I can't pay ten percent.
Boiardo. You will pay—and in cash.
Rigo. I can't. What do we get for the money?
Boiardo. There are a lot of mouths to feed in city hall. I take care of the mayor and the city council and anybody else that needs taking care of.

Rigo testified that he tried to work the kickbacks down to five percent, but that Boiardo told him: "Look what happened to Killam [Elson T. Killam, a consulting engineer who had formerly held city contracts.] He's not in Newark [any more], and he's going to sweat a long time before he gets what the city owes him." Under Boiardo's pressure, Rigo said, he eventually agreed to pay the ten-percent kickbacks.

After receiving the first of his payments from the city, Rigo testified, he began paying the kickbacks to members of Boiardo's group and directly to Public Works Director La Morte. Later, however, payments from the city to Rigo started lagging. Rigo testified he complained about the problem to La Morte, who sent him to Addonizio. The mayor, in turn, told him to see Boiardo. Even this incredible situation—the mayor of the nation's thirteenth largest city referring a contractor to a Mafia leader about collecting debts from the city—did not faze Rigo. He dutifully went to Boiardo, who complained that Rigo's kickback payments themselves were lagging. Rigo testified he told Boiardo that he hadn't been able to keep up the kickback payments because of the city's delay in paying him. He said Boiardo told him: "Pay the ten percent or I'll break both your legs!" Anxious to keep his legs intact, Rigo scraped together $30,000—which he testified he put in a paper bag and handed to a member of the Boiardo group, codefendant Ralph Vicaro.

Rigo said he continued making kickbacks through Boiardo and his subordinates for several years, and periodically was granted new contracts by the city. Eventually, he testified, La Morte told him during a conversation at city hall that Boiardo was in a "sensitive situation" and could no longer handle distribution of the kickbacks to Addonizio and other officials. He quoted La Morte as telling him that Boiardo was "desirous of me making payments" directly to the officials involved.

At the time, Rigo was seeking a city contract for work on a new project in the city's watershed area. He testified La Morte told him that, in order to get the contract drawn and the appropriations for the work approved, he would have to pay Addonizio and the eight city councilmen $10,000 each. In addition, La Morte wanted $25,000 for himself because he was "the department head" approving the contract. La Morte felt that Corporation Counsel Schiff "should have something, too," Rigo said. Prosecutor Stern asked whether he wanted to make these payoffs.

"No," Rigo replied. "But if we didn't we'd have lost God knows how much money and, in addition, there was always the fear."

He said he began making the demanded kickbacks in stages directly to the officials, and the watershed contract was awarded to him. Consulting a diary in which he had made coded entries referring to the kickbacks, Rigo ticked off a seemingly endless list of payoffs. A $5,000 payoff to La Morte, for example, was indicated with the code letter "S"—representing La Morte's nickname, "Sonny." A $2,000 payoff to Addonizio was noted in the diary as "P plus 2"—with the letter "P" standing for the mayor's code name, "the Pope." Rigo testified he had made that payoff to Addonizio in the mayor's office with nobody else present. When prosecutor Stern asked him to identify the payoff recipient, Rigo pointed across the courtroom and Addonizio rose from his seat with a faint smirk. On the same day he paid Addonizio the $2,000, Rigo said, he paid the eight city councilmen $1,000 each.

And, although Boiardo was no longer handling distribution of the kickbacks to the officials, the Mafioso and his associates continued to get a cut of the bribery proceeds. Rigo testified he handed over $10,500 to codefendant Ralph Vicaro for the Boiardo group, among other payments. Later, he said, he went to city hall with a paper sack containing additional payoffs for the public officials. He took with him his secretary, Norris Whitehead, and his bookkeeper, Charles Fallon. They counted up the money "in a little back room in the public works department" and put it in envelopes marked with appropriate initials, Rigo said. He and Fallon then distributed the money to the recipients—including Addonizio, La Morte, and the councilmen.

During his conversations with Addonizio, Rigo testified,

Addonizio explained why he had retired from Congress and run for mayor. He said the mayor told him: "There's no money in Washington, but you can make a million dollars in Newark." (If the quote can be accepted as true, it would seem to indicate that Addonizio lacked ingenuity while serving in Congress. For, as later chapters of this book will show, there are also millions to be made in Washington by crooked politicians who play ball with the Mob.)

In any event, there seemed little doubt that Addonizio had prospered in the mayor's office. All told, Rigo testified that he had paid $253,500 in kickbacks to the mayor, other officials, Boiardo and members of the Mafia leader's group. In addition, he described numerous contributions he had made to political campaigns in New Jersey, New York and elsewhere. He told, for example, of giving Boiardo $10,000 in cash for use in Addonizio's 1966 mayoralty race. He said he had also made a $15,000 contribution to an unsuccessful campaign by Abraham D. Beame (now New York City comptroller) for the New York mayoralty. At the same time, Rigo testified, he was able to convert checks for another $15,000 into cash at the Beame campaign headquarters for use in making kickbacks in Newark. (Both Rigo and other witnesses explained that obtaining cash for untraceable payoffs was a major problem confronting contractors involved in the Newark kickbacks.)

Under cross-examination, Rigo conceded that he had made what appeared to be an illegal $1,000 contribution to the 1968 campaign of President Nixon and Vice President Spiro T. Agnew. In response to an appeal for funds, he said, he had mailed a $1,000 check from his contracting firm, Constrad, Inc., to the Nixon-Agnew campaign committee. One of the defense attorneys, Thomas Wadden, pointed out that Federal law prohibits corporations from making contributions to election campaigns for Federal offices. The law provides that any corporate officer who consents to such a contribution and any person who accepts it is subject to a year's imprisonment and a $1,000 fine. "Willful" violation of the law increases the penalty to a possible ten years in prison and a $2,000 fine. Rigo testified that he was unaware of the law when he sent the contribution. Any possibility of his prosecution for violation of the law seemed to be ruled out by the fact that the government had promised him immunity from prosecution for any crime about which he testified in the Addonizio case. As for possible prosecution of those who accepted the check for the Nixon-Agnew campaign, that also seemed unlikely since the endorsement on the check consisted merely of a rubber-stamped impression reading: "Nixon-Agnew Committee."

The cross-examination of Rigo developed further testimony indicating that he had taken pains to maintain liaison with both Republican and Democratic officials. While making contributions to both parties and paying kickbacks to members of Addonizio's Democratic administration, he said, he kept a local Republican official, Miss Jean Hunt, on his company's payroll "for several years" although she did no work. When he became frightened by threats from the Mob and decided to blow the whistle on those taking part in the kickback scheme, he said, he asked for help from Walter Foran, Republican chairman of Hunterden County. Foran put Rigo in touch with a White House aide, who made an appointment for him with Justice Department officials in Washington. That appointment resulted in his agreement to become the government's star witness in the case against Addonizio.

During the cross-examination, Rigo admitted that he

had falsified bills submitted to the city as part of the kick-back scheme. He testified that the city still owed him $1.9 million for unpaid bills and that he had sued to collect the money. "I've sat here and admitted to padding these things," he told defense attorney Wadden. "I think I've thrown the whole thing [the $1.9 million] out the window."

Other prosecution witnesses substantiated parts of Rigo's story and provided further testimony about kick-backs to Addonizio and his codefendants. After the prosecution rested its case, Addonizio took the stand in his own defense—becoming the only defendant to testify in the case.

Addonizio denied all the charges of wrongdoing, claiming repeatedly that Rigo and other witnesses against him had lied. He denied that meetings in his city hall office described by Rigo and others had ever taken place. He also denied taking any kickbacks, having knowledge of any or making the statement that he had left Congress to run for mayor because "you can make a million dollars in Newark." Under cross-examination by prosecutor Lacey, however, Addonizio conceded maintaining a long-time friendship with Mafia leader Boiardo. He admitted attending by invitation Boiardo's wedding twenty years earlier, at which the best man was Gerardo "Jerry" Catena, a member of the Mafia's national commission. He also admitted dining with Boiardo and attending parties with him in New York, Puerto Rico, and Florida during the five years preceding the trial. Addonizio never satisfactorily explained why, as a congressman and mayor, he felt justified in carrying on a friendship with a high-ranking Mafioso.

He testified that, on various trips to Puerto Rico and Florida, his hotel bills and "perhaps" some of his gambling losses had been paid by "old personal friends."

Among these friends, he said, were Vincent Salerno, owner of a Newark optical firm; Herman Gering, who sold his plastics business "a few years ago for several million dollars" to Monsanto Chemical Company and had recently died; and Harold Lockheimer, a wealthy real-estate and construction executive.

Despite having such moneyed friends and despite having more than $45,000 in available cash in his bank accounts, Addonizio conceded under Lacey's questioning that he had "borrowed" $14,000 from Paul Rigo during the summer of 1968. He said he had given Rigo promissory notes for the money and had paid them off in 1969. But Lacey drew from him the admission that the promissory notes had not been given at the time of the original "loan"—that they had been drawn up some months later and backdated. Lacey contended that the notes had been a subterfuge—a belated effort to make the transaction appear normal after a grand jury had begun investigating Addonizio's dealings—but Addonizio insisted no irregularity had been involved.

Since Addonizio was the only defendant to take the stand, the presentation of the defense case was limited. The few witnesses called by the defense were unable to rebut much of the prosecution case. One, in fact, unexpectedly bolstered the government's case. The witness, Ferdinand J. Biunno, former business administrator for the city of Newark, had been called by the defense in an attempt to cast doubt on Rigo's testimony. Instead, Biunno generally supported Rigo and provided information, not covered in Rigo's testimony, that further damaged the defense cause. Biunno testified that he and former Public Works Director La Morte, while on city payroll, had allowed Rigo to pay for airline tickets, lodging, and other expenses when they and their wives attended a convention in Miami. Prosecutor Lacey introduced evidence that La Morte had collected expense money from the city for the trip, even though Rigo had paid his way.

After the defense rested its case, defense attorney Bernard Hellring argued on Addonizio's behalf in his jury summation that the outcome of the trial came down to whose word should be believed—Addonizio's or Rigo's. While characterizing Rigo as a liar, Hellring said of Addonizio: "He took the stand readily and voluntarily. He never flinched, he never hesitated, he never double-talked. He bared his life." Referring to the fact that Addonizio had admitted gambling at both casinos and race tracks, Hellring argued: "He told grimly and forthrightly of his Saturdays at the race track." The defense lawyer said Addonizio had also been forthright in discussing his association with Boiardo, despite the political risks involved. He reviewed Addonizio's years in Congress and the mayor's office and "his exemplary life" with his wife and six children. "His record stands untouched except by the charges in this case," Hellring said. By contrast, he described Rigo as a man devoted to "high living" and "booze for everybody"—a man who "padded his bills to the city."

Other defense attorneys argued that, while money had changed hands between Rigo and some of the defendants, there was no extortion involved. "Rigo paid with a smile," said defense lawyer Patrick Wall, representing Boiardo subordinate Ralph Vicaro. Thomas Dyson, representing Boiardo aide Joseph Biancone, argued that the payoffs were "mere voluntary payments, unaccompanied by fear of financial loss." He said they were paid "willingly and happily, because there was enough [money] for all and not subject to inspection by Internal Revenue." John W. Noonan, representing former City Corporation Counsel Philip Gordon, said the testimony was "entirely consistent with voluntary payments." Noonan said Gordon had admitted in a signed statement that he had taken $8,000 from Rigo while serving as corporation counsel. "Rigo wanted to be on good terms with Gordon because he had a good thing going," Noonan argued. All the defense lawyers contended that there was a difference between accepting a bribe and extorting one. The defendants were not charged with accepting bribes but with extortion, they pointed out.

Prosecutor Lacey, in his summation, countered that the defendants had been guilty of "cold-blooded, calculating, contemptuous corruption in the largest city of this state." Describing Addonizio as "a man of easy conscience and flabby pride" and a "frequenter of casinos and race tracks," Lacey said the defense had suggested that Addonizio had "built a wall of ignorance" around the mayor's office. "But the stench of corruption would have penetrated any such wall," he argued. Lacey said the defendants had belonged to two mutually supporting groups—one composed of racketeers headed by Boiardo and the other composed of public officials headed by Addonizio, who were "insulated and protected" by Boiardo's group. Lacey pointed out that, in leaving Congress, Addonizio had said publicly he was returning to his home town to save it from deterioration. Not only did the deterioration continue during Addonizio's mayoralty, Lacey said, but "in a few years this conspiracy was flourishing."

The jury deliberated the case for five and a half hours, then found all the defendants guilty on all sixty-four counts in the indictment. Addonizio slumped in his chair, with his head in his hands, as the verdict was announced.

"I can only say I'm terribly disappointed," he said outside the court. "I testified on the stand and I told my story. The jury evidently didn't believe me."

On July 22, 1970, Addonizio and his codefendants stood before Federal District Judge George H. Barlow for sentencing. The judge declared sternly that Addonizio had committed crimes of "monumental proportion that tore at the very heart of our civilized society and our form of representative government." As Addonizio bowed his head, Barlow continued: "It is impossible to estimate the impact of these criminal acts upon the decent citizens of Newark and, indeed, of this state in terms of their frustration, despair, and disillusionment. "How can we calculate the cynicism engendered in our citizens, including our young people, by these men? How does one measure the erosion of confidence in our system of government and the diminished respect for our laws occasioned by these men? These very men who, as government officials, inveighed against crime in the streets pursued their own criminal activities in the corridors of city hall."

Barlow said the enormity of Addonizio's guilt could "scarcely be exaggerated" because "an intricate conspiracy of this magnitude could never have succeeded without his approval and participation." Any good works Addonizio might have done during his years of public service must be disregarded in considering the seriousness of his crimes, the judge said. "These were no ordinary criminal acts. These crimes were not the product of a moment of weakness nor inspired by the defendants' financial circumstances nor the result of some emotional compulsion. Rather, they represented a pattern of continuous extortion over a period of many years, claiming many victims and touching many more lives. Moreover, the corruption disclosed here is compounded by the frightening alliance of criminal elements and public officials."

The judge then sentenced Addonizio, La Morte, and Biancone to ten years in Federal prison and Vicaro to twelve years. Gordon was given a lighter sentence, at least partly because he had admitted taking money from Rigo. The defendants, still professing their innocence, filed appeals and vowed that they would ultimately be vindicated. They are out on bail, pending the outcome of their appeals, at this writing. For Addonizio, the conviction and sentence were not the only setbacks resulting from the case. During the trial, the voters of Newark had cast him out of office—rejecting his re-election bid and electing a former city engineer, Kenneth Gibson, as mayor. Gibson, the first Negro mayor in the city's history, said after two months in office that he'd discovered the corruption of the previous administration had been much greater than he'd suspected. He said his aides had found that virtually every contract signed by the city in recent years had been inflated by at least ten percent to allow for kickbacks to officials. And, although he had pledged to clean up the administration, he soon learned that the Mob was counting on business as usual at City Hall. Within weeks of taking office, Gibson said, he was offered $31,000 in bribes—including $15,000 to appoint a man favored by racketeers as police director. Gibson said he had turned down the offers, but that there were still many men holding city office who showed no intention of giving up their alliances with the underworld.

Meanwhile, in other cities across the state, fresh developments almost daily showed that the Mob's grip on politics, government, and law enforcement was just as strong elsewhere as in Newark. "No one is immune," said Andrew F. Phelan, director of New Jersey's State Investigation Commission. "Organized crime has affected the lives of every man, woman, and child in New Jersey."

In the city of West New York, New Jersey, Mayor John R. Armellino pleaded guilty in 1971 to conspiring with Joseph "Joe Bayonne" Zicarelli, the Mafia boss of the northern Hudson County area, to protect Mob gambling operations. Armellino admitted taking payoff of $1,000 a week from Zicarelli. The mayor was sentenced to four years in prison and Zicarelli drew a twelve-year term. In a separate action, Zicarelli was indicted on charges of evading Federal taxes on more than $1 million worth of income during a two-year period. In still another case, Zicarelli was indicted with the Republican chairman of Hudson County, John B. Theurer, on charges of conspiring to gain the appointment of a county prosecutor who would protect the Mob's gambling interests. Theurer pleaded guilty, but Zicarelli pleaded not guilty in both the conspiracy case and the tax case. The charges against him are still pending at this writing.

In Jersey City, Mayor Thomas J. Whelan and seven other public officials were convicted in 1971 of conspiring to extort money from companies doing business with the city and county governments. There was testimony that they extorted at least $182,000 by delaying the movement of materials, equipment, and manpower to construction sites until the money was paid. There was also testimony that they caused $700,000 worth of bearer bonds to be transported illegally from an investment banking house in New York to Jersey City. The defendants, insisting they were innocent, appealed their convictions and are free on bail at this writing while their appeals are pending. Also indicted in the case was former Jersey City Mayor John V. Kenny, the Democratic boss of Hudson County and one of the most powerful political figures in the state. His case was severed from that of the other defendants because he was ill at the time of their trial. Kenny has pleaded not guilty, and his case is pending at this writing.

In the small town of Old Tappan, Police Chief Charles G. Schuh and all four other members of his police force were indicted in 1970 on charges of taking payoffs from a Mafia enforcer, Vincent "the Chin" Gigante. A prosecutor said Gigante paid the money to obtain information about an investigation of his Mob activities being conducted by another law-enforcement agency. Gigante had previously been tried and acquitted on charges of trying to assassinate gambler Frank Costello, but had served time for his part in the narcotics operations of the late Mafia "boss of all bosses," Vito Genovese. He had been described as one of Genovese's top lieutenants and had continued to hold an important position in the Mafia family headed by Genovese's successor, Jerry Catena. Gigante and the police officers pleaded not guilty to the payoff charges. Their cases are pending.

In Long Branch, the State Investigation Commission charged during lengthy hearings that the Mob dominated local government and law enforcement. A former Long Branch city manager, Richard J. Bowen, who had been fired because he had not worked "harmoniously" with the city council, testified at the commission hearings that he had been offered his job back by Monmouth County Mafia boss Anthony "Little Pussy" Russo. Bowen said Russo told him he "controlled" the city council and could order the city manager's reinstatement. If Bowen returned to City Hall, Russo was quoted as saying, there would be "plenty for everybody—a piece for everyone." Long Branch Mayor Paul Nastasio told the commission he had no knowledge of organized crime in the city, but then admitted that one of his chief political supporters was Attilio Agnellino, owner of a lounge frequently used as a meeting place by Mafia figures. Commission Chairman William Hyland charged at the hearings that "prominent organized crime figures were operating in Long Branch in an atmosphere of relative security from law-enforcement pressure."

In Elizabeth, Union County District Court Judge Ralph De Vita was convicted in 1970 of obstructing justice by offering a $10,000 payoff to a prosecutor to dismiss a case against two underworld figures charged with bookmaking and attempted bribery of a policeman. Prosecutor Michael R. Imbriani testified that De Vita told him the indictment against the defendants "has got to be killed" and that, if it were, "there are ten big ones in it for you." De Vita resigned his judgeship and was disbarred after his conviction.

In Trenton, Mafia leaders from various areas—including Jerry Catena, Angelo Bruno of Philadelphia (whose rackets territory includes parts of New Jersey) and "Little Pussy" Russo—were ordered jailed for contempt when they refused to testify before the State Investigation Commission about their political connections. Other high-ranking Mafiosi, such as Frank "Big Frank Condi" Cocchiaro, went into hiding to avoid having to testify before the commission about political corruption. In September 1971 the U.S. Court of Appeals for the Third Circuit in Philadelphia ordered Catena released and held that New Jersey's witness-immunity law was unconstitutional. Catena's imprisonment had followed his refusal to testify even after being given immunity from prosecution. But the appeals court ruled that New Jersey's law failed to give Catena the blanket immunity required by the Constitution—that it merely protected him against being prosecuted on the basis of his own testimony. If other independent evidence could be obtained about the acts described in his testimony, he could still be prosecuted. U.S. Supreme Court Justice Byron White prevented Catena's immediate release, however, by ordering him kept in jail until the Supreme Court decides the issue. The high court is still considering the case at this writing.

The Mob's blatant control of politics in New Jersey moved Federal prosecutor Frederick Lacey to charge that "the plunder was unmatched by anything in my experience." His investigations led him to conclude that virtually no area in the state was free from rackets domination. He summed up his feelings in six words that might well stand as the credo of Mafia bosses and crooked politicians not only in New Jersey but wherever the Mob seizes power: "Everything has a price on it!"

[4]

Marcus, the Mob,
and the Stud Duck

If there were a hall of fame for Mafia corrupters, a special place of honor (or perhaps dishonor) would no doubt be reserved for a stocky, black-haired, bespectacled mobster named Antonio Corallo. Within a span of seven years, Corallo managed to enmesh himself in three sensational bribery prosecutions involving no lesser figures than a New York State Supreme Court judge, a Federal prosecutor, a key aide to New York Mayor John V. Lindsay, and Democratic Party power broker Carmine De Sapio. Those three prosecutions represented merely the cases in which Corallo got caught. There is no way of telling how many other political fixes he arranged, only to escape undetected.

Until he ran into a string of setbacks in the bribery cases, escaping unscathed had long been the hallmark of Corallo's criminal career. During a thirty-two-year period, he had been arrested fourteen times but convicted only once—and even then let off with a wrist-slapping sentence. His ability to duck out of the clutches of the law had become so renowned that he had won the underworld nickname "Tony Ducks."

Corallo followed a long, rocky road on his journey from sidewalk hoodlum to Mafia fixer with entrée to the paneled offices of the politically powerful. Born on February

12, 1913, he grew up in the tough East Harlem section of Manhattan—breeding ground of numerous Mob figures. As an adolescent, he won a reputation as one of the roughest brawlers in the neighborhood, a young man to be trifled with only at serious peril. The reputation was to stick with him for years. He was arrested for the first time at the age of sixteen, on a charge of grand larceny. As he would do many times later, Corallo beat the rap. His boldness, toughness, and talent for outsmarting the law soon brought him to the attention of Mafia leaders, who recruited him for their organization after giving him a series of criminal assignments to carry out as an entrance examination.

Once in the Mob, Corallo branched out into a wide variety of criminal operations—including labor racketeering, strong-arm enforcement for mobsters with garment-industry interests, loansharking, and narcotics. He was arrested occasionally, on such charges as robbery and larceny, but each time slipped off the hook. When he finally drew his first court conviction, after police caught him with a $150,000 cache of narcotics, a judge handed him a mere six-month jail sentence. After his release, he rose steadily through the Mafia ranks—eventually becoming an underboss in the New York family headed by Thomas "Three Finger Brown" Luchese. It was assumed by many that he would ultimately succeed Luchese as the family boss.

Gradually, Corallo increased his power in the labor rackets until he controlled five Teamster Union locals and various locals of other unions, including the Toy and Novelty Workers Union, the Painters and Decorators Union, the Food Handlers Union, the Conduit Workers Union, and the United Textile Workers. Workers in many of these unions were victimized by "sweetheart" contracts arranged by Corallo and cooperative employers. Some em-

ployers put Corallo on their payrolls to intimidate their
workers into accepting substandard wages and working
conditions. In most cases, Corallo didn't even have to use
strong-arm tactics; the mere knowledge that he was in ca-
hoots with the employer was enough to frighten the workers. When Senator John McClellan's labor rackets committee launched an investigation into Corallo's activities, it
heard testimony that one employer hired Corallo to go
into his place of business once every two weeks or so "and
glare at the employees." The employer added: "All Corallo had to do was enter and just look at them, and that
was enough to keep them at their work." Corallo was
called before the committee, but pleaded the Fifth
Amendment 120 times.

He had become so successful in labor racketeering and
other criminal operations that Mafia boss Luchese gave
him the additional responsibility of serving as the family's
chief corrupter. In that capacity, Corallo moved smoothly
into the netherworld in which mobsters, politicians,
judges, and law-enforcement officers meet on common
ground. Despite his knockabout background, Corallo was
a slick article. He dressed fashionably (favoring dark suits,
shirts with French cuffs and conservative cuff links), spoke
softly and gave the impression of possessing an extremely
quick mind. Before long, he was on a first-name basis with
scores of influential New York political figures. When the
Mob needed a political favor, Corallo was invariably on
the scene—with a fat bankroll.

In 1961 he took on a particularly sensitive assignment.
An associate of the Mob named Sanford "Sandy" Moore,
who had operated a huge jukebox distributing business,
had been indicted on bankruptcy-fraud charges for trying
to hide some of the assets of his defunct company. (The
Mafia and its associates are deeply involved in the jukebox

industry and other coin-machine businesses in various parts of the country, including New York.) Moore realized the FBI had the goods on him and the chances of evading conviction were very slim, but he was determined to avoid a prison sentence. He sought Corallo's help and, with the aid of others, they set about trying to fix the case. In some jurisdictions, that would have been a relatively simple matter for a man with Corallo's connections and talent for corruption. But Moore's case was to come up in Federal district court, and Federal judges were reputed to be virtually impervious to bribes.

As a result, Corallo and his cohorts decided to try to fix the case by other means. They bribed the prosecutor, Elliott Kahaner, chief assistant United States attorney for the Eastern District of New York. Their plan called for Moore to plead guilty and for Kahaner then to recommend that Federal Judge Leo Rayfiel give him a suspended sentence. The plotters feared, however, that Kahaner's recommendation alone might not be sufficient to persuade the judge to let Moore off that easily. So they bribed a prominent New York figure, State Supreme Court Justice J. Vincent Keogh, to join the scheme. Keogh went privately to Rayfiel and, speaking as one judge to another, urged him to give Moore the suspended sentence. (There was never any implication of impropriety by Rayfiel.) Keogh was the brother of Congressman Eugene Keogh, a close political ally of then-President John F. Kennedy. Participants in the bribery scheme said Congressman Keogh was present with his brother at several discussions of the attempt to get Moore a suspended sentence, but Federal authorities insisted the congressman had done nothing illegal.

The plot backfired when word that attempts had been made to fix the case leaked to two other Federal judges, who passed on their information to Judge Rayfiel. Instead of giving Moore the suspended sentence, Rayfiel handed him a three-year prison term. An investigation was launched into the bribery plot. Moore agreed to cooperate with the investigators, in return for a reduction of his prison sentence to one year.

The investigation resulted in the indictment of Mafioso Corallo, Judge Keogh, and prosecutor Kahaner on charges of conspiracy to obstruct justice. Needless to say, the purported criminal association of a State Supreme Court judge and an assistant chief Federal prosecutor with a mobster of Corallo's ilk created a furor. At their trial, Moore and other witnesses testified that a total of $35,000 in bribes had been paid to Keogh and Kahaner. They told how Corallo had helped concoct the plot and raise the bribe money. The three defendants were found guilty and sentenced to two years in prison.

After serving his stretch, Tony Ducks Corallo stepped back into his old Mafia corrupter's role as if he had never been gone. His Mob associates did not hold against him the discovery of the Moore case plot. The fact that Corallo had been able to "buy" two officials as prominent as Keogh and Kahaner was seen as evidence of his high-level connections; the failure of the scheme was blamed on factors beyond his control.

How to Find a Pigeon

When John Lindsay took office as mayor of New York in 1966, Corallo started looking for a pigeon in the new administration—someone who could be corrupted on behalf of the Mob. He soon found his man in James L. Marcus, one of the administration's brightest young stars, who not only held high office but was also a close personal friend of Lindsay. On the surface, Marcus appeared an unlikely choice as a target for corruption. He seemed to have everything going for him—good looks, intelligence, social position, impressive family connections, and the prospect of a brilliant career in public office. His associates had no way of predicting that he would jeopardize all this by consorting with the likes of Tony Ducks Corallo.

Beneath the surface, however, there was a side to Marcus that made him vulnerable; he had been living a lie for years. Although he told friends he had a law degree, the fact was that he had never even been graduated from college. After attending fashionable eastern prep schools, he had dropped out of the University of Pennsylvania in an attempt to make some quick money. His business career had been more ambitious than successful. He claimed an impressive background of corporate positions in the investment field—and he talked constantly about phenomenal money-making operations in which he was involved—but the fact was that he had been associated with a string of very small and notably abortive ventures. Nonetheless, he talked a good game and convinced many of his associates that he was a highly successful businessman. This impression was heightened by the fast social company in which he traveled. He had married well; his wife was the former Lily Lodge, daughter of former Connecticut Governor John Davis Lodge and niece of 1960 Republican vice-presidential candidate Henry Cabot Lodge. Through his wife and her relatives, Marcus met and formed friendships with many politically and socially prominent persons. Among them was John Lindsay, an old friend of Mrs. Marcus.

In 1965, when Lindsay launched his drive for the mayor's office, Marcus joined his campaign staff as an unpaid volunteer. He carried out a number of special assignments with energy and tact, impressing Lindsay as a man who could get things done. When Lindsay became mayor, he appointed Marcus as one of his unpaid special assistants and gave him a variety of trouble-shooting assignments. It was assumed at first that his private business interests were so successful that he didn't need a salary from the city. Actually, Marcus was plunging in the stock market and losing thousands upon thousands of dollars at the time—but Lindsay was unaware of it. The mayor gave Marcus responsibility for solving an acute water shortage facing the city, and he responded with an effective plan that tapped extra supplies from other municipalities. Next, Lindsay assigned him to deal with problems in boisterous sections of Greenwich Village and the Times Square area. Again, Marcus performed well. He was fast earning a reputation as one of the most efficient men in the administration. As one top city official put it: "He was so very, very competent. He was not a guy who shoots off his mouth, who acts first and thinks later. The mayor had a good deal of confidence in his judgment. He did job after job without flap or fuss."

Meanwhile, the friendship between Lindsay and Marcus flourished. The two men and their wives were often seen together socially. When Mrs. Marcus gave birth to a son, Lindsay became the child's godfather.

By September 1966 the mayor decided that Marcus deserved a promotion and a salary from the city. He appointed Marcus to a $30,000-a-year job as commissioner of water supply, gas, and electricity. Moreover, he soon announced that he had even bigger things in mind for his appointee. Lindsay was in the process of reorganizing the city government, and planned to create ten super-agencies that would have enormous powers. He disclosed that Marcus was in line to head one of the super-agencies, the Environmental Protection Administration, which would in-

clude the Department of Water Supply, Gas, and
Electricity, the Sanitation Department, and the Department of Air Pollution Control.

To casual observers, all seemed to be going swimmingly
well for Marcus. But, unknown to such observers, Marcus
was in deep trouble. His financial investments had continued to be disastrous, he was in desperate need of
money, and his city salary did not begin to fill the gap in
his bank account. His financial problems were compounded by the fact that he felt obliged to keep up the pre-
tense that he was independently wealthy.

In an attempt to solve the problems, Marcus turned to
several recently-found associates. One of them was a shad-
owy character named Herbert Itkin, a labor lawyer whom
Marcus had met while seeking labor support for Lindsay's
mayoral campaign. Itkin's activities went far beyond the
mere practice of law. He had all sorts of mysterious connections with such assorted figures as racketeers, politicians, foreign officials, spies, and financiers. He acted as a
middle-man, for a fee, in lining up borrowers who wanted
to make loans from Teamster Union pension funds. He
registered with the Justice Department as an agent representing such foreign clients as the government of the Dominican Republic, and an exile group calling itself the
Provisional Government of Haiti. Moreover, he served as
a secret informer for both the FBI and the Central Intelligence Agency.

Marcus, evidently impressed with Itkin, became embroiled in a series of business ventures with him. Among
other things, they formed a company called Conestoga Investments, Ltd., while Marcus was still working on Lindsay's campaign. Conestoga was registered in London,
where Itkin visited frequently on business, and used Itkin's
law office as its New York address. Itkin and Marcus per-

suaded outsiders to invest in Conestoga, saying the firm
was involved in numerous profitable operations in the un-
derdeveloped countries of Africa. Among the projects they
mentioned were a housing project in Mauritania, a power
dam in Sierra Leone, and a beef distributorship in Mali.
Despite the impressive talk, however, Conestoga was as
unsuccessful as Marcus's other ventures. He quickly lost
more than $100,000, mostly borrowed from other people.

But, through Itkin, he met other men he hoped could
bail him out of his financial troubles. Itkin introduced him
to Daniel Motto, president of a New York local of the
Bakery and Confectionery Workers Union, and a member
of the union's seven-state Northeast District Council. During World War II, Motto had been convicted of racketeering in the black-market sale of gasoline ration coupons.
His union had later been expelled from the AFL-CIO for
engaging in corrupt practices. Notwithstanding this background, Motto served on the board of directors of the
American-Italian Anti-Defamation League, whose main
goal was to halt use of the term "Mafia" by news media
and law-enforcement agencies.

Motto, in turn, introduced Marcus to Tony Ducks Corallo. After Marcus went to work at City Hall, he pleaded
with Itkin for financial help. Itkin referred the problem to
Motto, who then consulted Corallo. The situation was
made to order for a Mafia corrupter such as Corallo—a
chance to get his hooks into a city official with the power
to award contracts worth millions of dollars. Corallo and
Motto listened to Marcus's tale of woe and immediately
offered to lend him money. The rate of interest they proposed was exorbitant—two percent a week—but the desperate Marcus snapped at the bait. At first, he took
$10,000 to pay off his most pressing creditors. Corallo told
him plenty more would be available if he needed it. A few

days later, Marcus borrowed another $40,000. Corallo
wanted the loans repaid, of course, and wanted the hefty
interest payments as well. But his real interest, more than
any profit he would make on the shylocking deal, was in
getting a hold on Marcus. He fully expected that Marcus
would be unable to keep up regular payments on the
loans. And, the more Marcus fell behind, the more indebted he would become to the Mob. He would then be
forced to do Corallo's bidding at city hall.

Matters developed just as Corallo had expected. While
using some of the borrowed money to satisfy creditors,
Marcus invested much of it in the stock market in an attempt to make a quick financial comeback. He bought
1000 shares in one company at $96 a share and, a week
later, another 1000 shares at $106 a share. The purchases
were made on margin, with Marcus putting up more than
$40,000 in cash. Later, the stock dropped more than forty
points and Marcus was pressed for more margin. Again,
he borrowed money from Corallo.

The time had come for Corallo to start cashing in on his
investment. Marcus was about to award a city contract for
draining and cleaning the 700-million-gallon Jerome Park
Reservoir in the Bronx. Since the project was considered a
high-priority emergency job, city regulations empowered
Marcus to give the contract to any firm he chose—without
taking competitive bids. Corallo had just the firm in mind
for the job. It was S. T. Grand Inc., headed by Henry
Fried, who was active in politics and no stranger to New
York City scandals. Nine years earlier, it had been disclosed that Fried had paid a city councilman $30,000 four
days after the city agreed to use a product called "fly ash,"
marketed by Fried, in mixing construction concrete. During the resulting investigation, Fried resigned a state job to
which he had been appointed by then-Governor W. Aver-

ell Harriman—membership on the commission that supervises New York state prisons. Two of Fried's brothers, Richard and Hugo, both ex-convicts, were vice presidents of S. T. Grand Inc. Despite their records and Fried's involvement in the scandal involving the councilman, the firm did considerable work for New York City and other municipalities in the metropolitan area.

But it wanted more city work than it was getting—presenting another situation made to order for Corallo. Working with Itkin and Motto, Corallo put the squeeze on Marcus to award the reservoir-cleaning contract to the Grand firm. Although some estimates were that the job should be worth only about $500,000, Marcus agreed to pay Grand $835,000. Corallo, of course, had not acted on behalf of Grand out of the goodness of his heart. He had a kickback deal in the works. The plan called for Grand to make a payoff amounting to five percent of the total value of the contract—with two percent going to Marcus and one percent each to Corallo, Itkin, and Motto.

At first, Henry Fried balked at paying the kickback. But then he received a visit from an associate of Corallo, Joseph Pizzo, who describes himself as a labor consultant. Fried would later describe Pizzo in court somewhat differently, as follows: "He was connected with Cosa Nostra, a muscle man who wouldn't hesitate to put the arm on anybody. I know if he came up to me and gave a command, I would have to adhere. I remember forty-ton, fifty-ton cranes dropped overboard into the river." Fried said Pizzo insisted the kickback be paid and told him: "I don't want any trouble with you. . . . If I make up my mind, you know what could happen. I could slow down your drill runner, your laborers, your engineers; it could cost you $100,000." Fried agreed to pay.

There was eventual testimony that periodically, as the

Grand firm received payments on the reservoir job from the city, Fried turned over kickback money to the plotters. The money was carried from Grand's office to Itkin's office by Fried's lawyer, Carl D'Angelo, a former assistant district attorney in Manhattan and the son of one of Marcus's predecessors as commissioner of water supply, gas, and electricity. At Itkin's office, the money was taken from D'Angelo by Motto, who then carried it to Corallo. After taking his cut, Corallo had the remainder of the money distributed to the others. All told, Fried paid $40,000 in kickbacks on the reservoir job. When the job was completed, Marcus and Mayor Lindsay flew to the reservoir in a helicopter amid great fanfare for a reopening ceremony. Marcus even went so far as to write an article about the efficient handling of the job for a magazine called *The American City*. The article, entitled "How to Clean a Big Reservoir," boasted: "Because of the magnitude of the job, we awarded it to an experienced and well-equipped contractor."

Corallo viewed the $8,000 he made on the reservoir deal as the mere down-payment on a potential bonanza that could be reaped through the manipulation of Commissioner Marcus. He quickly began making other demands on Marcus. Seeking a killing in real estate, he asked Marcus for inside information on property the city planned to condemn, lease, or rezone. To protect various rackets in which he was involved, he urged Marcus to use his influence with the Police Department to have certain precinct commanders transferred.

Even more important, Corallo and others involved in the reservoir-cleaning plot next concocted a scheme to extort money on construction contracts from New York's giant utility firm, Consolidated Edison Company. Commissioner Marcus, whose jurisdiction gave him broad powers over Con Ed's activities, would force the utility to award contracts to Henry Fried's S. T. Grand Inc. As in the reservoir deal, Fried would kick back a percentage of the profits to Corallo, Marcus, and Itkin. In the Con Ed case, however, there would be a prominent new figure among the conspirators—Carmine De Sapio.

Once the most powerful Democratic Party boss in New York state and an influential figure in national politics, De Sapio had given up his official party positions—but remained active as a string-puller behind the scenes. The other plotters called De Sapio into the affair because the Con Ed scheme would be extremely complex, requiring the sort of political sophistication he could provide. To some, it seemed odd that a prominent Democrat such as De Sapio would be involved in a conspiracy capitalizing on the corruption of a prominent Republican such as Marcus—serving in Lindsay's Republican administration. But Marcus later explained: "Political influence comes from strange directions." Once again, there was evidence that the Mob cares little for party lines, as long as it can get its bidding done.

The initial stages of the plot involving Con Ed as described later in a Federal court trial, centered around the utility's urgent need to provide New York City with more electricity. Con Ed wanted to build a new transmission line in Westchester County, north of the city limits, over an aqueduct right-of-way owned by the city. To do so, it needed a permit from the city, and Commissioner Marcus would decide whether the permit should be issued. The conspirators planned to use Marcus's decision-making power as a lever to force Con Ed to grant construction contracts to Fried's company. Fried and De Sapio would subtly indicate to Con Ed officials that De Sapio controlled Marcus. Meanwhile, Marcus would hold up approval of the permit until Con Ed awarded Fried the desired contracts.

It was contemplated that this would be just the beginning of a long-range extortion plan. Witnesses would later testify De Sapio assured the other plotters: "There's millions to be made if you handle it right, and I know how to handle it." A luncheon meeting was set up between De Sapio and a Con Ed vice president, Max Ulrich, at Manhattan's swanky L'Aiglon restaurant. De Sapio offered to serve as a sort of referee between Con Ed and Marcus's department. He said he "knew the department and Con Ed were two vital organizations in supplying lifeblood to the city" and had heard that relations between them were not particularly good. Since he had "a lot of experience in governmental works," De Sapio said, he might be able to help Con Ed in its troubles with the city. Ulrich replied that Con Ed would welcome all the help it could get.

Later, Marcus told Itkin that Con Ed wanted a letter from him permitting the company to start work on the Westchester transmission line. Itkin met with De Sapio to discuss the request. De Sapio cautioned Itkin that things had to be done "my way" and that "in this type of work we have to be very sophisticated." He said Marcus would have to "hold up that letter" until De Sapio okayed it. De Sapio feared that Marcus lacked the nerve to stick it out during the lengthy time it might take to consummate the extortion plot. Itkin explained that, despite the loans from Corallo, Marcus was still caught in a financial bind that had him "wild." In that case, De Sapio said, he could arrange a $25,000 payment to ease Marcus's crisis—but Marcus "must be patient."

Itkin, who had been serving as an FBI informer for the previous four years, secretly kept the FBI posted on all the developments concerning Marcus's involvement with Corallo, De Sapio, and the other conspirators. Using equipment provided by the FBI, Itkin covertly recorded some of his conversations with the plotters. Among them was a discussion of the Con Ed scheme with Marcus and Corallo at Itkin's apartment. The recording included numerous references to De Sapio's role in the conspiracy.

After this conversation, De Sapio and Fried had lunch with another Con Ed vice president, Gerald Hadden, who was in charge of the company's construction projects. Hadden complained that Con Ed still hadn't been able to get Marcus to approve the start of work on the transmission line. De Sapio, knowing the company had already told Marcus it would settle temporarily for a letter from Marcus if the construction permit were not immediately available, asked Hadden what was needed. "Would a letter do?" Hadden replied that it depended on what sort of letter it was. "I'll see what I can do," De Sapio said.

A short time later, assured that Con Ed would come through with the contract awards for Fried's company, De Sapio telephoned Itkin and gave him a coded message to have Marcus send the letter. "You can send that insurance policy out," De Sapio said. Marcus followed the order.

Itkin visited De Sapio's apartment four days later and De Sapio gave him an initial payment of $5,000 in cash. The following week, at De Sapio's office, Itkin received another $2,500. "Let's just see and make sure everything goes right," De Sapio told Itkin. "I have to get it all back from Henry Fried before I pay any more out." When Itkin returned to De Sapio's office for still another payment, De Sapio complained that Marcus had written Con Ed a "terrible letter." As a result, he said, "Henry decided we are only going to get $20,000." De Sapio planned to keep $7,500 of the $20,000 for "all the work" he had done, but turned the remainder over to Itkin. All told, Itkin received $12,500 from De Sapio—which he shared with his confederates. The assumption was that these were merely the first installments on what would eventually be enormous payoffs from a continuing plot to shake down Con Ed.

But the fact was that the conspiracy had just about reached the end of its road. The FBI apparently intended to encourage Itkin to continue playing along with his confederates while it gathered additional evidence, but an unexpected development forced the Federal men to move ahead of schedule. Two men who had invested money in the firm operated by Marcus and Itkin, Conestoga Investments, Ltd., filed a complaint with Manhattan District Attorney Frank Hogan about Marcus's handling of the company's funds. Hogan took the complaint before a grand jury and notified Mayor Lindsay that Marcus was under investigation. Lindsay questioned Marcus, who assured him that Hogan's investigation stemmed from a dispute with a former partner about expense accounts in Conestoga and had nothing to do with city business. Nonetheless, Lindsay instructed his investigations commissioner, Arnold Fraiman, to begin checking on Marcus's affairs.

With three investigations of Marcus being conducted simultaneously, the FBI and Federal prosecutors decided to act quickly before the waters became muddied. Evidence concerning Marcus's involvement with Corallo, Itkin, and others in the reservoir-cleaning case was immediately presented to a Federal grand jury. Meanwhile, Marcus resigned his city job—still insisting to Lindsay that he had done nothing wrong.

Six days after Marcus's resignation, the Federal grand jury indicted him with Corallo, Fried, Motto, and Itkin on charges of violating the anti-racketeering laws in the reservoir scheme. (Itkin's inclusion in the indictment was intended to prevent the other defendants from suspecting that he was an FBI informer.) News of the indictment hit the Lindsay administration like a thunderbolt. Marcus was the highest-ranking New York City official in decades to be involved in a scandal. And his involvement with a Mafioso such as Corallo struck some officials as virtually unbelievable. The indictment was all the more sensational because Lindsay and his aides had tried to create the impression that they had lifted city government high above the image of dirty politics that had long pervaded New York.

Mayor Lindsay, clearly jolted by the scandal, commented: "If the charge in the Federal indictment is true, then it's clear that Mr. Marcus lied to me, lied to Commissioner Fraiman, and lied to District Attorney Hogan. To say that in that event I have been ill-served and the public also is an understatement, obviously. I consider this a betrayal of a personal and a public trust."

Marcus, after briefly contemplating suicide, decided to tell all to the FBI, plead guilty, become a government witness and throw himself on the mercy of the court. Meanwhile, word leaked out that Herbert Itkin was actually an FBI informer. Less than a month after the return of the indictment, FBI agents arrested two men—one of them a lawyer—on charges of plotting to murder Itkin. The defendants in the murder-conspiracy case were Robert Schwartz, an attorney who was also under indictment in a stock-fraud case, and Robert Roden, an ex-convict who had formerly been a professional light-heavyweight boxer. Schwartz conceded he had been involved in financial dealings with Itkin, but both he and Roden denied knowing anything about a murder plot. Federal authorities charged, however, that the two men had tried to hire someone to kill Itkin to prevent him from testifying in the

Marcus case. A court complaint filed by the authorities said that Roden had met several times with a man who turned out to be another government informer and had offered the man money to murder Itkin. The first offer was $1,500, but the bounty was later raised to $2,500. The informer told FBI agents about the offer and was instructed to play along with the plot until the arrests were made. Assistant United States Attorney Michael Fawer charged at a preliminary hearing in the case that the murder conspiracy was so "well plotted" and so far along that "all that had to be done was the pulling of the trigger." Schwartz and Roden pleaded not guilty and the case is still pending at this writing. In the stock-fraud case, Schwartz was found guilty of using stock he did not own as collateral for a loan. He was fined $2,500, but is currently appealing the conviction.

The sensation created by the indictment in the city reservoir case and the arrests in the murder-conspiracy case was further compounded by a later indictment charging De Sapio, Corallo, and Fried with conspiracy in the Con Ed case. De Sapio was an even better-known figure than Marcus, both in New York and on the national scene. Moreover, his involvement with Corallo, coming on the heels of Marcus's indictment with Corallo, pointed up the Mob's ability to do business with both top-echelon Democrats and Republicans in New York. Other indictments followed, charging Marcus in the state courts with conspiracy and taking bribes.

Marcus and Itkin became the government's chief witnesses against the other conspirators in both the reservoir case and the Con Ed case. Both prosecutions were successful. In the reservoir case, Corallo was sentenced to three years in prison, Fried to two years and Marcus to fifteen months. In the state court cases, Marcus was sentenced to three concurrent one-year terms. In the Con Ed case, De Sapio got two years and Corallo got four and a half years. (Fried was found to be too ill to stand trial in the Con Ed case.)

During the Con Ed trial, Assistant U.S. Attorney Paul Rooney emphasized that the kickback scheme involving the transmission line was "peanuts" compared with more grandiose plans concocted by the conspirators—plans that were foiled by the revelation of the Marcus scandal. Next, Rooney charged, the De Sapio-Corallo combine intended to get its hooks into a $100 million nuclear power plant that Con Ed planned to build on Storm King Mountain near Cornwall, New York. The kickback projected on that job was $5 million, Rooney said, and the transmission-line deal was intended simply to set the "ground rules" for the bigger caper. "This is a case of big-time corruption," Rooney said. "This is corruption at the highest level. This is sophisticated corruption. This isn't four guys sitting in the back of the bar, plotting."

Screen Test for a Duck

While the stakes were higher and the names were bigger in the Marcus case than in many other cases of local corruption, the pattern followed was typical. As one Mob corrupter told this writer: "Marcus was exactly the kind of pigeon we look for; he was vulnerable and could be controlled because he was desperate for money." The Mob, he explained, is constantly hunting for frailties in public officials—weak spots that make them susceptible to corruption.

"Money isn't the only motive in the guys we do business with," he said. "Sure, we look for people who need dough. Maybe a guy's in hock to a shylock, the way Marcus was.

Or maybe he likes to gamble or play the market. But we get lots of other guys over the barrel through old-fashioned blackmail. We catch the pigeon with a broad or doing something stupid while he's drunk, and we threaten to expose him unless he plays ball. After he agrees, we keep him on the hook with money—but the blackmail is what gets him on the hook in the first place."

The corrupter told this writer about one case in which he used a combination of blackmail and an appeal to vanity in order to get rid of a politician for trying to double-cross the Mob. "I created this guy as a politician," the corrupter said. "He was a nobody—working on a two-bit job with nothing to do with politics. I picked out a public office for him, got him nominated, paid all his campaign expenses, put his posters all over town and got him elected. At first, he couldn't do enough for me and my friends. Let us run all the rackets we wanted—bookmaking, policy, crap games, whorehouses. We paid him off every week, just like clockwork. But, after a few years, he started getting greedy. He tried to screw us every which way. Not only wanted to double the size of the payoff; wanted to let another syndicate come in to compete with us.

"When we told him we wouldn't sit still for that, the son of a bitch raided a bunch of our joints. Got himself a bunch of publicity—the knight on the white horse, cleaning up the town. Well, hell, we'd had it with him. Some of our guys wanted to put out a 'contract' on him, but I persuaded them that knocking him off would just bring us more heat than we could afford. So they told me I had to figure out some other way to get rid of him; I had created him and now I had to eliminate him.

"Well, this guy's weakest point was that he had the big head about being God's gift to the women. He was a handsome bastard, and the broads really did flock around him. He loved playing the stud duck in the puddle. A couple of times he'd let slip to me that he'd always had a secret yen to be a movie star. I thought he was kidding, but he said he meant it. People had been telling him for years that he was better looking than some of the Hollywood glamour boys, and he believed it.

"I'd laughed about it at first. Hell, he couldn't even read a political speech worth a damn; I didn't see how he'd ever be able to act. But, when the time came for me to figure out some way to get rid of him, the movie-star business gave me an idea. I had a connection on the West Coast with a racket guy who secretly owned a piece of one of the movie studios; he'd originally been involved in the movie unions and then got cut into the management. He knew everybody worth knowing on the Coast, and a lot of people owed him favors. I got him to send a big-name movie actor to see me. I won't tell you the actor's name, but he's one of the biggest guys in the business—produces his own pictures.

"I told this actor I wanted him to offer our politician a long-term contract to act in some of the movies he was producing. I didn't care if the politician never appeared in a picture; I just wanted to get him out of town. The actor was hesitant—gave me a lot of crap about screen tests and that kind of stuff. He hadn't even met the politician at that point, so I arranged a party where they could meet. It was in a suite of rooms at a hotel owned by one of the guys in our syndicate. Before the party, I arranged to 'bug' the suite with a half-dozen hidden microphones. The damned place was 'wired' so well you could have heard a fart on the tape recordings.

"I had the party stocked with whores, and the thing developed into a goddam orgy. By the end of it I had everybody leave except the actor, the politician, and a few of the broads. Naturally, I got some choice material on the tapes. Later, I played the tapes for the actor—threatening to make them public if he didn't cooperate. I didn't play the tapes for the politician; figured I'd hold them in reserve in case the movie-contract deal didn't get him out of town.

"When the actor offered him the Hollywood deal, the politician bit like a fish on a worm. He didn't even want to bother with details in the contract. By God, he'd wanted to be a movie actor all his life and now he was going. He resigned from office, packed his stuff and left. Of course, when he got out there, he fell right on his ass. He never got into a picture, and they found some fine print in his contract to get rid of him. But he was too proud to come home. He found some half-assed job on the Coast and has been there ever since. We picked out another guy we could control and elected him to the vacant office. We haven't had a bit of trouble since then."

The Good Citizens of Youngstown

It is only rarely that the use of blackmail by Mob corrupters to neutralize uncooperative officials comes to public notice. More often, it is successfully concealed or, at least, kept in the realm of unproved suspicion. One case of apparent blackmail was blamed by insiders for the resignation of a reform mayor who tried to clean up the racket-dominated city of Youngstown, Ohio. The mayor, George Oles, had been one of Youngstown's most wealthy, respected and prominent businessmen. Throughout most of his life, Oles had taken no part in politics. But, disgusted by rampant racketeering and corruption, he ran for mayor with a pledge to throw the rascals out of city hall and into jail. He was elected by a large majority, and promptly set to work on fulfilling his pledge. He fired corrupt officials by the dozen, shook up the police department, and forced the arrest of mobsters who hadn't seen the inside of a police station in years.

The cleanup, however, lasted a mere matter of months. After serving only one year of his term, Oles mysteriously resigned as mayor. The Mob resumed operations as usual and corruption again ruled the city's politics. Oles is now dead, and his resignation has never been fully explained. But those in the know say mobsters got something on the mayor and threatened to expose him if he didn't bow out. For a man whose reputation had previously been unblemished, the fear of possible scandal apparently was sufficient to cause a strategic retreat.

With Youngstown reopened to the Mob, a series of Mafia power struggles ensued for control of the rackets. Gambling alone was a $4.5 million-a-year business in the city. Rival Mob factions seized control at various times, only to be overthrown in a wave of bombings and shootings. An attempt was made to end the violence and bring the warring factions together at a meeting of 150 Mafia leaders from all sections of the country, secretly convened in a motel at Worcester, Massachusetts. But the effort failed, and the violence resumed. During one period, there were eighty-one gangland bombings. The public was generally indifferent to the warfare, consoling itself with the notion that the only victims were no-good bums and that innocent people were left alone.

But that myth was shattered by the eighty-second bombing. A Mafia boss named Charles "Cadillac Charlie" Cavallaro left his home one day to drive his two sons, Charles, Jr., twelve, and Thomas, eleven, to a practice session of their football team. Despite Cavallaro's status in the Mob, his sons were among the most popular children in their neighborhood. When Cavallaro turned on the ignition switch in his car, a tremendous explosion shook the area. The blast disintegrated the lower half of Cavallaro's body and blew the top half into his yard. Thomas, seated beside him, was also killed. And Charles, Jr., seated against the right front door, was trapped in the wreckage with his left hip crushed by the impact of the explosion.

No longer could the citizenry of Youngstown delude itself with the idea that gang warfare spared the innocent. One young boy was dead and his brother was crippled. A public outcry brought a new reform drive to the city. Clergymen and civic leaders demanded an end to the corruption and racketeering. The Mob temporarily shut down its rackets operations. Federal agents arrived in town, seeking evidence against both mobsters and crooked politicians. But, within a couple of months, the reform fervor began to fade. Once the heat had died down, the Mafia bosses passed the word to their underlings to reopen the bookie joints, the policy gambling, and other rackets. Citizens who had been tempted to provide information to the Federal agents had second thoughts. The Cavallaro bombing remained unsolved and eventually was almost forgotten.

A county grand jury, however, began a lengthy investigation of the ties between the Mob and local politicians and law-enforcement officers. The grand jury found that, once the racketeers reopened their operations, their gambling business quickly returned to the $4.5 million-a-year level. "On the basis of evidence submitted to us, it would appear that many of our citizens and many of our law-enforcement officers have little or no respect for the gambling statutes of this state, and this situation has permitted the professional gamblers to operate almost unmolested," the grand jury said in its report.

The panel lambasted politicians who sought favors from

the Mob. It described "show raids" and "accommodation arrests" made to give the appearance that gambling laws were being enforced. Actually, however, the racketeers had been tipped off in advance to the raids and arranged for their subordinates to be arrested and let off with small fines. There had been a virtually complete breakdown in enforcement of laws against racketeering, the grand jury charged.

"The testimony has been sufficient to reflect a deplorable condition which indicates that many police officers and public officials . . . were guilty of the utmost dereliction of their duties," the panel reported. "Crime of the stature with which we are presently confronted could not have developed without the total indifference, acquiescence, or direct permissive assistance of some politicians and law-enforcement officials."

Playing into the hands of the mobsters and corrupt officials, the grand jury said, was the attitude of the citizenry. "This grand jury feels that the general public of this area cannot escape their share for this blame in the breakdown of law enforcement. From testimony we have heard, we find that citizens and citizens' committees and other groups, with few exceptions, have made no real effort to get in touch with any local law-enforcement body or to act as a watchdog over the activities of the various law-enforcement agencies. . . . One of the principal reasons for this laxity is the apathy of the ordinary citizen toward law enforcement. Too many 'good citizens' simply do not want to get involved."

Such apathy and reluctance of "good citizens" to get involved are hardly confined to Youngstown. They open the gates to racketeering and corruption of local government in city after city across the American landscape. Since local government is closest to the people, it is there that the average citizen has his greatest opportunity to challenge the conspiracy between the Mafia and the politician. If the citizen fails at the local level, it becomes increasingly difficult for him to combat the conspiracy at the state and Federal levels. And it is at these levels, as succeeding chapters will demonstrate, that the Mob is currently concentrating its campaign to seize illicit power.

[5]

The Affairs
of the States

The Southern Gentlemen

Sitting behind his office desk, the man could have passed for a typical business executive. He was dressed immaculately and conservatively. His desk was well-ordered, bearing a neat stack of correspondence, a note pad, a pen-and-pencil set, two telephones, and a large cigarette lighter that tossed a torch-like flame. Standing against a wall were charts, maps, and aerial photographs depicting various real-estate and construction projects.

But the man behind the desk was not a typical business executive. He was Carlos Marcello—frequently described in such terms as "the Mafia boss of the South," "the most powerful man in Louisiana" and "one of the most important racketeers in the country." For reasons of his own, Marcello had agreed to be interviewed by this writer. Several interviews took place in Marcello's home city of New Orleans and elsewhere; they were among the few on-the-record discussions of this sort ever granted to a writer by any reputed top Mafia leader.

As will be seen, Marcello makes no bones about his racketeering background, although he disavows the title of Mafia boss and claims he has operated within the law in recent years. It is clear that his history represents a classic case of a syndicate racketeer profiting enormously from political manipulation at the statewide level and from infiltration of legitimate business. For many years Marcello has had the power to make the wheels turn in the state government of Louisiana. His influence has also been strong in the governments of other Southern states. To appreciate how he came to exert such political domination, it is necessary to know something about his background and the milieu in which he rose to power.

Marcello was born on February 6, 1910, in Tunis, North Africa. His parents, originally from Sicily, emigrated to the United States and settled in New Orleans when Carlos was eight months old. At that time the Mafia was already firmly entrenched in New Orleans and had strong ties with prominent politicians and businessmen. Although Marcello denies knowing it by the name Mafia, it is clear that he became acquainted early in life with members of the syndicate. He saw corruption and lawlessness all around him, so it was not surprising that he turned to crime at an early age.

His name first showed up on a police blotter at the age of nineteen when he was arrested on a charge of being an accessory in a bank robbery but beat the rap. Six months later, however, he was convicted of assault and robbery in a chain grocery store holdup and was sentenced to nine to fourteen years in state prison. Paroled after serving fewer than five years, Marcello began displaying a knack for getting political strings pulled. He somehow arranged for Louisiana Governor O.K. Allen, a stooge of Huey Long, to give him a full pardon. Other arrests followed—on such charges as assault, robbery, and Federal tax evasion—but none of them stuck until he was caught selling twenty-three pounds of marijuana in 1938 and sentenced to a year in the Atlanta Federal Prison.

After his release, Marcello returned to New Orleans and moved from narcotics into other rackets. He joined forces with Sylvestro "Silver Sam" Carollo, then the Mafia boss of Louisiana. With Carollo's approval, Marcello began operating slot machines, gambling casinos, bookie joints, a horse-race wire service, and other rackets traditionally controlled by the Mob. Payoffs to public officials and law-enforcement officers were necessary, so Marcello cultivated close ties with influential politicians—ties that he would later broaden and refine until he was considered by many the most powerful behind-the-scenes figure in Louisiana politics.

Marcello's rise in the Mob was speeded by his association in the gambling rackets with Frank Costello, a New York Mafia boss who had been invited by Huey Long to set up operations in Louisiana, and with such other mobsters as Costello aide "Dandy Phil" Kastel and underworld financial wizard Meyer Lansky. Together, they ran both slot-machine ventures and a plush gambling casino called the Beverly Club, just outside New Orleans. When Silver Sam Carollo was deported to Italy in 1947, Marcello succeeded him as the Mob boss of Louisiana. He forged additional alliances with important mobsters from other states and extended his influence far beyond the boundaries of Louisiana. His racing-wire service, for example, supplied results to the Mob's bookmaking operations in such states as Illinois, Indiana, Michigan, Florida, Kentucky, Texas, Alabama, and Mississippi. While broadening his criminal empire, Marcello also expanded his corrupt alliances with politicians and law-enforcement officers.

A long-time nemesis of Marcello, Aaron M. Kohn, managing director of the Metropolitan Crime Commission of New Orleans, described the racketeer's criminal and political operations this way in 1970 during testimony before a congressional committee: "Marcello and his growing organization developed their capital or bankroll through extensive gambling, including casinos, slot machines, pinball, handbooks, layoff, football pools, dice, card games, roulette, and bingo; also, narcotics, prostitution, extortion, clip-joint operations, B-drinking, marketing stolen goods, robberies, burglaries, and thefts. Their criminal enterprise required, and had, corrupt collusion of public officials at every critical level—including police, sheriffs, justices of the peace, prosecutors, mayors, governors, state legislators, and at least one member of Congress."

This corruption was accomplished in a variety of ways. In some cases, there were direct cash payoffs. In others, huge campaign contributions were made. Sometimes, for example, Marcello picked up virtually the entire tab for a campaign for governor or other statewide office. In still other cases, he delivered large voting blocs to favored candidates. An insight into Marcello's technique for political manipulation was provided by a hard-fought gubernatorial election in Louisiana. The candidates in the Democratic primary runoff, which was equivalent to election, were former Governor Jimmie Davis and the late New Orleans Mayor deLesseps Morrison. Marcello had maintained excellent relations with both Davis and Morrison and wanted to keep things that way. Rather than choose between the candidates, he found a way to back both of them. He became the chief contributor to Davis's campaign fund. Meanwhile, two of his associates became Morrison's main financial backers. No matter who won, Marcello was sure of keeping close ties with the incoming governor. Davis was elected, and later took official actions that benefited Marcello's empire.

While operating his rackets and establishing his dominance in the political world, Marcello also made heavy investments in legitimate business. Among his business interests were motels, restaurants, taverns, banks, truck dealerships, real estate, housing subdivisions, beer and whiskey distributorships, shrimpboat fleets, shipbuilding, finance companies, taxi and bus firms, sightseeing lines, linen-supply companies, gasoline stations, souvenir shops, phonograph-record distributorships, and electrical-appliance stores. In his real-estate ventures, Marcello bought up thousands of acres of property valued in the millions of dollars. He also acquired two Holiday Inns, built a $1 million motel called the Town and Country on the main highway between downtown New Orleans and the city's airport and operated another motel by the same name outside Shreveport, Louisiana.

By the spring of 1970, several problems had developed for Marcello and led to his decision to be interviewed by this writer. For one thing, he had been convicted of assaulting an FBI agent and was given a two-year prison sentence in a case in which he claimed he had gotten a bum rap—a view that was supported by some legal observers. The case was on appeal, and Marcello felt his side of the story had not been adequately aired. For another thing, the Louisiana Legislature—prompted in part by a *Life* magazine article charging that Marcello "controlled the state of Louisiana . . . with little interference from public officials or police and indeed often with their help" —had appointed a special committee to investigate organized crime. The committee's chief focus was on Marcello's purported domination of the state's politics and government. Marcello claimed the legislative investigation was part of a concerted harassment campaign aimed at "crucifying" him and that here, too, his side of the story was being ignored.

Among the charges the committee announced it would investigate were:

- That Marcello's control of state officials enabled him to amass vast riches at the public's expense.
- That officials of the State Revenue Department allowed Marcello and his associates to evade many thousands of dollars in state taxes.
- That former Governor Jimmie Davis took official action to help Marcello.
- That Tom Ashy, a state racing commissioner, was a Marcello associate and a bookie in Lafayette, Louisiana.
- That, perhaps most importantly, Marcello had been allowed by officials to use public funds to increase enormously the value of his real-estate holdings. This allegation centered around Marcello's ownership of a 6000-acre tract called Churchill Farms, a few miles southwest of New Orleans in Jefferson Parish (County). The tract consisted chiefly of swampland, worth an estimated $1 million.

But real-estate experts estimated that, if the property were diked and drained, it would increase in value to about $60 million. Rather than spend his own money on the necessary drainage project, *Life* charged, Marcello persuaded officials of the state and Jefferson Parish to do the work. Former Governor Davis, in one of his last official acts before leaving office, signed a contract authorizing the state and a regional flood-control agency to share $1 million in construction costs for a levee designed to protect the low-lying perimeter of Churchill Farms. The contract also called for a $500,000 payment to Churchill Farms as compensation for use of Marcello's land to build the levee. When the levee was finished, drainage work was begun with the installation of massive pumping equipment. It was charged that this work would benefit only Marcello's property and would eventually cost the taxpayers at least $2.5 million. Despite the fact that Marcello's land would increase in value by an estimated $59 million, it was said, his only cost would be an annual drainage tax of $264. Moreover, there were predictions that the value of Churchill Farms would be further increased if the Federal government went through with preliminary plans to route a six-lane superhighway, the Dixie Freeway, through Marcello's acreage.

With the legislative committee's investigation in progress and the appeal still pending in the case involving the purported assault on an FBI agent, Marcello sent word to this writer that he was willing to be interviewed. Arrangements for the interviews were made through an intermediary, a syndicate racketeer who had previously provided this writer with information about the Mob. "I've given Marcello a 100-percent guarantee on you," the racketeer said. (The underworld uses what it calls a "guarantee" system, in which one mobster recommends a third party to another mobster under a rating system ranging from zero to 100 percent. The rating refers to the person's trustworthiness. If someone with a high-percentage guarantee betrays the person to whom he's recommended, it's up to the person making the recommendation to murder him. As the racketeer who served as an intermediary in this case put it: "We bury our own mistakes." The 100-percent guarantee given this writer did not bind him to write favorably about Marcello, but rather to abide by the ground rules for the interviews and to report Marcello's remarks fairly.)

The arrangements for the interviews were made in utmost secrecy. After flying to New Orleans, the writer was instructed to check in at the Rowntowner—a motel operated by one of Marcello's associates—and await further word. He was not to let anyone know where he was staying or to make any telephone calls. Following a half-day wait, the intermediary appeared and said that things were "still being worked out." He directed the writer to remain in the motel room, then left without saying when he would return or where he could be reached. He did not come back until the next day.

"Let's go," he said. He drove with the writer to Marcello's Town and Country Motel at 1225 Airline Highway. After another wait of more than an hour, which was spent drinking cup after cup of coffee in the motel restaurant, the intermediary was summoned to the telephone. He then led the writer to Marcello's suite of offices, situated in a separate one-story building behind the motel. Two attractive secretaries were on duty in a reception room. One of them ushered the visitors into Marcello's private office.

Marcello rose from a black leather chair behind his desk, shook hands, offered his guests seats, then buzzed a secretary on the intercom phone and asked her to bring in some coffee and soft drinks. The impression he gave was anything but sinister. The swarthy face that had usually seemed angry in news photographs was now relaxed. The voice was soft, though husky. Marcello's entire demeanor throughout the interviews appeared designed to suggest an aura of respectability.

When he returned to his chair, he pulled it close to the desk and sat absolutely erect—an apparent attempt to look taller than the five-feet three-inches that have given him the underworld nickname "The Little Man." The front of his wooden desk was adorned with a carving of a helmeted gladiator's head, framed by Marcello's initials. The room contained numerous maps and charts of real-estate and construction projects in which Marcello was involved. The wall behind his desk, about fifteen feet wide and ten feet high, was covered with a rich, gold-covered drapery. (Marcello evidently has a fondness for gold. In his office bathroom, the plumbing fixtures—including the toilet-flush handle—are gold.)

At the outset, Marcello explained why he had agreed to be interviewed. "A lot of people have been tryin' to crucify me," he said. "They've been spreadin' a lot of crap about me. I figured it was time to tell my side of the story. I've heard a lot about you—that you're a straight-shooter—so I decided to tell it to you."

He was particularly indignant about repeated references to him as a Mafia boss. "All I ever hear is 'Mafia boss' or 'Cosa Nostra boss,' " Marcello said. "I don't know what they're talkin' about. Sure, I used to be involved in the rackets; I don't deny that. I know a lot of guys around the country who've been in the rackets. But the Mafia—I don't know a thing about it. I've read some of this crap about how the Mafia is supposed to have initiations, making guys blood brothers and all that mumbo-jumbo. Well, maybe that's how things are done in New York or Chicago. But I've never heard of anything like that in Louisiana. I don't come from Italy, much less Sicily, where the Mafia's supposed to have started. I was born in Tunisia. And I wouldn't know a Mafia or a Cosa Nostra from a Congolese tribesman."

He insisted that he had been out of the rackets, and involved solely in legitimate business, for more than ten years. "I'm makin' millions of dollars in real-estate, motels, restaurants and the rest," he said. "What the hell do I need gambling or narcotics or anything like that for? I'd be a fool to take the risk."

If that is so, he was asked, why do Federal officials and such men as Aaron Kohn, managing director of the New

Orleans Metropolitan Crime Commission, continue to accuse him of masterminding gambling operations and other rackets? "That Aaron Kohn is the biggest phony I've ever known," Marcello replied. "He's made a career out of harassin' me. His crime commission is nothin' but a money-making proposition for him. If I didn't exist, he'd be out of a job." (The crime commission is not a governmental body, but a citizens' unit. Kohn and a secretary are the only full-time employees. Over the years, there have been numerous exchanges of invective between Marcello and Kohn.)

Marcello's denial that he was a Mafia boss or that he had been involved in the rackets for the previous decade raised the question of how he had come to be arrested in 1966 while eating lunch with twelve other reputed Mafia leaders in the private dining room of an Italian restaurant in New York. The officers who made the arrests called the luncheon gathering the most important meeting of underworld leaders since the notorious Apalachin conference nine years earlier. Among those arrested with Marcello were Thomas "Tommy Ryan" Eboli, then acting boss of the late Vito Genovese's Mafia family; Michele "Mike" Miranda, a top lieutenant in the Genovese family; and Santo Trafficante, a Florida Mafia boss. The defendants were charged with consorting with known criminals, each other, but their cases were ultimately dismissed and a grand jury investigation of the gathering produced no tangible results. Nonetheless, the question remained: What had Marcello been doing with those men?

"That was my first trip to New York in about twenty years," Marcello said. "While I was there, I decided to see some of my old friends—so we all got together for lunch. Sure, some of these fellows have been in the rackets; that's how I knew them from the old days. But, if they're in the

Mafia, I don't know a damned thing about that. This was strictly a social gathering; that's all there was to it. But the first thing you know the cops and the newspapers and the television make it out to be a big deal—the same old 'Mafia' and 'Cosa Nostra' garbage. What's the matter with some old friends gettin' together for lunch? Who would you expect me to have lunch with in New York, Nelson Rockefeller? I don't even know the man."

It was on his return to New Orleans from New York that Marcello became embroiled in the altercation that resulted in his being charged with assaulting an FBI man. While in New York, he had posed agreeably for news photographers several times after his arrest. When he flew home, a crowd of newsmen—tipped off to his arrival time by the FBI—was waiting for him at the New Orleans airport. Two FBI agents, Patrick J. Collins, Jr., and Joseph M. Aviagone, assigned to observe and photograph the arrival, were in the crowd—posing as newsmen. When Marcello left the plane, he was surrounded by the crowd amid a popping of flashbulbs. Complaining that he had already posed for numerous photographers, Marcello snapped: "That's enough pictures. I'm the boss here." The newsmen backed off and stopped shooting pictures, but Agents Collins and Aviagone did not. Marcello, assuming they were members of the press corps, asked: "Are you looking for a lot of trouble?" Collins replied: "I can handle trouble." With that, despite the fact that Collins was nineteen years younger and ten inches taller than he, Marcello jabbed at the FBI man with his left hand—missing him—and then tried to throw a haymaker with his right. He was grabbed by his brother, Joseph, before he could cut loose the haymaker. The altercation ended there. Marcello's brother and other members of his party persuaded him to leave the airport without further incident. But within a week, al-

though no blows had landed and Marcello had no idea
Collins was an FBI man, he was indicted on a charge of
assaulting a Federal agent. At his trial, the judge explained
to the jurors that they could convict him even though he
hadn't actually struck Collins and hadn't known Collins
was an FBI man. The jurors found Marcello guilty and the
judge sentenced him to two years in Federal prison.

"Have you ever heard of such a chicken-shit case?"
Marcello said in the interview. "If my name wasn't Carlos
Marcello, do you think I would have even been indicted?
They couldn't get anything else on me—because I've been
strictly legitimate all these years—so they set me up for
this chicken-shit case. They didn't give me two years for
assaulting an FBI man; hell, I never touched him. They
gave me two years because of my reputation. Is that fair?
Is that what we call justice? But, if the case stands up on
appeal, I'll just have to go off to the can for a couple of
years. There's nothin' I can do about it."

At that point, the racketeer who had served as an intermediary in arranging the interview spoke up. "You know,
the Federal government has been harassing Carlos for the
last ten years—and it's all because of politics," he said. "In
1960, when Bobby Kennedy was managing his brother's
presidential campaign, he sent a guy down here to see Carlos. This was before the Democratic National Convention.
He wanted Carlos to use his influence to swing the Louisiana delegation for Kennedy at the convention. Carlos said
he was sorry, but that he'd already promised his support at
the convention to Lyndon Johnson. The Louisiana delegation went for Johnson. Even though Jack Kennedy got the
nomination and picked Johnson for Vice President, Bobby
was pissed off at Carlos and promised he'd get even. When
he became attorney general, the first thing he did was start
a campaign to put Jimmy Hoffa in the pen. The second

thing he did was go after Carlos's ass. The FBI, the Immigration Service, Internal Revenue—all the Feds—have been harassing Carlos ever since, even with the change of administrations from Kennedy to Johnson and now Nixon. Once these things get started in Washington, it's hard to stop them no matter who's President."

Marcello, who had sat silently through this account, was asked whether it was accurate. He replied that it was. Regardless of Robert Kennedy's motivation, it is a fact that he did launch an intensive harassment campaign against Marcello—a campaign that has been pressed by his successors as attorney general. This harassment included Marcello's deportation to Guatemala (only to return a short time later) and his prosecution on a variety of charges ranging from fraud to bribery, all of which had been overturned in the courts by the time of the interview except the assault case.

Since the story of Robert Kennedy's attempt to enlist his support lent credence to reports that Marcello was a powerful behind-the-scenes force in Louisiana politics—perhaps *the* most powerful force—he was asked to elaborate on his political role. "Sure, I've got plenty of political connections; I don't deny that," Marcello said. "I've been helping put people in office for years. I've spent a whole lot of money on campaign contributions and I've spread the word to people to support my candidates. What's wrong with that? I thought it was everybody's duty to take part in politics. I hear talk all the time that it's terrible that Carlos Marcello is supporting so-and-so for office. You don't hear that it's terrible that the banks or the utilities or the oil companies are supporting so-and-so. Hell, many of the big companies operating in Louisiana are run by outsiders. I'm a local fellow. I provide a lot of people with jobs. Why shouldn't I have the same right as these big companies to try to elect my friends to office?"

The question, of course, was what sort of strings were attached to his support of various candidates. "Well, naturally, I'm not goin' to support someone who's later goin' to go out of his way to try to hurt me," Marcello said. "In the old days, when I was involved in gambling, I'd try to elect a governor or mayor or district attorney who took a lenient position on the gambling issue. Today, things are different. I'm strictly involved in legitimate business. There are things government can do to help or hurt my businesses—licenses, zoning regulations, that kind of thing. Naturally, I expect my friends in government to do what they can to cut red tape and help me when they can. I'm not talking about anything crooked or underhanded—just doing what they can legitimately do, the same way they would for any constituent."

Perhaps, but did "any constituent" have the same access to influential officials as Marcello? "I don't know about that," he said. "But they have the same chance to make friends with politicians as I do."

He was asked how he had originally gone about obtaining political influence. Again, the intermediary spoke up. "You have to remember that, when Carlos and I were starting out in the rackets, just about the only money available for political campaigns in Louisiana and other Southern states was rackets money," he said. "These were poor states. There were no 'fat cats' around to finance political campaigns. If a guy wanted to run for any important office, the only place he could get enough money was from us. So we got control of the political machinery. We picked the candidates; we paid for their campaigns; we paid them off; we told them what to do. We even provided the poll-watchers and vote-counters. It didn't really matter how many votes a candidate got. What counted was how many votes we tallied for him."

Many of the politicians originally elected under that system, he explained, still hold office today. Over the years, they have continued accepting cash payoffs, campaign contributions, and political support from the Mob. Since the political machinery in Southern states has grown increasingly sophisticated, the intermediary said, racketeers now exercise more subtle political influence than in the past. "There are other ways to make a bundle of dough besides gambling and the other old-fashioned sort of rackets," he said. "Let me give you an example. A few years ago, there was an election for governor down this way. There were two candidates in the runoff. I put up just about all the campaign money for one of the candidates; a partner of mine put up the money for the other guy. No matter who won, the next governor would be beholden to us. We made just one demand on these candidates, and they agreed. We didn't ask for wide-open gambling or anything like that. What we wanted was the power to name the next state conservation commissioner. Sounds innocent, right? You'd think the conservation commissioner would be an unimportant guy—supervising parks and fiashing and hunting licenses and crap like that. But this election was in an oil state, and the conservation commissioner had the power to approve or reject the drilling of every oil and natural gas well in the state! After the election, we named the commissioner—and there were millions made through that appointment. With a deal like that, who the hell needs gambling?"

Although the intermediary had not identified Marcello as one of the participants in that piece of political chicanery, didn't the account lend credence to the sort of charges being investigated by the Louisiana legislative committee? Wasn't Marcello being accused before the committee of taking part in just such political manipulation?

"Let me tell you about that crap this committee is investigating," Marcello said. "It's full of lies. People take one little piece of true information, twist it around, add a lot of bullshit and come up with some charges that don't even resemble the truth. Look what's been said about Churchill Farms, for example. Supposedly, the story goes, I bought the property for a million dollars; that's wrong to start with. Then I'm supposed to have had some underhanded scheme in mind all the time to make a killing on the land. Also, I'm accused of being the only one who benefits from the drainage work done by the state. That's all a lot of crap. This is what really happened.

"Years ago, when I was still in the gambling business, one of the bookmakers who worked for me ran into a problem with a bettor. This bettor owed us $60,000 and he didn't have the money to pay us. He came in to see me, wanting to square things. The only thing he had that was worth anywhere near $60,000 was this piece of property— 6000 acres. It was nothin' but an alligator swamp then. It had been in his family ever since the Civil War. I didn't have any idea what the land was worth or what I'd do with it if I took it off his hands. But I told him I'd have it appraised and let him know. I sent some appraisers out there, and they told me they figured the land was worth maybe $54,000. I told the bettor I'd wipe out his debt if he gave me the land plus $6000 in cash. He raised the $6000 somehow, and we closed the deal.

"For years, that land was nothin' but a goddam white elephant to me. I couldn't do anythin' with it. The banks wouldn't give me a mortgage on it; they didn't want to risk publicity for dealing with Carlos Marcello. Nobody

wanted to buy the land from me; as I said, it was nothin'
but a goddam alligator swamp. So I was stuck with it.
Year after year, all I did was pay taxes on it.

"As the time went by, most of the property near downtown New Orleans was developed. The developers kept
pushing farther and farther into the outskirts of town. Naturally, as more and more land was used up, the property
values on the remaining acreage increased. So Churchill
Farms became more valuable—just like many other pieces
of property. All I did was hold onto this white elephant because I couldn't get rid of it, and then it luckily became
worth more money. I still don't know what I'm gonna do
with the place. I haven't made any money on it yet—not a
cent. But, if you believe some people, I've already made a
killing on it. Let me show you something."

With that, he drew open the gold-colored drapery covering the large wall behind his desk, revealing a huge aerial
photo of the New Orleans area. "This is Churchill Farms,"
Marcello said, pointing to a section of the photo marked
by a green-crayon border. "According to the charges,
Churchill Farms is the only property covered by the drainage project. That's a goddam lie. All these other areas are
covered, and I don't own any of them." He pointed to numerous parcels outside the green border. Marcello did not
deny that he had used his political influence to get the
drainage project approved. He said he had the same right
as any property owner to seek a public works project in his
area and insisted that other land-holders had also benefited. (Witnesses before the legislative committee, as will
be seen, later challenged Marcello's version.)

"Here's another thing," Marcello said. "The people
tryin' to spread this garbage about me make it look like I
used some kind of influence on the Federal officials to get
them to route the Dixie Freeway through part of Churchill

Farms. That's ridiculous. Just look at the picture and the map and you'll see how ridiculous it is." Pointing again to the aerial photo, Marcello indicated a narrow strip of land separating Lake Cataouateheon from the Mississippi River. "That land is all part of Churchill Farms," he said. "It's the only piece of land in the area between the lake and the river. So where else are they gonna build the freeway? If they don't put it there, they'd have to build a road right across the water. To tell you the truth, I wish to hell they could put it somewhere else. All it's gonna bring me is headaches. With the complaints about why they're puttin' the freeway through my property, I'll probably get some more heat from the Federal Government."

(Marcello's prediction was correct. A short time later the Justice Department launched an investigation of how the freeway came to be routed through Churchill Farms. It was disclosed that, if the original plan were followed, the government would have to pay Marcello $170,000 for a 300-foot-wide right-of-way through his property. A Federal highway official in Louisiana said when the Justice Department investigation was announced that the Churchill Farms route was the only logical one. "If Judas Priest himself owned some of that land, we wouldn't have any choice except to set a fair price and negotiate with him," the official insisted.)

In the interview, Marcello refused to identify any of his close associates in government—saying he wanted to avoid embarrassing them—but conceded they held high Federal, state and local offices. How high? As high as they go in Louisiana. These men include not only top state officials, but leading figures in both houses of Congress. Marcello reiterated that he had the same right as anyone else to cultivate political friendships. "If I've done anything wrong, let's see somebody prosecute me for it," he said. "But why should I have to apologize for who my friends are—for having friends who are politicians?"

As the interview drew to a close, Marcello gave this writer his unlisted telephone number. "Call me anytime," he said. "I'll be glad to talk to you." That brought up the question of how freely he felt he could speak on the phone. Wasn't he suspicious that his line might be tapped? "Hell, what if it is?" he replied. "I don't have anything to hide."

The session ended with agreement that further interviews could be arranged. Subsequently, this writer was approached by a law-enforcement official who said he had learned of the interview. He would not say how he learned of it, but he did say he knew that additional interviews were anticipated. With that in mind, he asked the writer to become an unofficial emissary to Marcello—offering him a possible deal in his case involving the purported assault on the FBI agent. The official needed a vital tidbit of information in a politically sensitive investigation he was conducting. He had reason to believe that Marcello—and perhaps only Marcello—could provide the information. If Marcello would cooperate, the official said, he might be able to help Marcello get a reduction of the two-year prison sentence in the assault case. He emphasized that Marcello would never have to testify about the matter, merely provide the information on a confidential basis.

This writer then arranged to meet Marcello in Houston, Texas, where a Federal judge had scheduled a hearing on motions for a new trial and a reduction of sentence in the assault case. (Marcello's case had been transferred to Houston on the ground that he could not get a fair trial in New Orleans because of long-standing unfavorable publicity there.) Several additional interviews took place in Houston, mainly concerning the assault case and Marcello's possible imprisonment. During these interviews, the offer of a possible deal with the law-enforcement official was discussed. When asked about the information the official wanted, Marcello made clear that he had the information all right. "What you're asking about happened quite a while ago," he said. But there was no question that it *had* happened, which was what the official wanted to know. Marcello made it equally clear, however, that he had no intention of cooperating with the official and did not want the information passed on—even if it might save him from prison or reduce his term. In short, he chose to abide by the underworld code of *omerta* (silence).

"I'm not anxious to go to the can," he said. "But I've been there before and, if I have to, I can stand it again."

At the hearing in the assault case, Marcello's attorneys presented new evidence supporting a claim that the FBI had illegally "entrapped" him by provoking the airport incident. The defense contended that the FBI had deliberately tipped off newsmen to Marcello's impending arrival at the New Orleans airport, so its men could infiltrate the press contingent and lure Marcello into a confrontation with the agents. Although conceding that there was some basis for believing this version, Judge John V. Singleton, Jr., ruled that Marcello's lawyers had not made a sufficiently strong case for reversal of the conviction. "When the Supreme Court and other courts rule that the government can set the stage [for a prosecution]—that it can lay the bait out—then entrapment is pretty hard to get at," Singleton said in denying the motion for a new trial. As for the motion to reduce Marcello's sentence, on the ground that a two-year term was excessive in a case in which no blow had even been struck, Singleton was equally unpersuaded. He gave Marcello forty-five days to get his affairs in order before surrendering to begin serving the sentence.

Later, however, the judge had a change of heart and reduced the term from two years to six months—citing the
circumstances of the case and Marcello's age. After Marcello's final appeal had been denied by the U.S. Supreme
Court, he surrendered and began serving his sentence on
October 14, 1970. He was released on March 12, 1971.

During his imprisonment, the legislative committee continued its investigation. Three witnesses testified at committee hearings that few persons other than Marcello had
benefited from the $2.5 million drainage project in the
Churchill Farms area. They said intense political pressure
was exerted to get the project approved, over their objections that the project was a blatant give away of public
funds. "It was public money and it seemed to me it was
being used for a private land-owner," said Ben Rome,
former president of a public flood-control agency that authorized the project. "The money wasn't there. The board
[of his agency] didn't have enough money to pay its staff."
Rome said he did everything he legally could to block the
project, but was eventually overcome by political pressure.
He said he was fired six months after his election to head
the agency because he persisted in attempts to cut public
expenditures.

Glen Long, who was attorney for the agency at the time
the project was under consideration, testified that the political pressure intensified during the waning days of Jimmie Davis's last term as governor. "Pressure was being
brought to bear from somewhere," Long said. "At what
level the influence was brought to bear, I don't know. All
of a sudden, it was an urgent, A-number-one project."
Long said Marcello and an attorney, Phillip Smith, made a
"social visit" to his home one night in an attempt to persuade him to drop his opposition to the project, but that he

refused. Despite such opposition, Governor Davis signed a contract authorizing the project on his last day in office.

An associate of Marcello's in Churchill Farms, J. F. Roy, told the committee that the drainage project had not originally been Marcello's idea but rather had been initiated by the State Public Works Department. This version was disputed, however, by department engineer Arthur Theis. "We had no such plans," Theis testified. "The Department of Public Works doesn't initiate any work." He said the department did the work only on orders from officials of other agencies.

The legislative committee, in its final report, concluded that Marcello had benefited materially from the use of public funds on the project. After hearing testimony on other subjects, it also concluded that the State Revenue Department had shown favoritism to Marcello and his associates in allowing them to evade state taxes. This favoritism raised "a suspicion of corrupt influence," the committee said. Special treatment had also been given by the department to Marcello's friend, Democratic National Committeeman Marshall Brown, the committee charged. The panel's report said the committee found it "hard to understand" why the chief Revenue Department attorney, Emmett Batson, had been kept in office even after other officials discovered he had not filed his own tax returns on time.

In testimony before the committee a Marcello associate, State Racing Commissioner Tom Ashy, conceded that he had placed bets "for friends" with bookmakers and had telephoned such bets to Racing Commission employees at tracks within the state. Telephone records introduced at the committee hearings showed that Ashy had made more than 100 calls in a year to Marcello's brother, Vincent. Ashy denied that there was anything improper about his relationship with Carlos or Vincent Marcello, insisting that he had never given them any special favors. He also denied that he was a bookmaker, but the committee found charges that he was a bookie to be "substantially correct."

As for allegations that Marcello dominated the state government, the committee found suspicion of corruption but said it had no firm evidence to sustain the charges. Cynics noted, however, that members of the committee were themselves part of the very state government that Marcello was said to dominate. They also pointed out that the committee had originally been appointed only in response to repeated complaints from outsiders about Marcello's political influence—and amid heated denials of such influence from state officials. Thus, it was considered hardly surprising that committee members—while reporting evidence of Marcello's influence in specific cases—would refrain from making a broad-scale finding that he controlled the state government in which they served.

Marcello, meanwhile, resumed operations as usual after his release from Federal prison. He showed no inclination to slacken the pace of his behind-the-scenes political manipulation.

Further allegations of political corruption in Louisiana arose in June 1971 when flamboyant New Orleans District Attorney Jim Garrison was arrested by Federal agents on charges of taking bribes to protect illegal pinball gambling. The Justice Department accused Garrison of taking up to $1,500 a month in payoffs. Nine other men, including two ranking policemen and several top officials of pinball machine companies, were also arrested. All pleaded not guilty and are awaiting trial at this writing. Garrison, vehemently denying the charges, said: "I've never accepted a dollar in my life." He claimed the arrest was an attempt by the Federal government to suppress his widely publicized attempt to prove that a conspiracy was responsible for the assassination of President John F. Kennedy.

The influence of organized crime on the government of Louisiana is paralleled in dozens of other states in all regions of the country.

Room at the Top

The Mafia has found that political connections at the state level often can make up for a failure to corrupt certain officials at the local level. Suppose, for example, Mob corrupters found themselves unable to buy protection in a city government. By some odd set of circumstances all the officials in that city were honest. The Mafia tried to operate there anyway and one of its key men was arrested. Since the local district attorney and the judges were also honest, there was no way to fix the case. The mobster was convicted and given a stiff prison term. Suppose, however, that the Mob had corrupted key officials at the state level —perhaps the governor or some of his most important aides. The governor, answerable to nobody on such matters, would have the power to pardon the imprisoned racketeer.

This hypothetical case is no mere daydream. Examples of just this sort of corruption are prevalent in many states. Pennsylvania, for instance, has had a long history of gubernatorial pardons to syndicate racketeers—a history traced in detail in a report issued by the State Crime Commission.

Item: The Federal government once tried to deport John S. LaRocca, boss of a Mafia family in southwestern Pennsylvania, on the ground that his record of criminal convictions made him an undesirable alien. Governor John Fine then pardoned LaRocca for the crimes of larceny, receiving stolen goods, and operating a lottery—thus clearing the mobster's record and making deportation impossible. Although the pardon was filed after hearings in the deportation case had been completed, Fine back-dated it to the period when the hearings were still in progress in order to thwart the Federal authorities.

Item: Joseph Frank Rosa, a *caporegime* (captain) in LaRocca's Mafia family, was also pardoned by Governor Fine. The crimes for which he was pardoned included bombing and illegal entry.

Item: Luigi Quaranta, a Mafia member, was pardoned by Governor George Earle for the crime of murder.

Item: Joseph Luciano, another Mafia member, was pardoned by Governor Earle in a robbery case.

Item: Nicholas Piccolo, a *caporegime* in Angelo Bruno's Philadelphia Mafia family, was pardoned by Governor James Duff in a robbery case.

Item: Frank S. "Blinky" Palermo, a Mafioso and notorious figure in the professional boxing world, was pardoned by Governor Duff for the crimes of aggravated assault and battery and operating a lottery. The pardon was needed so that Palermo could obtain a boxing manager's license. Later, Palermo was convicted on a Federal charge of interstate extortion involving boxing rackets.

Item: Felix Bocchiccio, a Mafia associate and friend of Palermo, was pardoned for a prison escape.

Item: John Wittig, the enforcer for a gambling syndicate, was given a commutation of his prison sentence for murder.

Item: Leo Kaminski, a leading racketeer in Erie, Pennsylvania, was given a commutation of his sentence for bribery and conspiracy by Governor George Leader.

Item: Louis Barish, a convicted murderer and an associate of a Pittsburgh Mafia family, was given a commutation of sentence.

State officials, as well as officials at other levels, use other means besides the pardon system to help mobsters who have fallen into the clutches of the law. Often, an official appears in court as a character witness for a racketeer—claiming the defendant is such a paragon of virtue that he could not possibly have committed the crime in question. If the mobster's guilt is so plain that such an appearance would be futile, the official may appear before the judge at the time of sentencing to plead for leniency. Usually, such an appeal is based on a claim that the defendant is an asset to his community, a good family man, and a churchgoer whose imprisonment would accomplish nothing. Since judges are creatures of the political system, often beholden to the officials who appear on behalf of the Mob, they find it hard to resist the pleas.

As in the case of pardons, Pennsylvania has long been notorious for such court appearances by public officials. The Pennsylvania Crime Commission, in its published report on organized crime, itemized a series of such appearances. When a mobster named George Barrow was tried on a racketeering charge, for example, his character witnesses included Congressman William A. Barrett, Delaware County District Attorney Raymond Start, a Pennsylvania mayor, a magistrate, a county commissioner, a city tax collector, and a former assistant Philadelphia police superintendent. When racketeer Ben Lapensohn was tried on a charge of conspiracy to defraud, his character witnesses included Philadelphia County Court Judges Adrian Bonnelly, Benjamin Schwartz, and Edward Kallick, Magistrate Harry Ellick, Philadelphia City Councilman George

Schwartz, Commissioner of Voting Registration Harold Salkind, former Philadelphia City Solicitor Frank Truscott, and sixty-seven other persons.

Pennsylvania State Representative Charles Caputo, a police chief and a former state trooper were among the character witnesses for Mafia *caporegime* Antonio Ripepi at an extradition hearing on a charge of assault and battery. State Representative Matthew Coppolino, Philadelphia City Council Minority Leader Thomas Foglietta, and City Councilman Benjamin Cucuroto were character witnesses for Mob loansharks Edward and James Datillo when they were tried on 209 counts of usury. State Supreme Court Justice Henry O'Brien, another judge, and a police chief were witnesses for former Assistant Pittsburgh Police Superintendent Lawrence Maloney when he was tried for tax evasion involving failure to report to the Internal Revenue Service bribes he had taken from racketeers.

Philadelphia County Court Judge Adrian Bonnelly, in addition to appearing as a witness for Ben Lapensohn, also testified at a deportation hearing on behalf of Russell Bufalino, boss of a Mafia family in northeastern Pennsylvania, and at a tax-evasion trial on behalf of a gambling czar named Abe Minker. A police chief and two of his officers were character witnesses at a naturalization hearing for Giaocchino "Dandy Jack" Parisi, a high-ranking member of the Buffalino family. Philadelphia City Councilman Raymond Alexander testified to the good character of Harry Riccobene, a member of Angelo Bruno's Mafia family, at a narcotics-trafficking trial. And Philadelphia Common Pleas Court Judge William Dwyer appeared at a tax-evasion trial on behalf of a top Mob loanshark, Frank Jaskiewicz.

Commenting on both the prevalence of gubernatorial

pardons for racketeers and the frequency with which public officials appear as character witnesses for mobsters, the
Pennsylvania Crime Commission charged: "The only logical conclusion that can be drawn . . . is that organized criminals in Pennsylvania have benefited from the method of
administering criminal justice. Whether through bribery,
political influence, or subtle manipulation of its processes,
the criminal justice system has operated more to the advantage of the racketeer than for justice and the safety of
society."

Corrupting the Courts

Pennsylvania is far from alone in the perversion of its
state court system for the benefit of the Mob. Parallel situ-
ations exist in many other states. In New York, it is common for Mafia bosses to hand-pick cooperative lawyers for
places on the important state court benches. Once, a wiretap picked up a conversation in which State Supreme
Court Justice Thomas A. Aurelio thanked Mafia boss
Frank Costello for obtaining the judgeship for him. "It
went over perfect," Costello replied. "When I tell you
something is in the bag, you can rest assured." Aurelio
again thanked the Mob boss profusely, then added: "I
want to assure you of my loyalty for all you have done. It's
undying." Although the wiretap was made public and resulted in a grand jury investigation, it came to naught and
Aurelio retained the judgeship. The Aurelio affair was no
mere isolated case; it was typical of a pattern that has
been followed many times in New York. The Mob's influence in selecting judges and corrupting their actions on
the bench is being investigated at this writing by the New
York Joint Legislative Committee on Crime.

Although the investigation has a long way to go, it has
already produced significant evidence of court fixes, politi-

cal interference in Mob cases, and a generally lenient approach to racketeers by numerous judges. Several witnesses, wearing hoods to protect their identities from the Mob, testified that the Mafia had paid off judges to dismiss rackets cases. One hooded witness, a hoodlum, testified that his Mafia superiors told him he didn't have to worry if he were ever arrested in Brooklyn because "we got judges on the payroll that can straighten it out one-two-three."

A study made by the committee staff disclosed that, although 536 organized-crime figures had been arrested for felonies in the New York metropolitan area during the previous decade, only thirty-seven had been sent to prison. Jeremiah McKenna, a committee consultant, said the study showed conclusively that mobsters fared far better in the state courts than other criminals not affiliated with the Mafia.

It is a common practice among lawyers representing the Mob to seek interminable delays in a racketeer's case until it comes up before a "friendly" judge. Since dockets are rotated periodically among the judges, it usually is only a matter of time before a cooperative judge gets the case. One New York mobster who apparently has had more than his share of "friendly" judges is a Mafia enforcer named Dominick "Mimi" Scialo. Since 1944, Scialo has been arrested fourteen times on charges ranging from felonious assault and rape to first-degree murder. But he has never been sent to jail. Excerpts from Scialo's police record show the monotonous regularity with which he has been let off the hook by the state courts:

10/5/44—Arrested on a felonious assault charge. Case dismissed 11/13/44.

5/27/47—Arrested on charges of rape and assault. Charges dismissed 6/18/47.

8/9/50—Arrested on a charge of grand larceny. Case dismissed 9/11/50.

12/3/50—Arrested on charges of felonious assault
with a gun and attempted robbery. Charges dismissed
12/13/50.

11/20/54—Arrested on a felonious assault charge.
Case dismissed 12/8/54.

3/14/55—Arrested on a felonious assault charge.
Convicted of a reduced charge, disorderly conduct,
and let off with a thirty-day suspended sentence.
Served no jail time.

10/7/55—Arrested on a gambling charge. Case dismissed 10/19/55.

7/27/59 and 3/29/60—Arrested on two charges of
first-degree murder. Both cases dismissed 12/1/60.

6/11/70—Arrested on a charge of criminal contempt for refusal to answer questions of a grand jury
investigating Mob infiltration of legitimate business.
Case still pending at this writing.

Of all the charges dismissed in Scialo's long underworld
career, the most noteworthy undoubtedly were the two
first-degree murder raps. Scialo, with accomplices, was accused of beating two young men to death with snow-tire
chains. The evidence disclosed that Scialo had previously
hired the victims—Bartholomew Garafalo, eighteen, and
Alexander Menditto, nineteen—to burn down a dance hall
in Boston. Although Garafalo and Menditto botched the
job, they insisted they be paid in full. When Scialo refused,
Garafalo and Menditto were said to have beaten him up in
a tavern and then added the indignity of shoving his head
into a toilet bowl and flushing the toilet. Later, it was
charged, Scialo and several accomplices waylaid the two
young men and beat them to pulps with the chains.

The victims were found in a vacant lot—Garafalo already dead and Menditto dying. Before his death, how-

ever, Menditto gave police a statement, signed in his hospital room, that implicated Scialo. On the basis of this statement and other evidence, Scialo was charged with the two murders. Later, Menditto's deathbed statement was said to have mysteriously disappeared from the district attorney's office. The charges were then dismissed. Circumstances of the dismissal, as well as those in the various other cases against Scialo, are among the facts currently under investigation by the state legislative committee.

Influence Peddling

There is a tendency among the uninformed to assume that the Mafia's corruption of state governments is confined to such urbanized states as New York and Pennsylvania. Not so. As one Mob corrupter with coast-to-coast influence told this writer: "I make as much money in Mississippi and Alabama as I do anywhere else." Pressed for details, the racketeer pulled from his billfold a business card that identified him as an official of a construction company with headquarters in Mississippi's state capital, Jackson.

"Mississippi is one of the last states in the country where the governor and his administration can give out construction contracts to just about anybody they want," he said. "My outfit's got contracts all over the state. We can get contracts in other states—in fact, we do—but it's a lot more complicated and a lot less profitable. There are a lot more people to take care of [bribe] and you have to go through the rigmarole of making sure you submit the lowest bid. Sometimes, you have to pay off competing companies to put in high bids. All of that cuts down on the profits. In Mississippi, you take care of a few select people and you've got it made. It's a lot simpler, and a lot more dough can be made."

As for Alabama, the corrupter said the Mob was "making a fortune" there on state control of liquor distribution. "You know, the governor of Alabama has the power to designate the brand-name of every bottle of liquor sold in the state. The state operates the liquor stores. For a price, we get the state to handle brands bought from companies that we control. Hell, we've got a license to steal. You should see some of the half-assed brands we peddle down there at premium prices. The customer doesn't have any choice; it's a monopoly situation. The only place he can buy booze is at the state store, unless he goes to a bootlegger—and we control most of the bootlegging, anyway. The governor of Alabama gets a salary of $25,000 a year, but in his four-year term he can pick up at least a million dollars in liquor payoffs. If he's making that much, you can imagine what kind of dough *we're* making."

Another generally rural state in which the highest councils of government have been corrupted has been West Virginia. In 1968, a grand jury indicted former Governor William W. Barron, State Road Commissioner Burl A. Sawyers, Deputy Road Commissioner Vincent Johnkoski, Finance and Administration Commissioner Truman E. Gore and two other men on charges of violating the Federal anti-racketeering laws. The defendants were accused of participating in a mammoth conspiracy to obtain bribes on numerous contracts awarded by the state.

The scandal centered around the colorful former Governor Barron, who had long been a controversial figure in West Virginia politics. Barron, the son of a Presbyterian minister, first won public office as mayor of Elkins (population 9000). From that modest beginning, he rose steadily to more important offices—including state legislator, state attorney general, and state liquor commissioner. If he had not been exposed to racketeers before—which is a big if, if it is in a state with a long history of corruption such as West Virginia—Barron got a full taste of Mob tactics as liquor commissioner. Just as in Alabama, mobsters have consistently played an important role in determining West Virginia's liquor policies. Barron emerged from the commissioner's job, however, without any taint of public scandal.

He was not so lucky in his campaign for governor. One of his opponents accused Barron during the campaign of offering him $65,000 to drop out of the race. What's more, the opponent produced a tape-recording of a conversation with Barron as proof. Barron admitted it was his voice on the tape, but claimed that only campaign expenditures had been discussed in the secretly recorded conversation. Whether the voters believed him or just felt that a slight trace of crookedness was to be expected in a West Virginia politician, Barron was easily elected.

During his term as governor, there were repeated rumors of broad-scale corruption in the state administration. It was not until he left office, however, that Federal investigators caught up with him. The indictment accusing him of violating the anti-racketeering laws charged that Barron had appointed Commissioners Sawyers, Gore, and Johnkoski to their state jobs as part of a bribery conspiracy. The defendants were accused of setting up dummy corporations in Ohio and Florida to serve as conduits for bribe money. Companies seeking business from the state were advised that they could obtain contracts by making payoffs, disguised as "consulting fees," to the dummy corporations.

After the payoffs had been received, the indictment said, the defendants rigged the bids to insure that the bribers received the contracts. Phony bids were arranged in the names of nonexistent firms to make the procedure appear legitimate. Contract specifications were drawn in such a way that only companies paying kickbacks could get state work. The prosecution charged the payoff money was funneled into the bank accounts of one of the dummy corporations in Florida, then split among the defendants.

Barron and his alleged confederates went on trial on August 13, 1968. Witness after witness testified about making payoffs to the dummy corporations and then getting state contracts. One witness said he paid five-per-cent kickbacks on all sales to the state. Another said he paid $29,000 to get contracts to supply the state with paint. Still another said he made payoffs on every load of stone he sold to the state for use in construction work.

In a verdict that took many by surprise—since the evidence against Barron seemed stronger than that against his codefendants—the jury acquitted the former governor but convicted Commissioners Sawyers and Johnkoski and two other men, an attorney named Bonn Brown and an automobile dealer named Alfred W. Schroath. (Testimony had shown that Brown and Schroath had incorporated the dummy companies and served as middlemen in finding firms willing to make payoffs.) The sixth defendant, Commissioner Gore, had his case severed from that of the others when his lawyer became ill during the trial. Gore, who pleaded not guilty, has not been tried as of this writing. Brown and Schroath were sentenced to four years in Federal prison; Sawyers and Johnkoski got two years.

But that wasn't the end of the story. Two and a half years after the trial, those who had been surprised by Barron's acquittal learned the apparent reason for the verdict. On February 20, 1971, Barron and his wife, Opal, were indicted on charges of paying $25,000 to the foreman of the trial jury to get him acquitted. The foreman, Ralph Buckalew, pleaded guilty and was sentenced to twelve years in

Federal prison. Facing the prospect that Buckalew would testify against him, Barron also pleaded guilty after persuading the prosecutors to drop the charges against his wife. U.S. District Judge John A. Field, Jr., sentenced Barron to twelve years in prison and fined him $50,000. "This was an offense that strikes at the very heart of the administration of justice," the judge said in pronouncing sentence. "I know that there were many things that would ameliorate the condition of the governor. I know that he was a desperate man. But this is not the time for this court to indulge in personal compassion." Barron began serving his sentence on March 29, 1971.

As a result of the Barron scandal, the West Virginia Legislature appointed a commission to investigate corruption in the state government and make recommendations on how to overhaul the state's procedures for dealing with private companies. Commenting on the Barron case, the commission said: "The appalling truth unfolded during the [racketeering] trial was that against these practices—all the wheeling and dealing, the influence peddling, the rakeoffs and kickbacks, the rigged bidding, and undercover deals—West Virginia and West Virginians were utterly helpless. The state government was not organized to detect and prosecute these crimes. It was scarcely constituted to suspect or guard against them. From the testimony during the trial, it appeared that, both in and out of government, there are men who think it perfectly proper to 'make a deal' in order to sell to the state."

There are indeed many such men bent on corrupting state government, not only in West Virginia but in most other states as well. And, as the next chapter will show, a large proportion of them represent a special constituency —the Mob.

[6]

The Fine Art
of Official Corruption

For three days in April 1971 many of the nation's leading experts on the Mafia met at a hotel in Houston, Texas, to discuss strategy for combatting organized crime. The occasion was the sixteenth annual conference of the Law Enforcement Intelligence Unit, an elite group of racket-busters from leading law-enforcement agencies throughout the country. Those attending the conference stood around the hotel lobby between formal sessions, talking shop. In one group was a handsome young lawyer named Martin Danziger, chief of the Organized Crime Program Division of the U.S. Justice Department's Law Enforcement Assistance Administration—the agency that provides Federal aid to state and local governments for use in fighting crime. Danziger pulled from his briefcase a thick brochure with a yellow cover bearing the prosaic title, *Guide for Discretionary Grant Programs.*

"You know, there's a helluva good untold story here," he told those standing around him, including this writer. "Nobody's been paying much attention to it." He was greeted with blank stares. If there was an untold story in that dry government brochure, filled with bureaucratic jargon, few of us in the group could imagine what it might be. But Danziger, undaunted, plunged ahead. Opening the brochure to page 82, he pointed to a passage of his agency's organized crime program headed "Statewide Corruption Control Units."

"Read that," he said. "Most people have been ignoring it." The passage began: "The objective of this program is to encourage the establishment of units to investigate and combat corruption at the state level of government. There is a need for most states to establish a separate unit with responsibility for, and full-time attention devoted to, the problem of official corruption." Danziger's implication was clear. The Mob's corruption of state governments had reached such epidemic proportions that the Federal government was now offering hundreds of thousands of dollars to the states to combat the problem. But state officials, reluctant to have anyone poke into their cozy arrangements with racketeers, were allowing the Federal funds to go begging.

Judging by past experience, however, corrupt state officials cannot hope to be entirely successful in covering up their dealings with the Mob. Despite zealous efforts to maintain a mantle of secrecy over such dealings, many of them have been discovered. Several of the more notable disclosures have involved corrupt alliances between state officials and the Mafia boss of New England, Raymond Patriarca.

For more than a quarter-century, Patriarca's headquarters in Providence, Rhode Island, has been the hub of a criminal empire that has sprawled across all of New England and exercised influence from Canada to the Caribbean islands. A key ingredient in Patriarca's exercise of power has been his control of political leaders. The first public exposure of this control occurred after he was convicted in Massachusetts of three crimes that could have brought him a maximum of twenty years in prison. A judge let him off with a combined sentence of only five years, but that was just the beginning of the story. After Patriarca had served a mere eighty-four days behind bars, then-Governor Charles Hurley granted him a full pardon on all three convictions. Hurley acted on the recommendation of his right-hand man, Massachusetts Executive Councilor Daniel H. Coakley, who had drafted the pardon petition and guided it through governmental channels.

The petition had ostensibly been signed by three clergymen who attested to Patriarca's good character. But, after the mobster had been pardoned, it was discovered that one of the purported clergymen didn't exist and that the other two had never heard of the petition—much less signed it. Although there was no way of revoking the pardon, a state investigating commission launched a lengthy investigation of how it had come to be granted in the first place. The investigation turned up evidence of Patriarca's close ties with Massachusetts political figures, most notably Executive Councilor Coakley. The commission found that Coakley had been guilty of "deceit and fraud" in pressing the pardon petition. As a result, the state legislature impeached Coakley and barred him from ever again holding public office. His impeachment was the first against any member of the Massachusetts governor's executive council in more than a century.

Further evidence of Patriarca's connections with state officials throughout New England was later uncovered when FBI agents secretly bugged the Mafia boss's Providence headquarters. For more than three years, the FBI's hidden microphone eavesdropped on Patriarca's conversations. Every few days, FBI men forwarded to their superiors summaries of the tape-recorded discussions. Excerpts from these summaries contained such reports as the following:

> Joe Modica [a Boston racketeer] contacted Patriarca specifically concerning the Berkshire Downs

Race Track, in which Patriarca allegedly has a financial interest. Patriarca told Modica to contact his friend who is allegedly extremely close to Attorney General Edward W. Brooke of Massachusetts [now a United States senator] and have him arrange to release the $100,000 bond that is being held by the Massachusetts court in connection with civil suits that have been heard in Massachusetts courts.

Henry Tameleo [a Patriarca subordinate] advised he contacted George Kattar and reiterated to Kattar that in order to operate he "must have the State." Kattar told him that he has arranged to pay off the state police and that he would furnish Tameleo the identities and the amounts paid to individual members of the state police. This apparently refers to a gambling operation that Kattar will open in Biddeford, Maine.

Patriarca said that he was contacting ———— [a state official whose name was not disclosed] to obtain the parole of Lee Santanielle and Lawrence Baione [both Mob lieutenants].

Roy French, a horse trainer, contacted Gennaro Anguilo [the underboss of Patriarca's Mafia family] through an intermediary, requesting assistance to obtain a state license as a horse trainer at the Rhode Island tracks. Patriarca indicated he would assist in this.

The FBI disclosed that among those "owned" by Patriarca were top officials in several state governments, a high-ranking court administrator, two licensing officials, a police chief and numerous state legislators. It also revealed that the going rate for corrupting high state officials in New England was $100,000.

One case in which Patriarca was unsuccessful in trying to corrupt a state official—and then resorted to an unusual means of retaliation—was uncovered by the FBI. Patriarca offered a $100,000 "campaign contribution" to Massachusetts Lieutenant Governor Francis S. Bellotti, who was running for governor. In return, Patriarca wanted a promise that Bellotti would protect his rackets if elected. Bellotti rejected the contribution. Patriarca responded by spreading word through subtle means to the public that the money had been accepted. The false rumors were a key factor in Bellotti's defeat in the gubernatorial campaign.

For every state official such as Bellotti who refused to play ball, Patriarca found several who were only too willing to cooperate. All of his political connections at the state level, however, were of virtually no use to him when Federal agents and prosecutors launched a major assault against his criminal empire. The Federal men got an important break when an imprisoned Patriarca subordinate, Joseph "the Baron" Barboza, decided he had been betrayed by the Mob and agreed to become a government witness. Two FBI agents, Dennis Condon and Paul Ricco, won Barboza's confidence and persuaded him to reveal a mother lode of information about Patriarca's operations. Among other things, Barboza told how Patriarca had ordered him to murder a gambler who had set up a dice game in Providence without Patriarca's permission. Since Barboza had crossed state lines in carrying out the murder, the FBI had jurisdiction in the case. On the basis of Barboza's testimony, Patriarca was convicted of interstate conspiracy to commit murder and sentenced to five years in prison. At this writing, he is serving his sentence at the Federal penitentiary in Atlanta, Georgia.

Other prosecutions of members of the Patriarca family followed the boss's conviction. These put a dent in the

Mob's operations, but the family has been able to continue functioning on a limited basis—with Patriarca still calling the shots by passing messages through the prison and underworld grapevines. Moreover, there is considerable doubt that Patriarca will have to serve his complete sentence. Barboza has now had a change of heart and has recanted testimony he gave in a trial involving several Patriarca aides. Patriarca's lawyers, contending that this recantation will exonerate Patriarca as well as the aides, are seeking the Mob boss's release. If he does win his freedom, it's a cinch Patriarca will try to benefit from his past miscalculation and go looking for Federal officials to join the state officials in his stable of corrupt allies.

One problem confronting those who seek to eliminate Mafia bribery of state officials is the lenient treatment often given by judges to those involved in corruption cases. In one classic case of this kind, a Mafia corrupter named Walter J. Plopi tossed a wad of bills on the desk of a Pennsylvania state senator in an attempt to persuade him to influence a newly elected prosecutor to protect gambling rackets. As a starter, Plopi promised to pay the prosecutor $2,000 a month to allow numbers racket operations in McKeesport. If the prosecutor "really wanted to play ball" and permit even wider gambling, Plopi said, the payoffs would be raised to $200,000 a year plus any money needed for future political campaigns. By prearrangement with the state senator, state police had been hidden in an adjoining room during the meeting with Plopi—tape-recording the entire conversation. After gathering sufficient incriminating evidence, the police burst into the office, arrested Plopi and seized the wad of bills he had thrown on the senator's desk. Plopi was convicted of attempted bribery, for which he could have received a stiff jail sentence. Instead a judge let him off with a mere $250 fine. What's more, the judge handed him back the wad of bills seized as evidence. After paying the $250 fine, Plopi walked out of court richer than when he had entered.

In New Jersey, the minority leader of the State Assembly, David J. Friedland, was accused of acting as a middleman in obtaining the dismissal of criminal charges against a Mafia enforcer and loanshark. Friedland's purported involvement with the Mob first came to light when Assistant New Jersey Attorney General William J. Brennan 3rd accused him of being one of three state legislators who were "too comfortable with members of organized crime." All three legislators issued denials, but the legislature appointed a special committee to investigate Brennan's charge.

As a result, the two other legislators accused by Brennan—State Senator Sido L. Ridolfi and Assemblyman John E. Selecky—were censured by the legislature. The only action taken by the legislature in Minority Leader Friedland's case, however, was to refer the charge against him to the state courts. A grand jury looked into the Friedland affair, but took no action. The State Supreme Court then appointed Superior Court Judge Alexander P. Waugh to conduct a hearing on the matter.

The hearing centered around Friedland's activities on behalf of John Di Gilio, a loanshark and enforcer for Joseph "Joe Bayonne" Zicarelli, the Mafia boss of northern Hudson County. A criminal complaint charging Di Gilio with attempted extortion had been filed by Julius Pereira, owner of an automatic car-wash business and head of a Young Democrats organization in New Jersey. Pereira accused Di Gilio of threatening his life and having windows at his car wash smashed because he had reneged on nearly $5,000 in usurious loans.

There was testimony at the hearing that Pereira agreed

to drop the charges after receiving a cash payoff from Di Gilio. There was also testimony that Assemblyman Friedland had served both as Di Gilio's lawyer in the case and as a go-between in arranging the payoff. A dual role in the case was also played by Norman Robbins, the municipal prosecutor for Woodbridge Township. Although the criminal complaint against Di Gilio had been filed in the court where Robbins served as prosecutor, he acted as Pereira's private counsel in the case. There was testimony that Di Gilio gave Friedland $6,500 in cash and that Friedland handed the money over to Robbins. Witnesses testified that the money was then divided among Pereira, Friedland, and Robbins and the case against Di Gilio was dismissed.

Judge Waugh ruled that Friedland had been guilty of impropriety in the case, but he had no power to take action against the legislator. His ruling was sent to the State Supreme Court for review and possible disciplinary action. On July 27, 1971, the State Supreme Court suspended Friedland and Robbins from practicing law for six months. In its decision, the court said: "It is impossible to come to any conclusion but that the proposed [cash] settlement was for the sole purpose of suppressing the criminal complaints [against Di Gilio]." The court ruled that Robbins had engaged in a conflict of interests and should have made clear to the judge in the Di Gilio case his conflicting roles as prosecutor and attorney for Pereira. Despite the Supreme Court ruling, Friedland, and Robbins continued to insist they had done nothing wrong.

On the very day that Judge Waugh issued his ruling in the Friedland case, another New Jersey legislator pleaded guilty to criminal charges in an unrelated matter. Assemblyman Peter W. Moraites, a former speaker of the Assembly, had been indicted on charges of accepting illegal fees for helping various companies obtain $2.4 million in "improvident" loans from a bank of which he was a director. The indictment, handed down by a grand jury investigating organized crime and official corruption, accused Moraites and a confederate of taking more than $66,000 for their part in arranging the poor-risk loans—which were not backed by proper collateral. Moraites, a former aide to U.S. Senator Jacob K. Javits of New York, was sentenced to sixteen months in Federal prison. In an emotional speech to his fellow legislators, he resigned from the Assembly. Although he had pleaded guilty, Moraites told them he was resigning "not because I did anything wrong but because I cannot operate effectively from jail." He received a standing ovation, and many legislators rushed up to throw their arms around his shoulders and shout expressions of continued support. On April 26, 1971, Moraites surrendered to begin serving his sentence.

Still another former New Jersey legislator is currently under indictment. Joseph Biancardi, a former assemblyman who also served as president of a Teamster Union local with Mob affiliations, has been charged with misuse of union funds. The indictment resulted from a nine-month investigation by a Justice Department organized-crime strike force. Biancardi and two other Teamster officials were accused of spending $15,497 in union funds for non-union purposes. Much of the money, the indictment charged, went for illegal contributions to New Jersey political campaigns—including those of officials involved in other corruption cases. Biancardi pleaded not guilty and is awaiting trial at this writing.

The Secret Spoils of Paul Powell

One apparently corrupt state official who will never come to trial—because the full extent of his chicanery did not come to light until after his death—was Illinois Secretary of State Paul Powell. When Powell died on October 10, 1970, he was considered so powerful a political figure that his body was laid in state in the Illinois Capitol on the same catafalque that had once borne Abraham Lincoln. The state's leading Democrats and Republicans paid him flowery homage, with Governor Richard B. Ogilvie declaring: "He was, above all, a man who demanded of himself a sense of honor that stood the test of service spanning four turbulent decades."

Two months later serious doubts were cast upon Powell's "sense of honor." A search of his belongings turned up $800,000 in cash, stuffed into shoe boxes, envelopes, and a bowling bag in one of his closets and in an office safe. Further investigation disclosed that the total worth of his estate was nearly $3 million. He had somehow managed to accumulate all this wealth despite the fact that his salary had never been higher than $30,000 a year in the thirty-six years he had held various state offices.

During his flamboyant political career, Powell had never made any secret of the fact that he was a staunch supporter of the spoils system. "There's only one thing worse than a defeated politician, and that's a broke politician," he said often. But, while he was alive, nobody suspected just how far from broke he was and no serious investigation of his activities was launched. Even when it was discovered that Powell had issued a special unlisted automobile license plate to Chicago Mafia boss Sam "Momo" Giancana, the incident was passed off as a minor peccadillo.

After Powell's death the discovery of his secret horde of wealth touched off major investigations by Federal and state agents. They discovered, among other things, that one of the chief sources of his riches was an alliance with Illinois gambling interests. One of his closest friends and business associates was found to be an ex-convict named Irwin "Big Sam" Wiedrick, considered the unofficial czar of horse racing in the Chicago area. In addition, it was discovered that Powell—while holding state office—was on the payroll of the Chicago Downs race track as a $20,000-a-year "consultant."

Before becoming secretary of state in 1964, Powell had served thirty years in the Illinois Legislature—including three terms as speaker of the House. An investigation of his legislative record disclosed that he had consistently sought to help the racing interests, keeping state taxes on the tracks low and profits high. His estate showed that he owned 23,000 shares of stock in various race tracks—not available to the general public—much of which he had been allowed to buy for only ten cents a share. The value of one such block of stock, 15,400 shares in Chicago Downs, is now placed at about $600,000.

Powell was also reportedly involved in a variety of other political rackets. For example, an Illinois investigative organization, called the Better Government Association, has charged that he took large payoffs from corrupt trucking industry leaders who wanted to avoid weight regulations. The association accused him, in addition, of accepting bribes to permit Illinois trucks to operate with cheaper out-of-state licenses—many made out to fictitious addresses. Meanwhile, Internal Revenue agents launched an investigation into reports that Powell required truckers to buy expensive tires from companies in which he held secret interests. Powell controlled 5000 state patronage jobs, and insisted that his appointees kick back part of their salaries to him. He also benefited personally, to the tune of at least $500,000, from testimonial dinners and political campaign funds—despite laws that prohibit converting campaign contributions into personal wealth.

How significant will be the results of the investigations begun after Powell's death is problematical. Thus far, the only charges filed have been against a former Powell aide, William Glenn, who has been accused by a state prosecutor of tampering with state records. State's Attorney Richard Hollis charged Glenn in a criminal complaint with concealing numerous records—including titles for motor vehicles, title applications, license-plate applications and "negotiable instruments." Glenn has pleaded not guilty and has not yet come to trial at this writing. What seems most significant is that, although the complete scope of Powell's activities did not surface until his death, many public officials knew bits and pieces of the story during his lifetime and yet took no action to expose him. Powell was fond of boasting: "My friends eat at the first table." Perhaps so many of his political friends were eating there that nobody dared kick the legs out from beneath the table.

Taking More Than the Sun

Another state in which officials and mobsters frequently feast at the same table of plenty is Nevada, the legalized gambling capital of the United States. Nevada officials have long maintained that strict government regulation keeps organized-crime figures from infiltrating casino operations in the state, but the fact is that this supposed regulation often has degenerated into a charade. In some cases secretly and in other cases rather openly, top Mob leaders have dominated both gambling and political operations in Nevada.

A prime example of the alliance between racketeers and Nevada politicians is provided by the assorted escapades of the state's former lieutenant governor, Clifford A. Jones. While serving both as lieutenant governor and as the Democratic national committeeman for Nevada, Jones was actively engaged as a gambling operator. He owned pieces of three major Las Vegas gambling casinos—the Thunderbird, the Pioneer Club, and the Golden Nugget. In the Thunderbird, Jones's secret partners—not listed, as required, in state tax records—included Jake Lansky, brother of the notorious Meyer Lansky, and George Sadlo, a long-time front man for Meyer Lansky. Sadlo and Jake Lansky had often operated illegal gambling houses together in Florida and other states. Lieutenant Governor Jones, in addition to maintaining his gambling interests, also practiced law while holding office. His law firm represented, among other clients, the estate of the late mobster Benjamin "Bugsy" Siegel.

Called before a congressional committee to explain what appeared to be a conflict of interests between his gambling operations and his position as the state's second highest official, pledged to regulate the gambling business, Jones contended he owed nobody an apology. He also defended Nevada's practice of allowing convicted racketeers to hold gambling licenses. This exchange followed between the investigating committee's chief counsel and Jones:

Q. Wouldn't you say . . . a great many undesirable characters, with bad police records, were engaged in gambling operations in the state of Nevada?

A. Well, of course. I could very definitely concur with you on that. Some of them are people who have been in the state long before I was here, so I wouldn't presume to pass upon their qualifications to conduct their business.

Q. Well, there had been a lot of people—

A. There were some people that you might say had police records and reputations of [illegal] gambling in
other places. But this seems to hold true, that people
who came here when the state started to grow, to
gamble in the gambling business, they weren't particularly Sunday School teachers or preachers or anything like that from out of the state. They were gamblers. In other words, they came here to gamble.

Jones's testimony underscored the prevailing ethic in
Nevada. While paying lip service to the principle of keeping the Mob out of the state's legalized gambling, officials
actually have thrown down the welcome mat for some of
the nation's most notorious racketeers. In Nevada scores
of top mobsters are treated as if they were respectable
businessmen. An indication of the ease with which a racketeer can win acceptance in the state was provided by an
incident involving Lieutenant Governor Jones. The *Las
Vegas Sun,* a newspaper seeking evidence of corrupt alliances between Nevada politicians and the Mob, hired a
noted undercover investigator named Pierre La Fitte to
come to Las Vegas and impersonate a big-time racketeer.

La Fitte, using the name Louis Tabet, arrived shortly
after a notorious brothel had been raided by FBI agents.
The brothel had long been provided with protection by
corrupt local officials, but they had been powerless to prevent the Federal raid. Tabet sought out the brothel's owners and offered to buy the place. While negotiations were
under way, he started making arrangements for renewed
protection from both local and state officials. In addition
to operating the brothel he pretended he also wanted a
gambling license—despite the fact that his phony identity
included a long criminal record. To help work out the de-

tails, local officials arranged for Tabet to meet Lieutenant Governor Jones. At the time, a gubernatorial election campaign was taking place in Nevada. Governor Charles H. Russell was seeking a second term. He was opposed by former Governor Vail Pittman, who was supported by Jones. When Tabet met with Jones, another man was present—Dick Kellogg, general manager of the brothel, who was supposed to retain his job when Tabet took over from the prior owners. The conversation, which took place in an office at the Thunderbird Hotel, was secretly recorded by Tabet. Excerpts from the conversation follow:

Tabet. Cliff, I'm going to let my hair down now. Ordinarily, in cases like this, where a man like me has to grease the wheels to eliminate the squeak, a witness is not desirable. But in this situation, Dick [Kellogg] being my right-hand man, I do not see the necessity of leaving him out of the office.

Jones. Dick's okay. There's a couple things I want to straighten out first. I haven't had a chance to check on you personally, Louis. It's okay to call you Louis, isn't it?

Tabet. Sure.

Jones [to Kellogg]. What did you find out about Louis's connections?

Kellogg. He's okay. He knows important people in Florida, Chicago, and other places.

Jones [to Tabet]. You have a record?

Tabet. Nothing recent. A few things when I was young—a little narcotics, bootlegging, murder, manslaughter.

Jones. Anything recently?

Tabet. Not in the past eleven years.

Jones. You're all right, but not until after the first of the year when Pittman takes office. After this election we're going to be stronger than ever. To make an application for a gambling license during election time would be poor judgment, especially with your criminal record. Wait until the first of the year; then we're going to boot Robbins Cahill out of his job. After that everything is going to be smoothed out.

Tabet. Cahill?

Jones. He's the secretary of the State Tax Commission. He's the big boss in Carson City [the state capital]. He says whether you get a gambling license or not. And what he says goes up there right now, but it's going to change damn quick after the election.

Tabet. Well, I've taken care of the county. [He then named several county officials he had agreed to pay off.]

Jones. You're with the right people. I talk for the state. Louie Weiner, my [law] partner, takes care of the legal end of the deals and the finances.

Tabet. Louie told me [during a previous meeting with Weiner].

Jones. Louis, believe me. I've been called a lot of names. But everybody in the state knows me and, believe me, I can deliver. Only one thing nobody ever called me and that's stupid.

Thus, with no investigation other than asking for a brothel manager's assurance that Tabet was "okay," the lieutenant governor was willing to guarantee a gambling license for a self-described mobster with a police record for such crimes as manslaughter and murder. When the *Las Vegas Sun* published a series of articles describing Tabet's exploits and his dealings with Jones and other officials, a major scandal erupted. The Clark County sheriff and a county commissioner were indicted on charges of accepting gifts and offers of money from Tabet in return for promising him protection. As for Cliff Jones, he resigned his position as Democratic national committeeman; he did not, however, resign as lieutenant governor. In time, the furor faded without any significant steps being taken to eliminate Nevada's collusion between officials and syndicate racketeers.

Later, Jones became involved in a variety of gambling and business ventures with assorted rackets figures and such political cronies as the discredited former U.S. Senate aide, Robert G. "Bobby" Baker. Among these ventures was a mysterious bank chartered in Nassau, the Bahamas, accused of acting as a secret conduit for Mob money— including cash illegally "skimmed" from Las Vegas gambling casinos to avoid payment of taxes. The bank, known as the Bank of World Commerce, was entwined in a myriad of complex financial transactions apparently designed to camouflage its operations. The president of the bank was an ex-convict named John Pullman, a long-time associate of Meyer Lansky. Pullman, who has renounced his American citizenship and now lives in Lausanne, Switzerland, has been identified by the Justice Department as the Mob's leading expert on use of secret Swiss bank accounts to hide rackets money. He has been accused of channeling millions of dollars in underworld money into Swiss banks for later investment in legitimate business.

Jones was one of the largest stockholders in the Bank of World Commerce. Among his associates in the bank, in addition to Pullman, was gambler Edward Levinson, head man of the Fremont Hotel in Las Vegas and "front" for mobster Joseph "Doc" Stacher. Money "skimmed" from Vegas casinos was traced through the Bank of World Commerce to Meyer Lansky.

Moreover, Cliff Jones, the Bank of World Commerce and some of the bank's owners were also involved in another apparent scheme to slip rackets funds out of the country through the use of an account in a savings and loan association in Maryland—a state noted for its lax regulation of such associations. Among those identified in public records as depositor-stockholders in Account 804 at the Anjon Savings and Loan were Jones; Ed Levinson; John Pullman; Charles D. Baker, former mayor of Las Vegas; Floyd Lamb, a Nevada state senator; Edward J. Barrick, part owner of three Las Vegas casinos; Ben Sigelbaum, a suspected cash courier for the Mob; and Irving Devine, a Las Vegas gambler whose wife has been suspected of acting as a courier. Like the Bank of World Commerce, Account 804 was linked through a confusing network of transactions with numerous other financial organizations—all apparently designed to hide the movement of money to such places as the Bahamas and Switzerland.

Cliff Jones's involvement with the notorious Bobby Baker concerned, among other things, the operation of gambling casinos at hotels in the Caribbean. Baker, protégé and long-time aide of Lyndon B. Johnson, had his hand in many a curious venture—both during and after his service as secretary to the Democratic majority in the U.S. Senate. Along the road that led him to scandal and imprisonment, Baker picked up numerous associates in the gambling rackets in Nevada and elsewhere. He tried to cash in on his connections in both the political world and the underworld by seeking to obtain casino concessions for his associates at resort hotels in the Caribbean. The specific target of his influence was Intercontinental Hotels Corporation, a wholly owned subsidiary of Pan American World Airways. The story of this affair was detailed in congressional hearings on Baker's activities.

Among the twenty-three foreign hotels operated by Intercontinental were three containing casinos—in Santo Domingo, the Dominican Republic; Curacao, Dutch Antilles; and San Juan, Puerto Rico. Pan Am considered the casinos lures for tourists, many of whom would use the airline to fly to the Caribbean, but the company had no desire to participate directly in the gambling operations. Except in Puerto Rico, where the law required the hotel owner to operate the casino, Pan Am wanted to lease the casinos on a concession basis to experienced gamblers. John Gates, board chairman of Intercontinental Hotels, was in charge of choosing the gamblers. He needed men familiar with the credit aspects of casino gambling—expert at both judging how much credit to extend and at collecting from losing bettors.

At this point Bobby Baker stepped into the picture. Through a Pan Am vice president who was familiar with Baker's political clout and the fact that the airline was subject to strict government regulation, Baker arranged an appointment with Gates. Baker appeared at Gates's office with Las Vegas gambler Ed Levinson, whom he described as a friend and client. Levinson had previously been involved with Baker in a series of business ventures. Baker told Gates that Levinson was interested in acquiring the casino concession at the Intercontinental Hotel either in Santo Domingo or Curacao. Although Baker denied having any personal interest in Levinson's bid, his usual technique was to take a cut of any business he helped a "client" obtain.

At the congressional hearing, Gates testified he explained to Baker and Levinson that other bids were already under consideration for the Curacao casino—one of them from Cliff Jones and Jones's partner, Jake Kozloff. Levinson responded that the Jones-Kozloff bid would be no problem. "We're all very close," he said, adding that he, Jones, and Kozloff could all operate the casino together. The meeting ended with an agreement that Gates would pursue the proposal with his associates.

At another meeting a month later, which Baker also attended, Gates told Levinson that his bid would not be considered if his brother, Louis "Sleep-out Louie" Levinson, were to be involved in the casino operation. The objection to Sleep-out Louie apparently stemmed from his long-time participation in an illegal gambling empire at Newport and Covington, Kentucky. But no apparent complaint was raised about the fact that Ed Levinson himself had also been involved in the Kentucky gambling empire in his early years and had been arrested five times—with one conviction—in gambling cases in such cities as Detroit and Miami. Assured by Levinson and Baker that Sleep-out Louie would have nothing to do with the Caribbean casino operation, Gates agreed to keep the bid under consideration.

About a month after that, a third meeting was arranged by Baker at Gates's office. This time, Levinson showed up with Cliff Jones and Jake Kozloff. By some accounts, Levinson said he was withdrawing his bid and leaving the way clear for the casino concession to be granted to Jones and Kozloff. But, only a day after the meeting, Gates wrote to his associates: "Messrs. Jones, Kozloff, and Levinson called on me yesterday in regard to the casino contract. They are going to present a joint bid." When the actual bid was considered, however, it was signed only by Jones and Kozloff.

Whether Levinson actually pulled out or merely decided he didn't want his name on the official papers has been a matter of speculation. It has long been a practice in Nevada for gamblers to hold secret interests in casinos, and this procedure has been carried over into gambling operations in the Caribbean. Levinson's decision to keep his name off the papers may have resulted from the fact that he was then under investigation by several Federal law-enforcement agencies. Moreover, Levinson would have faced problems in Nevada if he appeared as one of the recorded operators of the Curacao casino. Nevada officials had ruled that nobody holding a state gambling license could officially enter the gambling business in any other place. Thus, if he became officially involved in the Curacao operation, he might jeopardize his license for the Fremont Hotel in Las Vegas. Jones and Kozloff faced no such problem because, at least on paper, they had abandoned their Nevada gambling interests.

The government of Curacao at one point raised objections to the granting of the concession to Jones and Kozloff, but a way was found to circumvent the problem. Ultimately, Jones and Kozloff were given the Curacao concession. Later, they also were given leases on the casinos at the Embajador Intercontinental Hotel in Santo Domingo and the Quito Intercontinental Hotel in Quito, Ecuador.

As for Bobby Baker, he became embroiled in the scandal that exposed his influence-peddling, conflicts of interest and general wheeling and dealing. And, when he went on trial on charges of tax evasion, theft, fraud, and conspiracy, his further dealings with Cliff Jones became an integral part of the case. One count in the indictment charged that Baker conspired with Jones and another man, Wayne L. Bromley, to defraud the government of taxes by concealing the sources and recipients of $34,500. Jones and Bromley were named as coconspirators but not as defendants in the case. Jones denied any wrongdoing. Bromley testified at the trial that, during a Las Vegas meeting with Jones and Baker, it was arranged that a company controlled by Jones would send Bromley a check every month for $1,000. He would then cash the check and turn the money over to Baker, he said. Bromley said the payments to Baker were concealed and that Jones promised to reimburse him for any taxes he paid on them.

Asked whether he had performed any services for Jones's company, Bromley replied: "No, I did not." But Bromley had not kept the money. What services Baker had performed to merit the payments were never disclosed. In the end, Baker was found guilty on the charges involving Jones and Bromley and on numerous other charges. He was sentenced to one to three years in Federal prison.

While the case was being appealed and shortly before Baker surrendered to begin serving his sentence in early 1971, this writer interviewed him in Washington, D.C. While refusing to discuss the details of his dealings with Cliff Jones, Baker said: "I'm contemptuous of those who say about me, 'You know all those gamblers.' Sure, I know lots of gamblers in Nevada. Hell, yes, I do. But it's legal to be in the gambling business in Nevada. When I go out to Las Vegas, I don't even drop a nickel in a slot machine. I go out there on business—strictly business." Judging by past experience, it would be logical to assume that his "business" dealings in Nevada must be far more profitable than gambling. Baker's comment about the legality of Nevada gambling is typical of those made by apologists for the state. The standard line of such apologists, including many public officials, is that strict state regulation keeps organized-crime figures out of Nevada gambling operations. But the record shows that such claims are laughable.

Recent Federal investigations have revealed anew the deep involvement of the Mob in Nevada's gambling. For example, on March 25, 1971, a Federal grand jury indicted

Meyer Lansky and four other men on charges of conspiring to engage in illegal Nevada gambling and to conceal proceeds from the Flamingo Hotel in Las Vegas. Among the codefendants was Morris Lansburgh, president of Miami Beach Associated Hotels, which operates eight beachfront hotels in Miami Beach. Lansburgh also heads groups that own resort interests in Las Vegas, the Bahamas, Virginia, and elsewhere. The other codefendants were Samuel Cohen of Miami Beach and Samuel Belkin and Jerry W. Gordon, both of Las Vegas.

The indictment charged that Lansky held one of the original controlling interests in the Flamingo Hotel and its casino, although he was never officially listed in Nevada records as a gambling operator. While maintaining his secret interest, the indictment said, Lansky induced Lansburgh and Cohen to buy into the Flamingo and continue to give him a cut of the proceeds. Lansburgh and Cohen paid Lansky $200,000 initially and continued to make secret payments to him from 1960 to 1967, the grand jury charged. It also charged that the defendants "skimmed" about $2 million a year from the casino winnings and concealed them from the Internal Revenue Service. During the period covered by the indictment, the Flamingo casino was partly owned by the Albert Parvin Foundation of Los Angeles. Associate Justice William O. Douglas of the U.S. Supreme Court was the president and the only paid director of the Parvin Foundation until he resigned in May, 1969. An attempt was made by some members of Congress to impeach Douglas as a result of his connections with Nevada gambling through the foundation, but he was eventually cleared.

Whether Meyer Lansky will ever come to trial in the Flamingo case is doubtful. Shortly before his indictment, Lansky moved to Israel and is still there at this writing. He has refused to return to face the charges. Although the United States has an extradition treaty with Israel, it does not cover the crimes included in the Lansky indictment. In Israel, as he has done in the United States, Lansky has cultivated close ties with key politicians. Thus, he may be able to stay there indefinitely—out of the reach of U.S. authorities. The other defendants in the case pleaded not guilty and have not come to trial at this writing.

Within a month of Lansky's indictment, two other Mob figures were indicted in an unrelated case on charges of violating Federal laws arising out of their concealed ownership of the Frontier Hotel casino in Vegas. The racketeers were Anthony J. Zerilli—a captain in the Detroit Mafia family and son of Joseph Zerilli, a member of the Mafia's ruling national commission—and Michael S. Polizzi, also a captain in the Detroit family. Four other men were indicted with them, including a former Michigan judge, Arthur J. Rooks.

The indictment charged that Zerilli and Polizzi arranged for other men to act as "fronts" for them in operating the Frontier casino, since they could not get Nevada gambling licenses because of their Mob backgrounds. Zerilli and Polizzi conspired to have fictitious loans made to some of the other men in order to keep Nevada officials from learning the true ownership of the casino, the indictment said. These and other acts by the defendants were alleged to be violations of the Federal anti-racketeering laws. The defendants pleaded not guilty and the case is still pending at this writing.

Nevada officials often take a curious attitude toward Federal investigations that expose "skimming" and mobsters' secret ownership of casinos. Although state coffers are cheated along with the Federal treasury by "skimming" operations, Nevada's leading politicians seem to consider the unfavorable publicity created by Federal investigations a more serious problem than the loss of tax funds. In one notable case, an FBI investigation revealed that more than $1 million a month was being "skimmed" from Vegas casinos and finding its way to such men as Meyer Lansky, Chicago Mafia boss Sam Giancana, and Cleveland mobster John Scalish. The FBI planted hidden microphones in several casinos, which were particularly effective in the gathering of evidence. Nevada Governor Grant Sawyer, presumably in an attempt to protect his state's reputation, lashed out against the investigation. He ordered an attempt to prosecute FBI agents on charges of violating Nevada's law against electronic eavesdropping. Las Vegas District Attorney Edward G. Marshall, responsible for enforcing the laws against "skimming," instead bent his efforts toward investigating the FBI. Although the furor eventually blew over, the incident pointed up the proprietary interest Nevada officials take in protecting the gambling interests.

Once the Mob has succeeded in corrupting officials at the state and local levels, it seeks to complete the circle of political control by subverting the Federal government. Today, more than ever before, it is concentrating its efforts at the Federal level. Succeeding chapters will describe how this is being done and detail the grave threat it poses to the nation's political integrity.

[7]

The Big Fix

The not-so-fine art of political corruption has rarely been practiced with more finesse than by a paunchy, gravel-throated syndicate racketeer named Jack H. Halfen. Operating from a Texas base, Halfen paid public officials millions of dollars to protect gambling and other rackets in that state and elsewhere. Although he had political connections at all levels of government, it was at the sensitive Federal level that he proved particularly adept in corrupting officials who could not be reached by less resourceful Mob bagmen. In recognition of his services as a corrupter, Halfen was tagged during the 1950s with the sobriquet "The Big Fix." But not until recently, when he revealed details of his operations to this writer, did it become clear just how influential Halfen actually was—that his political associates included one man who eventually occupied the White House and another who made it to the United States Supreme Court.

Some of Halfen's bribes consisted of direct cash payments; others were made in the guise of campaign contributions. The money changed hands in such diverse places as the U.S. Capitol building and a hideaway known as Joe's Place at Reynosa, Mexico, frequented simultaneously by American politicians and mobsters. For their money, Halfen and his Mob associates received benefits

ranging from police protection and favorable court rulings
to help in killing anti-rackets legislation.

It takes an unusual breed of man to play the role of
Mob bagman—able to bridge the gap between the underworld and the political world. Jack Halfen is just such a
man. He has numbered among his cronies, on the one
hand, some of the leading political figures of our time and,
on the other, such notorious Mafia bosses as Frank Costello and the late Vito Genovese. Since Halfen's life pre-
sents a particularly revealing study of the politics of corruption, it is worth examining in detail.

Halfen was born on December 11, 1913, at Kansas City,
Missouri, into a respected family of business people and
ranchers. His father was a newspaper executive who eventually moved to Texas and went to work in the business
office of *The Houston Post.* As a boy, Jack Halfen was too
bright for his own good. With an IQ in the genius range,
he found school work unchallenging and dull. Bored with
the "square life," he ran away from home in his mid-teens
and joined a carnival.

While traveling with the carnival, Halfen learned from
older hands how to make counterfeit half-dollars from
pieces of scrap metal. He passed numerous bogus coins
before Secret Service agents caught up with him in a Texas
border town and arrested him. After being held temporarily in jail, he was sent on his way with a stern warning to
keep his nose clean. He didn't.

Instead, he quit the carnival and fell in with a gang of
young holdup men in San Antonio. He participated with
the gang in armed robberies at several grocery stores, and
was arrested again. Once more he beat the rap. By that
time, Halfen was becoming expert at either evading the
police or evading responsibility for his acts.

He drifted into bigger-time underworld circles in Texas

and Oklahoma—where his cronies included such despera-
does as Clyde Barrow, Bonnie Parker, and Charles "Pretty
Boy" Floyd. After a celebrated murder attributed to Bonnie and Clyde, one in which the victim was a lawman, Halfen was arrested by Dallas police. They had nothing on
him, however, and were forced to turn him loose. A short
time later he was arrested in Tulsa, Oklahoma, on a charge
of consorting with Pretty Boy Floyd. Again, he beat the
rap.

Shortly before Bonnie and Clyde were ambushed and
slain by a posse near Arcadia, Louisiana, Halfen got a tip
that the showdown would soon take place. He had a
buddy who was one of Clyde's closest friends. Since Clyde
had been holding some money belonging to Halfen's
friend, Halfen and the friend decided to rush to Arcadia
and try to recover the money before it was found by the
lawmen. A skilled pilot, Halfen borrowed a light airplane
and flew with his friend to Arcadia—arriving just before
the fatal shootout. They were too late to recover the
money, but arrived in time to see the bodies of Bonnie and
Clyde hauled into a small undertaking parlor that occupied a back room of a furniture store.

"That posse had really shot those poor bastards up,"
Halfen recalled years later in one of a series of interviews
with this writer. "Ol' Bonnie was flat-chested to begin
with—but they'd shot the tits right off her." After an un-
dertaker did some preliminary work on the corpses, he
asked whether anyone wanted to take pictures of them.
Halfen, who had a camera in his borrowed plane, snapped
several pictures. They are still in his possession.

A short time later Halfen got involved in a scheme to
pay off a key Oklahoma political figure on behalf of Pretty
Boy Floyd, who was on the lam from a murder charge. If
captured and convicted, Floyd faced a possible death sen-

tence. But Halfen arranged to pay the politician $10,000 with the understanding that Floyd would be let off with a minimum two-year prison sentence. To raise the $10,000, Halfen produced a short movie on Floyd's career, then toured Southwest theaters with Floyd's wife, Ruby. They showed the movie, Ruby made a little speech, and the pair collected the admissions fees for the secret Floyd payoff fund. Before the entire $10,000 could be raised the heat on Floyd became so great that he was ambushed and slain by FBI agents. Halfen turned the money he had collected over to Ruby.

His experience with the proposed payoff on Floyd's behalf started him on the road toward becoming a big-time bagman for the Mob. He learned early in life how to capitalize on the greed of politicians and lawmen. In the mid-1930s Halfen moved to Houston and set up a rackets headquarters. The town was wide open for gambling, vice, and virtually any other sort of racket. But the racketeers lacked cohesion, feuding constantly among themselves. Gangland murders were commonplace. Payoffs were made on a catch-as-catch-can basis by individual racketeers to individual politicians and lawmen, with no centralized control. Halfen put an end to this disorder by bringing the mobsters together in a well-oiled syndicate that enriched the Mob and the politicians for more than two decades.

Under the syndicate system, all payoffs were funneled through Halfen to the ultimate recipients. Senators, congressmen, governors, mayors, judges, and various other officials and law-enforcement officers were paid on a regular basis to protect the Mob enterprises. Halfen gradually expanded his operations to other areas in Texas and nearby states. In addition, he formed alliances with mobsters from more distant parts of the country. As the syndicate's rackets grew, so did the payoffs. By the 1950s, Halfen says, he was paying off about $100,000 a week in Houston alone.

To understand how Halfen could afford to make such enormous payoffs, it is necessary merely to glance at a few partial balance sheets of his syndicate. In Houston alone, the syndicate provided a racing-wire service to more than 200 illegal bookmakers. Each bookie paid at least $250 a day for the service; some paid as much as $500 a day. Thus, the syndicate's daily take from the wire service in Houston alone was upward of $50,000. Since there were 312 racing days a year, the annual gross totaled more than $15.6 million. Forty percent of the gross went directly to the out-of-state mobsters who provided Halfen with the service. Another twenty-five percent went for bribes. That left thirty-five percent for the Halfen syndicate.

The wire service was just part of the syndicate operation. The syndicate's most consistent moneymaker was the policy racket (known in other parts of the country as the numbers racket). Halfen and his associates controlled six major policy "banks." In Houston, these banks wrote an average of $75,000 worth of bets a day. Again, twenty-five percent of the take went for bribes. Another forty-eight percent went for overhead, such as salaries for runners, payments to winning bettors, and routine business expenses. The remaining twenty-seven percent was clear profit. Halfen's syndicate also operated 3000 slot machines and innumerable illegal pinball machines (the kind that paid winners in cash, not free games). In addition, the syndicate controlled betting on football, baseball, boxing, basketball, and election contests.

In Halfen's heyday, the racketeers dominated the election machinery in many parts of Texas. Even more than the oilmen and the giant construction companies looking for public works contracts, the racketeers served as financiers of political campaigns. They decided long in advance of elections whom they would run for office. Their money, influence, and other assets determined who would win various positions from the top to the bottom of the ticket.

Among those who benefited from this system was Lyndon B. Johnson. Halfen claims that he was a prime financial contributor and political supporter of Johnson's campaigns for both the House and Senate. He says he also made heavy contributions to the campaigns of numerous other members of both houses of Congress. Many of the congressmen and senators Halfen helped over the years took positions on legislation that could not have hurt Halfen's racket operations.

It not only took campaign contributions, but out-and-out payoffs, to solve some of Halfen's problems in Congress. For example, some congressman or senator was forever introducing a bill to make interstate transportation of slot machines a Federal crime. Or else someone was proposing legislation to increase the Federal tax on such machines from $10 a year to several hundred dollars. The tax on pinball machines, pegged at $5 a year, was also in constant danger of being drastically raised. Each time a threatening piece of legislation was introduced, Halfen collected a slush fund to combat it. He met with various senators and congressmen and handed them envelopes stuffed with thousand-dollar bills. The legislation invariably was killed in committee. Halfen jokingly accused members of Congress more than once of seeing to it that such legislation was introduced just so the slush funds would be raised. When a law was finally enacted to ban interstate transportation of slot machines, it came out full of loopholes.

Halfen says his friends in Congress also helped kill various proposals to curb interstate transmission of gambling information such as race results. It was not until after Halfen gave up his racing wire that such legislation was ultimately passed.

In addition to helping kill anti-rackets legislation, Halfen says, his congressional allies aided the syndicate by acting to head off or curb potentially embarrassing investigations. One example involved the late Senator Estes Kefauver's celebrated investigation of organized crime. Besides conducting sensational hearings in Washington, Kefauver took his committee on a tour of racket-infested cities. Halfen got word that the committee was planning to call hearings in Houston. Fearing that such hearings would generate intolerable heat on his syndicate, Halfen urged a powerful senator to use his influence to prevent the committee from coming to Houston. In the end, there were no Houston hearings. His Senate ally wrote Halfen, on official stationery, concerning his efforts on Halfen's behalf. The letter is one of numerous pieces of evidence of Halfen's connections with top-level political figures that he currently has stashed in various vaults.

On another occasion, Halfen prevailed upon a Senate leader for help in curbing a congressional investigation of tax-free charitable foundations. At the time, Halfen says, the Mob had on its payroll one of the nation's best-known syndicated newspaper columnists—who secretly lobbied in Washington on behalf of rackets interests. Every six months, racketeers throughout the country set aside one day's take from slot and pinball machines and delivered it to the columnist—half in cash and half in a check to his favorite charitable foundation. When a congressional committee began investigating such foundations, Halfen feared that he and other racketeers would be subpoenaed to testify. He particularly feared having to disclose the original sources of large amounts contributed to the charitable foundation, since tax problems might result. He asked the Senate leader to do what he could to see that neither Halfen nor any of his associates received committee subpoenas. In addition, he asked the senator's advice on whether to continue dealing with the columnist and his pet charity. The senator interceded on his behalf, seeing to it that neither he nor any of his associates were subpoenaed. The senator wrote Halfen, on official stationery, describing his efforts in guarded language and advising that it would be safe to continue dealing with the columnist. This letter is also locked in one of Halfen's vaults.

Halfen has carefully preserved various mementos of his social relationships with prominent political figures. There is, for example, 800 feet of movie film showing three couples—Lyndon and Lady Bird Johnson, Halfen and his wife, and former Harris County (Houston) Sheriff Neal Polk and his wife—together on a hunting trip. There are also still pictures of the Johnsons with the Halfens and of former Texas Governor Allan Shivers and his wife with the Halfens on another hunting trip. Additional still pictures show the Halfens with a Texas district attorney and other public officials.

Along with his rackets interests, Halfen participated in various legitimate businesses from time to time. He helped found a small airline, sold liquor and beer, and dabbled at trading in scarce commodities such as sweet syrups. Even in such enterprises he invariably found a way to skirt the fringes of the law and make use of his widespread political contacts.

Despite his political connections, he could not prevent the Internal Revenue Service from poking into his tax affairs. Although Halfen had several Internal Revenue officials on his payroll, they were powerless to help him when orders came down from Washington to launch a full-scale investigation during the early part of President Dwight D. Eisenhower's Republican administration. With the heat on his rackets operations, Halfen pulled up stakes in Houston and moved to Peru—where he operated a chemical plant and an airline.

In his absence, his was indicted by a Federal grand jury on tax-evasion charges on April 7, 1954. Besides accusing him of the criminal violations, the government also filed civil tax liens against Halfen that eventually totaled more than $1 million in back taxes, penalties, and interest. Although he could have fought extradition from Peru, Halfen agreed to return voluntarily to the United States and face trial.

Coincidentally, the man assigned to prosecute Halfen was Charles Herring, former congressional aide to Lyndon Johnson. After Herring had served with him in Washington, Johnson had arranged for his appointment as United States Attorney for the Western District of Texas. Although he was a Democrat and normally would have been expected to lose his patronage job under the new Republican administration, Herring was retained in office temporarily by Eisenhower. Today, Herring is a Texas state senator. In a recent interview with this writer, he confirmed many of the details of Halfen's career. "We knew, and proved, that Jack Halfen was a payoff man of unbelievably large proportions," Herring said. "But we never knew the identities of all those he paid. Jack wouldn't tell us. But Jack never told us any lies. He just wouldn't talk about most things. What he did say, though, was found to be true."

Halfen went on trial in the Austin court of U.S. District

Judge Ben H. Rice, Jr., a stern jurist with a reputation for handing out stiffer sentences than any other Federal judge in the country. Jurisdiction rested in Austin, the state capital, because all income-tax returns in Texas were filed there. After a jury was empaneled, the story of Halfen's role as "The Big Fix" immediately began to unfold. In rapid succession ten gamblers took the stand and testified that their payoffs to Halfen's syndicate on illegal pinball machines alone amounted to $5 to $7.50 per week per machine. They said the payoff money was called by its universally accepted underworld term—"the nut"—and was handed in cash in unmarked envelopes to a Halfen hireling, Thomas Jefferson Vondy. Halfen was the guiding genius and Vondy was secretary of a "protective organization" known as the Coin Machine Operators Association.

There was testimony that Halfen had organized the protective association, telling the operators it would take payoffs to keep the gambling devices in business and that they would have to kick into the syndicate to stay out of trouble. In addition to "the nut," the witnesses said, they were required to pay $1 per month per machine as association "dues."

A key prosecution witness, Robert T. Griffin, testified that he attended a meeting at which Halfen made a speech informing the machine operators what they would have to do to stay in business. "Halfen said members would have to pay dues on each machine or the machines would be confiscated by the police," Griffin said. "He said he would have to make payments to keep the officials off our necks."

Griffin testified that about eighty gamblers joined Halfen's syndicate and that all paid protection money. Later, he said, Halfen organized a second syndicate within the original syndicate—composed of sixteen of the initial members. The sixteen were the biggest operators in the Houston area. The plan was to "freeze out" other members of the original combine, which was considered too unwieldy for adequate control. "We were to form our own organization and have protection," Griffin testified. "The others would not." He said he had refused to join the elite group.

Another gambler, Clifford L. Swanson, testified he had also attended the meeting addressed by Halfen. Swanson said Halfen had a pistol beside him on a table during the speech. "I questioned him about how the grand jury was to be taken care of," Swanson testified. "He picked up the pistol and moved it and said: 'You take care of the machines. We'll take care of the rest.'"

Other witnesses testified that Halfen had a rule against placing the gambling machines near schools or churches and that he had decreed that profits would be split between the machine operators (sixty percent) and the owners of the locations where the machines would be placed (forty percent). Halfen's former subordinate, Thomas Jefferson Vondy, was called as a government witness. He testified that six gamblers alone had made payments to Halfen totaling $16,650 a week. Vondy said all payoffs were delivered to him at his downtown Houston office. He then took them to another office maintained by Halfen. Whenever a gambler failed to pay on time, he said, Halfen would call him and instruct him to press for a payment.

After Vondy had testified about delivering the "nut money" to Halfen, prosecutor Herring introduced as evidence a list of such payoffs. All told, he introduced evidence that Halfen had paid off at least $50,000 a week in Houston—not to mention other areas. Actually, Halfen now concedes that the Houston figure was $100,000 a week, but Herring was able to prove only $50,000.

Other witnesses supported Vondy's testimony about Halfen's payoffs. A former slot-machine operator, Frank Roy Martino, elaborated on the weekly assessments Halfen had established. "Halfen said if we wanted to get along with the boys we would have to pay it or else," Martino said. He did not identify "the boys." Another slot-machine operator who gave parallel testimony, Clarence M. Ribbink, was asked what the assessment money was intended to accomplish. "I guess you would call it 'for protection,'" Ribbink replied.

Next, the prosecution explored a purported $35,000 election bet that had been the subject of a running controversy. Involved in the supposed bet were Halfen, a former Houston constable named M. L. Fay Woolley, and a candy wholesaler named William D. Morse. Certain facts concerning the transaction were undisputed. It was agreed by virtually all concerned that $35,000 had been put into the safe of a prominent Houston restaurateur named Bill Williams and that the money was somehow connected with the outcome of a race for sheriff in Houston. It was also agreed that Williams had served merely as an "honest broker" in the transaction. What was disputed was whether the $35,000 represented a bona fide bet on the election or a bribe.

One version of the story was that the money represented a bribe from Woolley to Halfen's friend, Sheriff Neal Polk. This version held that Woolley had agreed to pay Polk to retire as sheriff and support Woolley, who was seeking the office. The bet was described as a mere sham—a device to enable Woolley to turn the money over to Polk.

The terms of the transaction, it was said, were these: Bill Morse, representing Woolley, put $17,500 into the restaurateur's safe. Halfen, representing Sheriff Polk, put another $17,500 into the safe. After the election, Halfen was to take all the money—for payment to Polk—if Polk were not re-elected. Morse was to take the money, for payment to Woolley, if Polk were re-elected.

As it turned out, Polk did not seek re-election. Thus, Halfen eventually got the $35,000 and claimed he handed the bulk of it to Polk. But it was not Woolley who was elected sheriff. He lost the race to a former policeman named C. V. "Buster" Kern, who was subsequently re-elected to several additional terms.

Woolley adamantly denied at Halfen's trial, however, that the transaction had been a sham or a bribe. He claimed it had been an actual bet on the election. Asked why he would make a bet in which he would win only if someone else were elected, he contended the bet was a means of protecting his interests in the event he lost the election. It was left for the jury to decide which version of the story was true.

The last prosecution witness was an Internal Revenue agent, Travis G. Howard, who had been assigned to investigate part of the case against Halfen. He testified that he had uncovered a payoff list prepared by the Coin Machine Operators Association—which represented only part of Halfen's operations during a brief period—showing that one group of pinball operators alone had turned over $108,675 to the syndicate in twenty-one weeks. Howard said he charged that amount to Halfen's tax return.

The prosecution, for the most part, avoided a Pandora's Box that would have been opened by questions about the recipients of Halfen's payoff money. It confined itself to the considerably narrower question of whether Halfen had actually handled the payoff money and failed to report it correctly on his tax return. During the trial, however, the names of a number of politically prominent persons were mentioned in one context or another. Among those whose names cropped up were Tom Clark, then an associate justice of the United States Supreme Court, and the late Albert Thomas, then an influential congressman from Houston.

In the main, although a number of his former rackets associates had testified against him, Halfen made clear in testifying in his own defense that he would not try to shove the blame off on others. He was willing to take the rap, rather than identify the recipients of his payoffs. Halfen claimed he kept all the money given him by the Coin Machine Operators Association. At the same time, in an attempt to bolster his defense, he contended that all the money he had taken in had been accurately reported to the Internal Revenue Service. His income from the association, he said, consisted of $50,000 a year in fees—far below the income claimed by the prosecution. For this money, Halfen testified, he served as a public relations man and lobbyist for the gambling interests. He said he had worked to gain greater acceptance of the coin-machine business, to straighten out internal feuds among the gamblers and to defeat legislation aimed at curbing such devices as slot machines and pinball machines.

When the names of Justice Clark and Congressman Thomas came up during Halfen's testimony, he did not volunteer information on the two men, but answered questions about them from the lawyers. He said he was involved financially with Thomas and other prominent Texans in founding Great Southern Airways—a forerunner of the current major Southwest feeder airline, Texas International Airways. After the airline was formed, the government offered to unload numerous surplus aircraft at bargain prices. Halfen said he and Thomas arranged for Great Southern to buy at least ten C-46 planes from the government at a cost of $8,600 each. But, before the purchase was completed, the bottom fell out of the C-46 market—to about $1,000 a plane. If Great Southern carried out the terms of its government contract, it would have been paying $86,000 for planes worth about $10,000.

Halfen testified that he and Thomas decided to have Great Southern renege on the deal and let the government pick up the planes for nonpayment. But the government threatened to sue to get the $86,000. Halfen testified he and Thomas worked out an agreement with Tom Clark, then U.S. Attorney General and later appointed to the Supreme Court, to settle the government claim for $2,500. Neither Thomas nor Clark was called upon at the trial to confirm this deal, which Halfen said was made in Thomas's Capitol Hill office. He testified the deal fell through because a memorandum written by Clark to other Justice Department officials was "mislaid." The government ultimately obtained a default court judgment demanding the full purchase price. In interviews with this writer, Halfen said he had other dealings with Thomas and Clark over the years.

Before Congressman Thomas's death, this writer questioned him about his relationship with Halfen. He conceded helping Halfen in various business deals, including those involving the airline. But he denied knowing Halfen was a racketeer and said he considered him a reputable businessman.

Justice Clark was also interviewed by this writer about the airline affair and other dealings he purportedly had with Halfen and Thomas. Clark said he did not recall Halfen, but that he was certainly a close friend of Thomas. He said this was not the first time he had been accused of having questionable associations. "I was once accused in Chicago of carrying a half-million dollars in underworld money in a big box to Washington," Clark said. "You know what the truth of it was? My wife loves blackeyed peas. And I'd picked up a box of blackeyed peas for her. And I carried it everywhere with me—put it on top of the air-conditioners in hotel rooms so the peas wouldn't spoil. That's all that was in the box, blackeyed peas."

In the Halfen trial, after describing his dealings with Clark and Thomas over the airplanes, Halfen blamed his tax troubles on his involvement with an Internal Revenue agent named Steve Werner. He said Werner had originally been assigned to investigate him after the squabble over the planes. The investigation resulted in the Internal Revenue Service filing a civil claim against him, covering years prior to those involved in the criminal trial. Halfen eventually settled the civil claim for a sum substantially lower than that originally demanded by the government.

After the settlement of the civil case, Halfen testified, Werner came to him and said that he had left the Internal Revenue Service to set up his own accounting practice. He offered to act as Halfen's personal tax consultant in the future. Halfen agreed. Werner then made out the tax returns that eventually resulted in Halfen's criminal prosecution. At the trial, Werner conceded filling out the returns. He said Halfen had paid him $650 for the work and expressed satisfaction with his services. Halfen claimed the payment was in the thousands of dollars, not the hundreds, and that he was scarcely satisfied with services that put him on trial in a criminal case.

By the time of the trial, Werner had abandoned his private practice and returned to work for the Internal Revenue Service. He admitted on the witness stand that during his original investigation of Halfen in the civil case he had tried to borrow $1,000 from Halfen. Asked about the propriety of trying to borrow money from a suspected tax cheat, he shrugged off the question as irrelevant.

Halfen, during his testimony, told his side of the "election bet" story. He testified he had kept only $500 of the $35,000 handed over to him—giving the remainder to former Sheriff Polk. He also testified he had frequently made bets on horse races and other sports events, but denied making his living as a bookmaker. He said he had financed a football betting operation, but claimed it had made him no substantial money.

Following his testimony, there was little more than the wrapping-up before the case went to the jury. Prosecutor Herring argued in his summation that Halfen was "a payoff man of astronomical proportions." He said the government had proved Halfen had paid off at least $50,000 a week to corrupt officials in Houston alone. "I'm not very proud of the conditions we've shown to exist," Herring told the jury. But since Halfen was handling such enormous amounts of money, Herring said, "the least he could do would be to pay taxes on it. . . . There wasn't but one man getting a rakeoff in this deal and that was Halfen. He was The Big Fix."

The jury deliberated only fifty-six minutes before finding Halfen guilty on all three counts filed against him. A week later, Judge Rice sentenced him to four years in Federal prison. After losing a series of appeals, Halfen entered Seagoville Federal Prison, near Dallas, in 1955.

At Seagoville, he was hounded constantly by visits from Internal Revenue and FBI agents—wanting to know who had received all those huge payoffs. They held out the possibility that Halfen would win an early release from prison if he cooperated, but he repeatedly told them to get lost.

By 1956, President Eisenhower was preparing for a re-election campaign. His Attorney General, Herbert Brownell, had masterminded his 1952 election victory and was seeking ammunition for the re-election race. Brownell was particularly interested in getting something on various Texas Democrats—foremost among them Lyndon Johnson—for use in the campaign. At the time, Johnson was Senate majority leader, the most powerful Democrat in Congress and considered by some the most influential Democrat in America.

Although Democrat Charlie Herring had been retained in office as U.S. Attorney for the Western District of Texas under the Eisenhower administration, a Republican had been given the patronage position as U.S. Attorney for the Southern District headquartered in Houston. Eisenhower had appointed to the post a bright young Harvard alumnus named Malcolm Wilkey. While book-learning smart, Wilkey was far from streetwise. Nonetheless, he was entrusted by Brownell with responsibility for poking into the possibility of digging up a scandal against the Texas Democrats.

Into the Halfen affair at this point entered a dedicated law-enforcement officer named J. Neal Matthews. A former Houston homicide detective and former Secret Service agent, Matthews was working at the time as a deputy U.S. marshal. He traveled extensively around the country transporting prisoners—among them Soviet spy Rudolf Abel, whom Matthews escorted from Texas to New York after his capture. Matthews visited Seagoville Prison frequently in the course of his duties. Early in 1956, while on one of these visits, he was told by an inmate that Jack Halfen wanted to see him.

On his next visit to Seagoville, Matthews spoke to Halfen, who complained about the constant harassment by Internal Revenue and FBI agents. Halfen was worried that word had got around the prison that he had turned stool pigeon, which wasn't true, and that other convicts might try to silence him. Though they had long been on opposite sides of the law, Halfen—in true Western-movie fashion—knew Matthews and trusted him. He talked candidly to the marshal. Before the conversation was over, Matthews asked what Halfen wanted in trade for cooperation with Federal agents. Halfen said that he would not inform on his Mob friends, but that some of his erstwhile cronies—particularly high-ranking politicians—had double crossed him. He said he might be willing to spill the details of his payoffs to them. In return, Halfen asked at first for an immediate parole. Later, after conferring with his attorney, he said he would take nothing less than a full pardon from Eisenhower. Matthews said he'd see what he could do.

When he returned to his home base in Houston, Matthews went to see U.S. Attorney Wilkey and told him of the conversation with Halfen. Wilkey phoned Attorney General Brownell's office and passed along the information. A series of high-level discussions ensued, involving Brownell, Wilkey, and Assistant Attorneys General David Irons and Warren Olney. As a result, Matthews was authorized to pursue the matter further.

Matthews returned to Seagoville, where the warden—on orders from Brownell—made his private office available for the marshal's second meeting with Halfen. Matthews told this writer in a series of interviews that the Justice Department had assigned him at that point to ask Halfen whether he could provide any incriminating information about four specific men. "The men were Lyndon Johnson, [House Speaker] Sam Rayburn, Tom Clark, and Albert Thomas," Matthews says. Halfen told him that he knew all four men and had political dealings with all of them.

But Halfen balked at what he considered the strictly political request to provide information only on these four men. He told Matthews that, even where he had incriminating evidence, he wasn't going to allow it to be used for a political hatchet job. He warned Matthews that it would be impossible to tell the story of his operations without discussing scores of top-level officials besides the four Matthews had named. "You and Wilkey are stirring some shit you won't be able to handle," Halfen said. "If you go into this very deeply, you're both liable to wind up working in Lower Slobovia."

Halfen told Matthews that he was particularly reluctant to discuss his relationship with Lyndon Johnson—especially at that time because Johnson was assisting in his efforts to get a parole. The senator, Halfen said, had written to the U.S. Board of Parole on his behalf, only to be rebuffed. (Copies of this correspondence are still in Halfen's possession.)

Matthews assured Halfen the Justice Department had pledged to conduct a thorough, impartial investigation—no matter what the political consequences. He said the four names were not the only ones in which the department was interested, merely those in which the department was most interested. Further negotiations ensued. Halfen's lawyers went to Washington to meet with Justice Department officials. Matthews met with Wilkey, who conferred with his Washington superiors.

Then, on June 21, 1956, Matthews returned to Seagoville to see Halfen. The warden's office was again made available. Halfen entered the office at 12:15 P.M. and left at 2:30 P.M. During those two and a quarter hours, Halfen provided Matthews with information that became what the late-show movies call political dynamite.

Matthews made a list of forty names from Halfen's information. The names were those of men about whom Halfen said he could, and would, provide evidence of corruption. But Halfen also insisted that he would protect his friends; some significant names were left off the list to comply with his wishes. Even so, the list was packed with headline names. They included influential members of Congress, governors, mayors, judges, state legislators, prosecutors, Internal Revenue and Customs agents, other law-enforcement officers, and administrative officials in local, state and Federal governments. Halfen provided Matthews with bits and pieces of information about most of those on the list—keeping other information for future bargaining power.

Matthews drove back to Houston from the prison and typed out the list of names and facts he had taken down in longhand at Seagoville. He then telephoned U.S. Attorney Wilkey's chief assistant, C. A. "Tony" Friloux, who is now in private law practice in Houston. Friloux met secretly with Matthews away from the Federal Building and Matthews gave him the list. "I gave the list to Malcolm Wilkey," Friloux told this writer. "That was the last I saw of it."

Others involved in the subsequent investigation say that Wilkey, anxious to get such red-hot information to Washington, sent the list in an open Western Union telegram to Brownell's office. Justice Department officials were understandably shocked that Wilkey had used open wires—rather than secret government channels—for the transmission of such politically sensitive material. One version is that Brownell considered Wilkey's move such a monumental blunder that he threatened to wash his hands of the entire affair.

But the Justice Department was in too deep at that point to withdraw before at least making some attempt to pursue the investigation. Additional negotiations took place. Halfen's lawyer conferred with Wilkey, then went to Washington for a meeting with Acting Attorney General Warren Olney, who was filling in for Brownell while the

Attorney General was on a trip through Central America with Eisenhower. He also talked to the chairman and vice chairman of the U.S. Board of Parole. As a result of these meetings, Halfen's lawyer expressed skepticism about the idea of a presidential pardon; the Justice Department, he came to believe, was promising more than it could deliver, if it were willing to deliver at all.

Still, the investigation rumbled ahead. Halfen continued to talk—though more gradually—to the Federal men. On orders from Washington, transmitted by Wilkey, Neal Matthews spirited Halfen from prison under a secret writ issued by Allen B. Hannay, chief judge of the U.S. District Court for the Southern District of Texas.

Matthews took Halfen from the prison on June 26 and did not return him until July 10. During that time, Halfen was shuttled among a series of county jails—where Matthews signed him in under an assumed name in an attempt to cover up his absence from Seagoville. The move from the prison was designed to make Halfen available for secret questioning by Wilkey and perhaps by a grand jury. Late one night, Matthews removed Halfen from the county jail at Wharton, Texas, and took him to Houston for a meeting with Wilkey in the prosecutor's office. Subsequent events are described in detail in a letter written by Halfen to Wilkey, with a carbon copy to Attorney General Brownell, after Halfen returned to Federal prison.

Halfen wrote to Wilkey:

> We discussed at that time [in Wilkey's office] what you wanted from me and, in turn, what you proposed to do for me. During this discussion you advised me that your investigation, up to that point, had led you to believe I could be of great assistance in clearing up many points and that you were willing to virtually guarantee me parole. . . .

Mr. Friloux [Wilkey's chief assistant] then suggested that we pick at random a person whose name
appeared on the list and that I relate what I knew of
this person as a sort of "sampling" arrangement, so
that your office would be able to evaluate my information—presumably as a guide to gauging its value
in later "negotiations" for my benefit upstairs. I declined to do this, feeling that I should discuss any further arrangements in the presence of my attorney,
whereupon we concluded this conference with the understanding that I would have my attorney present in
your office in a few days, at which time [Assistant Attorney General] David Irons would be in Houston. It
was felt that Mr. Irons would be in a better position
to state with some degree of certainty what position
the Attorney General's office might take.

My attorney arrived in Houston a couple of days
later and at that time I was again brought to Houston
late in the evening for a second conference with you.
However, we were advised that you had been called
to Washington for further discussions about this matter with the Attorney General, and my attorney then
made arrangements to meet you in Washington on
about the 19th or 20th of July.

Halfen's letter went on to describe further conversations
in which Matthews told him that Wilkey, the FBI and the
Internal Revenue Service had been ordered to proceed no
further until given new instructions by Brownell's office.
He told how he was returned to Seagoville by Matthews,
then taken by the deputy marshal to the La Tuna Federal
Prison near El Paso. At La Tuna, he said, Wilkey visited
him and questioned him in his attorney's presence. The
letter to Wilkey continued:

You stated that you were at present only interested
in discussing certain persons then holding public

office or employed by the Federal government. I advised you then that it would be difficult to discuss part and not all, as they were inexorably linked in a manner which would lead from one to the other. You then stated that the only thing you could offer me was the opportunity to tell what I really knew of these parties in the presence of the FBI, and after that agency had investigated and evaluated the substance of this that you would then probably feel that you might be able to get a pardon or parole for me if you felt that such would assist you in obtaining convictions.

I then stated to you that this was not our agreement and that I did not feel I should be held responsible for your office's ability to obtain convictions from my assistance. . . . During this conversation, you mentioned that you were going to be rather busy with your political activities [on behalf of the Republican national ticket] as well as the duties of your office. . . . Though you wanted to continue this investigation because you felt that the resultant publicity would have favorable effects on other investigations then in progress, you felt you would not be able to fully exploit same until after the national election.

At that time I requested only that you contact Mr. Warren Olney and endeavor to get a more definite commitment as to what the Attorney General's office expected of me—and what they were willing to do on my behalf. We then concluded our conference.

Wilkey later told Neal Matthews to inform Halfen that there would be further discussions with him. Meanwhile, the investigation continued on other fronts. Friloux says he telephoned Halfen's attorney in an effort to determine what sort of documentation Halfen had for his charges. "I wanted to be sure this guy [Halfen] was no fluke," Friloux says. "His lawyer, a respected member of the bar, told me Halfen really had the goods—that he had a bunch of documents, wire recordings, and so forth locked up in a safe." The evidence included secret wire recordings of conversations made during payoffs, letters from prominent politicians, other documents, and photographs.

After the assurances were received from Halfen's lawyer, Wilkey summoned a series of witnesses before a Federal grand jury—including some of the men on Halfen's list. Halfen was also subpoenaed. But, when the Justice Department refused to reaffirm its original pledge to get him a presidential pardon, Halfen balked at testifying. The grand jury investigation seemed at least temporarily stymied. Halfen was returned to La Tuna Prison.

Although the deal between Halfen and the Justice Department appeared to be deteriorating, Wilkey took another crack at Halfen. En route to the Republican National Convention in California, to which he was a delegate, Wilkey stopped off at La Tuna for three days of conferences with Halfen. He took two FBI agents from the El Paso field office to the prison with him. On the third day Wilkey repeated his earlier request for any possible information that might connect Lyndon Johnson with any illegal activities.

Halfen immediately accused Wilkey of playing politics —of wanting to investigate only those men, particularly Johnson, who stood most in the way of Republican control of the National political scene. Moreover, he accused Wilkey of breaking their original agreement. Wilkey denied either breaking the agreement or intending to whitewash any part of the case. He said the Justice Department merely wanted to check whether Halfen's information was worth pursuing. A heated argument ensued, and the two

FBI men had to jump between Halfen and Wilkey to keep them from coming to blows.

After the prison altercation, the Justice Department's interest in Halfen waned. Incredibly, the department never even turned over to the Internal Revenue Service any of its information on Halfen or the forty names on his list. Dan Goodykoontz, who was then agent in charge of Internal Revenue's Intelligence Division in Houston, told this writer he learned informally of the attempted deal with Halfen—but that neither Wilkey nor any other Justice Department official gave him any solid information to pursue. The grand jury investigation fizzled, producing no new indictments. (At the time of Halfen's original indictment in the tax case, the government had also obtained tax-evasion indictments against one of his gambling associates, Joe Steele, and against Sheriff Neal Polk and Houston Police Chief B. W. Payne. Steele was convicted. But, after numerous trial postponements during the period when the government was trying to make its deal with Halfen, the cases against Polk and Payne were dismissed following the breakdown of negotiations.)

Perhaps the only government man who refused to let the Halfen affair die was Deputy Marshal Matthews. He made periodic visits to Halfen in prison—more to try to make up for what he considered the Justice Department's betrayal than in the hope of producing new evidence. Matthews felt the Justice Department officials had treated Halfen shabbily. "They broke their word to Jack," Matthews says. "He was ready to keep his end of the bargain, but they wouldn't keep theirs."

In the end, Halfen served the remainder of his stretch at La Tuna—every last day of the four-year sentence. The information he had provided Matthews and other Federal men remained in the Justice Department files, constituting one of the most sensational sealed indictments in American political history.

After his release from prison, Halfen got involved in a variety of enterprises—some legitimate and others far from it. He became a partner in a construction company that relied heavily on political contacts in obtaining work. He was involved in various deals with swindler Billie Sol Estes. He smuggled guns and surplus American bombers, equipped with nose cannons, to Fidel Castro.

Although he got away with some of these escapades—such as running the guns and bombers—his luck finally ran out. In 1960, Halfen says, he concocted a plot to defraud the Western Union office in Las Vegas out of close to $500,000 through the use of forged money orders. But, before he could put the full plan into operation, he was arrested in 1961 on charges of passing a couple of the forged money orders. He stood trial on one charge in Fort Worth and on the other in Oklahoma City. He was convicted in both cases and given three-year and ten-year prison sentences, to run concurrently. Sent first to Leavenworth Federal Prison, he was later transferred to La Tuna.

By that time John F. Kennedy had taken office as President and Lyndon Johnson as Vice President. Kennedy's brother, Robert F. Kennedy, was serving as Attorney General. Robert Kennedy's assistant attorney general in charge of the Justice Department Organized Crime Section was a veteran racket-buster from New York named Edwyn Silberling. It was suggested to Silberling that, since Halfen then faced the prospect of serving ten years in prison, he might be willing to cooperate in a new investigation of political corruption in return for the chance of an early pardon or parole. Despite the fact that such an investigation might embarrass Vice President Johnson and other Democrats, Silberling wanted to pursue it.

But he never got the chance. Silberling and his aides had just finished prosecuting a group of Democratic office-holders on corruption charges in Indiana and New York. The prosecutions had proved politically troublesome for Attorney General Kennedy, since many of the defendants had been influential supporters of his brother's presidential candidacy. Silberling told this writer that, when he first presented Robert Kennedy with the evidence against the corrupt New York Democrats, Kennedy replied: "Damn it, I told my brother I didn't want to be Attorney General." As a result of the problems created by the Indiana and New York prosecutions, Silberling says, Kennedy ordered him not to initiate any further investigations with political overtones. Thus, he was unable to open a new investigation of the Halfen case. Silberling resigned a short time later.

In the absence of a deal with the government, Halfen faced the possibility of remaining behind bars until 1971 or, even with time off for good behavior, until 1968. Instead, he was unexpectedly paroled in the summer of 1966. He concedes that some of his influential political friends interceded on his behalf with the U.S. Board of Parole, but he refuses to identify them. At the time of his parole, Lyndon Johnson was President.

Following his parole, Halfen went into the farm and ranch supply business in Matagorda County, Texas. He later gave that up to become a partner in a company specializing in highway construction. With a Republican administration now in office in Washington, prospects seem stronger than in the recent past that the Halfen affair might come under renewed investigation. The passage of time has not significantly reduced the explosiveness of the evidence. Many of those who took payoffs from Halfen are still on the public payroll. Moreover, it is still possible for the government to file criminal tax-evasion charges against those involved and to try to collect millions of dollars in unpaid taxes. In tax-fraud cases, the law provides that the statute of limitations does not begin to run out until Federal authorities become fully aware of the fraud. Tax experts say Halfen's partial disclosure to Federal men of the details of his payoffs was not sufficient to make the statute of limitations begin running out in potential cases against the bribe recipients. Thus, charges could be filed at any time.

As for Halfen, he has once again fallen into the clutches of the law. At this writing, he is in jail—under circumstances that will be described in a later chapter of this book. Once again, there is a chance for investigators to try to make a deal to get him to talk about the payoffs he made. The next move is up to the Federal men.

[8]

The Pipelines
to Capitol Hill

Charles Siragusa is a tough little man with a wispy mustache who has spent most of his adult life fighting the Mafia. For many years, he was the U.S. Narcotics Bureau's chief agent in Europe—an expert on the Mob's international drug operations. Later, he served as deputy director of the Narcotics Bureau in Washington. Today, he is executive director of the Illinois Crime Commission, where much of his work involves exposing corrupt alliances between racketeers and public officials.

"There's something that's puzzled me for a long time," Siragusa told this writer in a recent interview. "I hear all the time about this program or that program to investigate the Mob's connections with local officials and state officials. But I never hear of any program to combat corruption of Federal officials by the Mob. I know, from my years in the Federal government, that plenty of corruption goes on there. A certain number of Federal officials are always being corrupted, along with the local and state officials. But there doesn't seem to be any organized system for dealing with corruption at the Federal level."

Other experts on the Mafia echo Siragusa's comments. They point out that the FBI, as will be seen later in this chapter, does investigate on a piecemeal basis some suspected acts of corruption by Federal officials. The Internal

Revenue Service, also on a limited basis, has jurisdiction in corruption cases where taxes are evaded. But there is no central Federal agency—corresponding to the investigation commissions set up by many states and some large cities—to serve as a constant watchdog against corruption.

The government's lack of zealousness in policing its own ranks is all the more puzzling in view of the Mob's recent efforts to step up enormously its corruption of officials at the Federal level. With the Federal government constantly enlarging its influence on American life, racketeers have found it increasingly essential to control top national officials. Some law-enforcement experts point out, as an example, that the Mob can consistently deliver the votes of at least twenty-five key members of Congress; others say that estimate is far too low.

Naturally, great pains are usually taken to conceal ties between congressmen and the Mafia, but occasionally evidence of these links bursts into the open. One such case involved a congressman from Chicago, Roland Libonati, who hired as his chief aide the son-in-law of Chicago Mafia boss Sam "Momo" Giancana. The son-in-law, an attorney named Anthony P. Tisci, represented Giancana in a court fight with the Federal government while on the congressional payroll. In addition, he had contacts with other racketeers besides his father-in-law. Congressman Libonati also had more than a nodding acquaintance with various mobsters.

Before entering Congress, Libonati served twenty-two years in the Illinois Legislature—six as a representative and sixteen as a state senator. There, he was a leader of the so-called West Side Bloc, a group of legislators noted for serving the interests of the Mob. Formed during the heyday of Al Capone, it was originally known as the Capone

Bloc; after his death, though its name changed, its connections with syndicate racketeers remained intact.

Libonati himself has conceded being a friend of Capone. During his first congressional race in 1957, he was asked about the friendship by a newsman. "Mr. Capone showed me great respect as a person of Italian extraction who represented one of the pioneer families in Chicago," Libonati replied. "And naturally . . . I treated him with like respect, as I would treat any American. Let's put it this way: He treated me with great respect and admiration and I never did anything not to merit his respect. You know, politically, that man was not a politician. If people treat me nice, I treat them nice." Asked about modern-day mobsters Tony Accardo and Paul "the Waiter" Ricca, Libonati said he considered them "charitable" and "patriotic" fellows.

Once, Libonati was photographed at a Chicago Cubs baseball game with Capone and a Mob assassin named "Machine Gun" Jack McGurn. "I was very proud when he [Capone] asked me at the ball game to speak to his son," Libonati later explained. "And, under the circumstances, today I would still be proud to speak to any man's son."

While serving in the Illinois Legislature, Libonati practiced criminal law—often representing Mob clients. In the legislature itself, he frequently supported measures helpful to the racketeers and opposed anti-crime bills proposed by the Chicago Crime Commission. One law favored by the Mob, which was rammed through the legislature by Libonati and eight other members of the West Side Bloc, proved a financial bonanza for the sponsoring legislators. The measure authorized harness racing at a track called Sportsman's Park. After the law took effect, it was learned that Libonati and the eight other legislators or their wives held stock in the race track. They had bought thousands of shares at the insider's price of ten cents a share. Within two years, they made a profit of 1650 percent.

When Libonati entered Congress in 1958, he promptly appointed Anthony Tisci as his chief aide. While Tisci was on the congressional payroll, his mobster father-in-law became embroiled in one of a series of legal battles with the government. Giancana was being kept under virtually constant surveillance at the time by FBI agents. He filed suit, seeking an injunction to halt the surveillance. Tisci not only represented Giancana in the court case; he also argued passionately in a television interview that his father-in-law's constitutional rights were being violated. The case ended in a partial victory for Giancana, with the judge placing limits on the manner in which future surveillance could be maintained by the FBI. One of the limitations imposed was that, when Giancana was playing golf, the FBI men must stay at least two foursomes behind him on the course.

Congressman Libonati, not content with allowing Tisci to represent Giancana while the government was paying his salary, got into the act himself. He introduced a bill in Congress that sought to make it a crime for Federal agents to keep mobsters and other suspected criminals under surveillance. The bill proposed that violations be punishable by imprisonment for up to ten years and fines up to $5,000. Discussing the proposal on a television newscast, Libonati said: "Yes, I know Giancana. Of course, my bill would cover him. It would cover anyone whose constitutional rights were violated in surveillance or investigation. And I'll tell you something: There's a lot of interest in my bill." There may have been a lot of interest, but the measure never got off the ground.

Meanwhile, some of the activities of Libonati himself were under surveillance by FBI agents, as were those of some of his associates. Information gathered during these surveillances was compiled by the Justice Department in a series of secret reports.

One such report said that a top Chicago mobster, Murray "the Camel" Humphreys, had been spotted by FBI agents when he arrived in Washington, D.C., by airplane on May 23, 1960. The agents tailed Humphreys to the Woodner Hotel. He later left the hotel carrying a package about five-inches by three-inches by two-inches, wrapped in blue and white gift-wrapping paper. Humphreys then proceeded by taxicab to 224 C Street Northeast, which the report described as "the local address for Congressman Roland Libonati." After spending about an hour at Libonati's residence, the report said, Humphreys left and "was not observed to be carrying any package." He then returned to the Woodner Hotel and entered a room registered to Murray H. Olf, described as "a reputed big-time gambler and a Syndicate Washington lobbyist." Later that night Humphreys went to the Hamilton Hotel, where he made a call on one of the house phones and was soon joined by Congressman Thomas J. O'Brien in a small room off the lobby. (O'Brien, a Chicago political ally of Libonati, had sponsored a successful drive to get Libonati appointed to the powerful House Judiciary Committee.) After meeting with O'Brien for about twenty minutes, Humphreys left the hotel. He returned to Chicago the next day.

Another Federal report disclosed that Libonati visited the Federal prison at Terre Haute, Indiana, on August 24, 1960. The visit had been approved in advance by the U.S. Bureau of Prisons in Washington. After inspecting the prison, the report said, Libonati asked to see mobster Paul "the Waiter" Ricca, then serving time for tax evasion. A Bureau of Prisons employee accompanied Libonati during the entire visit. Despite his presence, the report said, Libonati hugged and kissed Ricca when they met.

The report said that Murray Humphreys had made the arrangements with Libonati for the visit with Ricca. It said agents learned that Humphreys later talked to Ricca, who said he was very happy about Libonati's visit. In November 1960, the report said, Humphreys was described as communicating frequently with Libonati in an attempt "to expedite the early release" of Ricca from prison. Ricca later was released after serving twenty-seven months of his three-year sentence.

Another report said that Humphreys and his Mafia associates were becoming increasingly concerned about Federal investigations. They particularly feared attempts would be made to deport top mobsters who were aliens. The report said Humphreys had been meeting with Libonati to discuss the problem. As a result, it said, Libonati had been trying to get the U.S. Immigration and Naturalization Service to support a bill barring the deportation of any alien whose son had ever served in the U.S. armed forces.

Further evidence of dealings between Humphreys and Libonati was provided in a subsequent report. The report said that FBI agents spotted Humphreys talking with Congressman O'Brien in a corner of the Hamilton Hotel lobby on February 17, 1961. Humphreys then left the hotel and went to Libonati's residence. Another report said that Humphreys had acted on behalf of Libonati's pet charity in discussions with John T. O'Brien, international vice president of the Teamsters Union. It said Humphreys had asked O'Brien's help in getting the union to make a large annual contribution to a camp for underprivileged boys situated on part of a 188-acre farm owned by Libonati near Colona, Wisconsin. Such a contribution, the report said, would be intended to show appreciation to Libonati for helping the union in some unknown manner relating to a congressional investigation of the monitors appointed by a Federal court to supervise Teamster activities.

In January 1963 Libonati announced that he would not run for re-election the following year, saying his decision had been prompted by the illness of his wife and his desire to return to his Chicago law practice. There were indications, however, that other factors influenced his decision. A secret Federal report commented: "Congressman Roland Libonati stepped down on orders from Sam Giancana. . . . Giancana had already selected Frank Annunzio to replace Libonati. Annunzio will follow dictate of Mob."

Annunzio, a former Illinois state labor director, did indeed succeed Libonati in Congress. But, before Libonati left office, he managed to make additional waves as a lame duck. He introduced a resolution demanding that the House Judiciary Committee investigate what he described as the "persecution" of Teamsters Union President James Hoffa by the Justice Department. The proposed investigation seemed clearly intended to embarrass Robert F. Kennedy, who had spearheaded the government's numerous investigations and prosecutions of Hoffa. At the time Libonati introduced the resolution, Kennedy had recently resigned as Attorney General to run for a U.S. Senate seat in New York.

Congressman Emanuel Celler, chairman of the Judiciary Committee, refused at first to allow the committee to consider the resolution. Celler charged that Libonati's resolution had actually been drafted by the Teamsters. It developed that a batch of legislative proposals distributed by Teamster representatives at the 1964 Democratic National

Convention had contained one document virtually identical to the Libonati resolution. Celler accused Libonati of acting as a stand-in for Hoffa in the Teamster president's feud with Kennedy.

Nonetheless, Libonati succeeded in mobilizing support for the resolution within the committee and forced Celler to bring the issue to a vote. The Libonati forces mustered eighteen votes to fourteen for Celler's side. A couple of weeks later, in a subsequent vote, the committee modified Libonati's original proposal to provide for an investigation of the Justice Department without referring specifically to Hoffa. The revision, intended to serve as a compromise, did not mollify Celler. "This might be called the Hoffa resolution," Celler said. "Nobody asked for the investigation except those involved with the Teamsters Union." The investigation, timed to coincide with Kennedy's senatorial campaign, failed to prevent his election.

When Libonati retired from Congress, Frank Annunzio faced only token opposition in the election to succeed him. Annunzio coasted to victory, collecting eighty-two percent of the votes. He retained Giancana's son-in-law, Anthony Tisci, as chief aide in the congressional office. In fact, Annunzio even raised Tisci's pay from $13,000 to $19,000 a year. In mid-1965, Giancana and Tisci were called to testify before a Federal grand jury investigating organized crime in Chicago. Tisci pleaded the Fifth Amendment in three appearances before the grand jury, but Annunzio refused to fire him.

A crime-fighting civic group called the Better Government Association called on the Chicago Bar Association to recommend Tisci's disbarment because of his refusal to testify. In the ensuing furor, Tisci resigned his congressional job—saying his doctor had urged him to do so because of a heart ailment. Congressman Annunzio, in accepting the resignation, seemed to discount the health factor. "I'm hoping for the day when the American people will mature to the point that the sins of the father are not heaped upon the children," Annunzio said.

But Tisci's Fifth Amendment plea and subsequent events made it questionable whether the sins were those of his father-in-law alone. Two months after Tisci resigned, Federal agents tipped off police in St. Louis, Missouri, that their city would soon be the site of a meeting of top Midwest mobsters. The police learned that the invitation list for the gathering included such notables as Chicago's Tony Accardo, St. Louis kingpin Frank "Buster" Wortman, and Kansas City's Nick Civella. They also learned that the agenda for the meeting covered such subjects as Nevada gambling ventures, political machinations, and Mob takeovers of labor unions. Shortly after the meeting convened, it was raided by the police. And among those found at the meeting was none other than Anthony Tisci.

Later, Tisci bought an expensive house in Tucson, Arizona, and divided his time between there and Chicago. Tucson was a gathering place for numerous racketeers from all parts of the country. During the summer of 1968, violence flared several times in Tucson—and Tisci's home was one of the targets. On the night of July 4, two shotgun blasts were fired at the house. One shattered Tisci's picture window and the other riddled a parked car, but nobody was hurt. Two weeks later, two dynamite explosions rocked a nearby ranch owned by Pete Licavoli, one of five members of the Mafia's ruling council in Detroit. And, the night after that, a bomb was hurled at the Tucson home of Joseph "Joe Bananas" Bonanno, exiled former boss of a New York Mafia family.

Curious Friendships in Arizona

Arizona was also the scene of a set of curious friendships between leading rackets figures and one of the country's most prominent politicians. The politician was Senator Barry Goldwater, the 1964 Republican presidential candidate. The rackets figures included Willie Bioff, a convicted extortionist, and Gus Greenbaum, a gambling kingpin. Bioff and Greenbaum both had homes in Phoenix, but were deeply involved in various Las Vegas gambling ventures.

Greenbaum had lived in Phoenix since 1928. During the Prohibition era he became one of Arizona's leading bootleggers. He later became a big-time bookmaker, operator of a racing-wire service and eventually the state's organized crime boss. He dealt regularly with such out-of-state mobsters as Tony Accardo, Jake "Greasy Thumb" Guzik, Charlie Fischetti, and Mickey Cohen. When Benjamin "Bugsy" Siegel was murdered, the Mob needed someone to take over the gambling operations at Siegel's Flamingo Hotel in Las Vegas. Greenbaum was tapped for the job.

The Flamingo had been operating in the red under Siegel's management, but Greenbaum quickly turned it around. In his first year, it showed a $4 million profit. Among his frequent visitors at the Flamingo was Barry Goldwater. Greenbaum had been a close friend of Goldwater in Phoenix, where Goldwater had served as a city councilman before his election to the Senate. After Greenbaum took over the Flamingo, Goldwater often enjoyed his hospitality in a lavish suite at the hotel. Goldwater's brother, Robert, also became a familiar figure in Las Vegas—gaining a reputation as a high-rolling gambler.

Greenbaum ran the Flamingo for seven years before ill health—a combination of asthma, ulcers, and overwork—made him decide to leave. Over the strenuous objections of his Mob associates, who feared their profits might dip in his absence, he moved back into full-time residence in Phoenix. He fell in with Willie Bioff, who had settled in

Phoenix after pursuing a rackets career in Chicago, New York, Hollywood, and elsewhere.

Before arriving in Phoenix, Bioff had been involved in various rackets—chiefly concerning labor union corruption—with some of the nation's top Mafia figures. In one New York case, he was convicted of violating the Federal anti-racketeering laws and handed a ten-year prison sentence. He then made a deal with the government, turning informer on some of his Mob associates in return for clemency. With the help of his testimony, Federal prosecutors obtained an indictment charging nine Chicago mobsters with conspiring to extort $1 million from three Hollywood motion-picture companies. One of those indicted, Frank "the Enforcer" Nitti, committed suicide before the trial. Seven of the other eight, including Paul "the Waiter" Ricca, were convicted and imprisoned. Bioff, who had naturally fallen from favor with some Mob elements because of his testimony, deserted his old haunts and moved to Phoenix.

There, in addition to forming a friendship with Greenbaum, he soon became a close pal of Senator Goldwater. He and Goldwater were often seen together in public. The senator flew Bioff in his private plane to parties in various parts of the Southwest. Bioff contributed money to Goldwater's campaign coffers. When newsmen discovered the friendship between the two men, they asked Goldwater for an explanation. He replied heatedly at first that he had no idea his friend was a notorious racketeer, claiming he knew him by the name William Nelson—not Bioff. Later, however, Goldwater changed his story. He said he was making a study of the labor movement, and that Bioff was helping him explore union racketeering.

Meanwhile, events contrived to draw Gus Greenbaum back to Las Vegas—taking Bioff with him. A new casino-hotel called the Riviera had opened there, but had run into financial troubles almost immediately. Mob leaders, recalling Greenbaum's success at the Flamingo, decided to persuade him to take over the Riviera. Tony Accardo and "Greasy Thumb" Guzik visited Phoenix and put the proposition to him. Greenbaum turned it down, saying his health wouldn't permit him to return to the hectic Las Vegas pace. Accardo and Guzik implied that it might not be healthy, either, to thwart the Mob's wishes, but Greenbaum shrugged off the threat and sent them on their way.

Several days later Greenbaum was visited by his brother, Charlie, and Charlie's wife, Leone. They told him Leone had received a threatening phone call from a man who said he and his friends planned to teach Greenbaum a lesson. Greenbaum told his brother and sister-in-law there was nothing to worry about, but Leone was sufficiently frightened that she subsequently reported the threat to the police. A few nights later, Leone was found murdered in her Phoenix home. The case was never solved. Gus Greenbaum got the message and returned to Las Vegas to take over the Riviera.

Bioff went with him, to assume responsibility for providing entertainment at the Riviera. Greenbaum figured that Bioff's Hollywood connections would enable him to book headline acts at bargain prices. Although the new combination succeeded in making the Riviera a money-making proposition, the Mob was not entirely happy. Some of the mobsters involved behind the scenes in the Riviera were allies of the Chicago racketeers against whom Bioff had testified in the $1 million extortion case, and still held a grudge against him. Tony Accardo sent his top gunman, Marshall Caifano, to Vegas to tell Greenbaum to get rid of Bioff. Greenbaum refused, although Caifano warned there might be dire consequences. Bioff continued working with Greenbaum, shuttling frequently between the Riviera and his Phoenix home.

A short time after Caifano's visit to Greenbaum, Bioff left his home, stepped into his car, turned the ignition key and was blown to bits by an explosion. Police said a tried and true Mob murder weapon—a dynamite bomb wired to the car's starter—had been used. Their investigation also turned up information about the Caifano threat. In backtracking on Bioff's movements during the period before the murder, they learned that he had last visited Las Vegas two weeks earlier. He and his wife had returned to Phoenix with Barry Goldwater in the senator's private plane. The police, however, were never able to solve the murder.

After Bioff's slaying, relations between Greenbaum and his Mob backers grew constantly more strained. The Riviera, which had been making money steadily, started losing. The losses continued over a period of months, and the Mob's profits dropped sharply. Greenbaum's silent partners began to suspect that he was cheating them—"skimming" casino winnings off the top before making the official count that was reported to them.

Marshall Caifano made another visit to the Riviera to see Greenbaum, but Greenbaum kept ducking him. Such behavior naturally aroused even greater suspicion among the mobsters. Ultimately, Caifano forced a showdown, confronted Greenbaum and told him the Mob wanted him out; he must sell his twenty-seven-percent share in the Riviera and give up its management. Ironically, after going to the Riviera under duress in the first place, Greenbaum now refused to leave. And the Mob, which had initially insisted on his taking over the hotel, now adamantly insisted that he get out "or else." Greenbaum stood his ground, hiring two bodyguards and remaining at the Riviera.

When he decided to spend a few days with his family in Phoenix, however, he left the bodyguards behind in Las Vegas. That decision cost not only his life but that of his wife as well. Shortly after his return to Phoenix, Greenbaum and his wife were found murdered in their home. Greenbaum's pajama-clad body was lying across the twin beds that had been pushed together. His throat had been slit so severely that his head was almost separated from his body. The remains of his wife, Bess, were found in another room. Her throat had also been cut. Her hands had been tied behind her back. On the floor beside her body was a bloody butcher knife resting on a plastic bag that her killer had apparently used to prevent blood from splattering on his clothing.

Police theorized that Mrs. Greenbaum had been slain only because she could identify her husband's killer or killers. Since nothing was missing from the home, robbery was ruled out as a motive. There were reports that two Mob killers had arrived in Phoenix by chartered plane from Florida the day of the murders and left immediately afterward. But the murders, like those of Greenbaum's sister-in-law and Willie Bioff, went unsolved.

The Greenbaums were given an impressive funeral at which a rabbi eulogized the racketeer as a man who "gave of himself humbly and simply, without notoriety." Among the mourners was Senator Goldwater.

In a recent interview, this writer asked Goldwater about his relationships with Greenbaum and Bioff. The senator did not deny being on close terms with both men, but claimed that their friendship had been over-emphasized by "unscrupulous" persons. Beyond that, Goldwater declined to discuss the subject.

The Ambitious Aide

Mafia corrupters have found that it is not always necessary to deal directly with a congressman or senator in order to get their way in the halls of Congress. Government is so complex today that members of Congress cannot possibly keep up with all the details of communications, requests, recommendations, and inquiries that pass through their offices. They must rely to a great extent on the advice of their aides. Often, they authorize aides to act in their names. Under such circumstances, if a sufficiently influential aide can be corrupted, it becomes virtually unnecessary to corrupt the member of Congress himself.

One sensational case involving the corruption of an extremely influential congressional staff member broke into the open in 1970 with the indictment of Dr. Martin Sweig, chief administrative aide to House Speaker John W. McCormack of Massachusetts. Indicted with Sweig was Nathan M. Voloshen, a seventy-two-year-old lawyer-lobbyist and long-time friend of McCormack. The indictment charged them with perjury and conspiring to misuse the influence of McCormack's office for the benefit of various Voloshen clients—including several men identified as either members or associates of the Mafia.

Sweig was accused of lying when he told a grand jury that he had never heard of an imprisoned Mafia gambling expert named Salvatore "Sally Burns" Granello, that he had never talked to Voloshen about Granello and that he had never made telephone calls about him to the U.S. Bureau of Prisons and the U.S. Board of Parole. Actually, it was charged, the intercession of Sweig and Voloshen had halted the scheduled transfer of Granello from the Federal Correctional Institution at Danbury, Connecticut—considered a "country club" by prisoners—to the tougher Federal prison at Lewisburg, Pennsylvania. Voloshen was said to have received $5,000 for his efforts on Granello's behalf.

Sweig was also accused of lying to the grand jury when he denied he had ever heard of a convict named Manuel Bello or had ever telephoned the chairman of the New York State Parole Board in an attempt to aid Bello. Officials identified Bello as a close associate of New England Mafia boss Raymond Patriarca. In addition, Sweig was accused of lying when he told the grand jury that he had never heard of a New York labor racketeer named Jack McCarthy and had never talked to Voloshen about him. It was charged that Sweig actually had tried to halt an investigation into alleged mail fraud by a labor publication with which McCarthy was associated and had made telephone calls in Speaker McCormack's name, saying McCarthy was a friend of McCormack and seeking to obtain the admission of McCarthy's son to the University of Delaware.

Other counts in the indictment charged Sweig with perjury in denying that he had made telephone calls seeking to obtain a hardship discharge from the Army for a client of Voloshen; in denying that he had telephoned the U.S. Bureau of Prisons about a prisoner being held in Los Angeles; and in denying he had called the Bureau of Prisons or the U.S. Board of Parole about other Voloshen clients.

The indictment jolted official Washington, since it charged that the authority of the nation's third highest office had been abused for the benefit of Mafia characters and other criminals. Although there was no indication that Speaker McCormack had personal knowledge of the alleged wrongdoing, it was undeniable that the prestige of his office had been seriously tainted. McCormack suspended Sweig without pay when the allegations were made public, but expressed confidence that his aide had merely been guilty of an "error in judgment."

Others viewed Sweig's actions far more severely. Sweig could hardly be called a babe in the political woods. He had worked for McCormack for twenty-four years, was earning $36,000 a year (extremely high for a congressional aide), supervised a large staff and was given broad latitude to act on his own authority in the speaker's name. While he held a Ph.D. in history from Georgetown University, he was far from an ivory-tower political scientist. He had been involved in the rough-and-tumble of Capitol Hill life long enough to know "an error in judgment" from a criminal act.

When the case against Sweig and Voloshen was called for trial in New York, where the alleged perjury had been committed, Voloshen pleaded guilty. Sweig, however, pleaded innocent and went to trial before a jury of eight men and four women. There was testimony early in the trial that, although Voloshen held no government position, Sweig regularly allowed him to use one of McCormack's offices to make telephone calls and to confer with clients and representatives of government agencies. Witnesses said Voloshen frequently made a point of telling people on the phone that he was calling "from the speaker's office"— sometimes leaving the impression that McCormack supported specific lobbying activities in which he was involved.

Russell G. Oswald, chairman of the New York State Parole Board, testified that Sweig had telephoned him on November 15, 1968, to seek the release of Mafia associate Manuel Bello, then serving time at Clinton State Prison for trying to dispose of $100,000 worth of stolen securities. Sweig said he was calling at the request of Speaker McCormack, Oswald testified. He said Sweig told him that two congressmen from Bello's home state of Massachusetts had advised McCormack that Bello "was very ill with a heart condition and could receive better care outside" prison. Sweig went on to say that Bello "would be in no future difficulty if he were released and returned to Massachusetts," Oswald testified. Evidence introduced at the trial disclosed that Bello was a client of Voloshen, who had visited him in prison at least four times.

Oswald testified he told Sweig "that I was very much surprised that the speaker or the speaker's office would be interested" in Bello's case. He said he informed Sweig that Bello was "closely involved with Raymond Patriarca of Providence, Rhode Island, and there is much more of a devastating nature about him in the folder." Rebuking Sweig for intervening on Bello's behalf, Oswald told him: "I would suggest to the speaker that he divorce himself completely from any interest in this case because I would hate to see an illustrious career ruined."

Six months before receiving the call from Sweig, Oswald said, he had received another call from a man who identified himself as Speaker McCormack. (McCormack later denied making the call and the implication was left that Sweig might have done so, using the speaker's name.) In the conversation, Oswald said, his caller sought a parole for millionaire financier, Edward M. Gilbert, imprisoned for a swindle that had cost defrauded stockholders more than $2 million. The man who identified himself as McCormack said he had known Gilbert's father "very favorably and felt that this [younger] Mr. Gilbert had a fine reputation except for his present difficulties and, when released, would be in no more difficulties," Oswald testified.

Other witnesses testified that Sweig had intervened with the U.S. Bureau of Prisons and the U.S. Board of Parole to prevent the transfer of Mafioso "Sally Burns" Granello from the correctional institute at Danbury to the prison at Lewisburg. Granello, considered one of the Mafia's top experts on gambling and loansharking, was serving time for tax evasion. A close associate of Meyer Lansky and Florida Mafia boss Santo Trafficante, Granello had also served time for extortion and had been indicted on charges of taking kickbacks on an $863,000 loan made by the Teamsters Union pension fund to a hospital in Midland, Texas. While he was imprisoned in the tax case, his son, Michael, was murdered—reportedly for failing to show proper respect for his Mafia elders. Granello ultimately left prison with a vow to avenge Michael's murder. Instead, he met the same fate as his son. His bullet-riddled body was found stuffed in a rented car parked on Manhattan's Franklin D. Roosevelt Drive.

In the Sweig trial, several witnesses testified that Speaker McCormack's name had been used in an attempt to obtain the discharge from the Army of a young man whose father previously had paid Voloshen $1,500 to try to prevent his induction. The soldier, Gary Roth of Lawrence, New York, received a hardship discharge three months after his induction on the ground that his deaf-mute brother-in-law could not carry on a family business without him. Roth, his father, his father-in-law, and four Army officers testified that Sweig had made calls to the officers, saying McCormack was a close friend of the Roth family and supported the soldier's discharge.

The dramatic high point of the trial came when Speaker McCormack—seventy-eight years old and serving his last term in Congress before retirement—took the witness stand. Tall, pale and white-maned, a veteran of forty-two years in the House, McCormack was an imposing figure in the courtroom. As he entered the witness box, he spotted Sweig at the defense table, smiled and waved to him before sitting down. Sweig stood, bowed slightly and returned the smile.

McCormack testified that if Sweig and Voloshen had misused the authority of his office, he had been unaware of it at the time. Asked how that could have happened, he replied: "I'm not an inquiring fellow." McCormack explained that he had two offices on the same floor of the Capitol—one in his capacity as speaker and one as representative of the Ninth Congressional District of Massachusetts. He said he rarely visited the district office, leaving virtually its entire management to Sweig. He had no idea, he said, that Voloshen had been using the district office to confer with clients and government officials. But he described Voloshen as a friend of twenty years' standing, whom he generally saw at least once or twice a week.

As for Sweig, McCormack testified that the defendant had begun working for him as a young man and become a "devoted" assistant. He said he had given Sweig the top job on his staff and allowed him to pick his own title—chief administrative aide to the speaker. Sweig was authorized to sign some correspondence in McCormack's name and to make appointments for constituents and friends of the speaker with government agencies. But McCormack emphasized that Sweig was not authorized to pretend on the telephone that he was the speaker.

The chief prosecutor, Whitney North Seymour, Jr., United States Attorney for the Southern District of New York, questioned McCormack about various telephone calls made to officials by a man identifying himself as the speaker. During each call, a request had been made concerning a case pending before the officials. Two of the officials had later written letters to McCormack confirming the calls. Seymour showed copies of the letters to McCormack. The speaker denied making all of the calls and testified he had not seen one of the letters at the time it was received. He said he had seen the other letter, had been puzzled by it and had asked Sweig about it. The letter was from an Army colonel, responding to a call ostensibly made by McCormack to request Gary Roth's hardship discharge. McCormack said, Sweig told him he had not made such a call in the speaker's name. "He said the colonel must have been mistaken," McCormack testified.

The other letter of confirmation was from Chairman Oswald of the New York State Parole Board, saying "it was very nice to have had the opportunity" to talk to McCormack on the phone about the case of imprisoned swindler Edward Gilbert. McCormack testified he had made no such phone call and had not been shown Oswald's letter until Federal authorities began investigating Sweig and Voloshen. He also said Sweig had never passed on to him Oswald's advice that the speaker should refrain from any efforts to obtain a parole for Mafia associate Manuel Bello. As for the calls Sweig had made to halt the prison transfer of Mafioso "Sally Burns" Granello, McCormack testified: "I know nothing about the Granello case."

Another witness, a discredited securities dealer named Michael Hellerman, testified that he had met with Voloshen to seek help in ironing out troubles he'd been having with the Securities and Exchange Commission. During the meeting, which took place in McCormack's district office at the Capitol, Hellerman said Voloshen told him: "We can do anything in Washington—anything short of murder." Hellerman would later be indicted on charges of being a prime mover in a fraudulent scheme to take over a

Florida investment company with the help of three Mafia leaders. The government would charge that efforts had been made by still another congressional aide to fix the case. That affair, which touched off a new congressional scandal, will be discussed in a later section of this chapter.

When the prosecution rested its case in the Sweig trial, the defense presented only seven witnesses—opening and closing its case the same day. Defense attorney Paul T. Smith, who previously had told the jury that Sweig would testify in his own behalf, changed his mind and kept the defendant off the stand. He said he did so because he had concluded that the prosecutors were "lying back, waiting for Dr. Sweig to take the stand, and hoping they could convict him on his own testimony." Among the witnesses Smith did call were three congressmen who testified that Sweig had an excellent reputation on Capitol Hill.

One of them, Representative Robert L. Leggett of California, went to great lengths in testifying that it was considered routine for congressmen and their aides to do favors for constituents and other citizens. "The whole country is my constituency," Leggett testified. He said he had no hesitancy about letting citizens—even those working on behalf of clients—use his office, his telephones, and his services on "Federal-type business." He also encouraged them to make long-distance calls on his phones as long as his $10,000-a-year telephone allowance lasted, he said. "I even tell people from my district to call me collect until the allowance is used up. I tell my staff to be as hospitable and courteous as possible. I often tell people, 'make yourself at home.' Taxpayers pay for this and deserve to be made to feel at home. I do all sorts of things to be accommodating."

Among the things he did to be accommodating, he said, was to telephone Federal judges and prosecutors about criminal cases at the request of defense lawyers. Such calls, Leggett testified, were "not to tell them to violate their oaths of office" but to obtain or provide information, suggest settlement of a case or pass on the advice that a potential defendant was "a pretty good guy." He made similar calls, he said, to representatives of numerous other government agencies. "I have very little trepidation about calling anybody," Leggett said. "We have to work very fast on a great many matters. We get 500 letters a day and we have to handle them every day if we want to get reelected. We get so many inane requests. Some people want us to do everything from fixing a traffic ticket to handling a sewer problem."

Another defense witness, a Boston salesman named Peter J. Cloherty, testified that he often had Sweig make appointments for his engineering and architectural firm with government officials. Among the agencies with which Sweig had arranged such appointments, Cloherty said, were the U.S. Bureau of Public Roads, the Agency for International Development, the Army Corps of Engineers and the World Bank. When in Washington, he said, he often used the facilities of Speaker McCormack's office and "might tell people, two or three people at home, that they could reach me there." The defense clearly intended to show through the testimony of Cloherty and Congressman Leggett that the use of McCormack's office by Voloshen had not been nearly so unusual as the prosecution contended.

After resting his case, defense attorney Smith argued to the jury that Sweig had merely carried out his duties as a "devoted" aide to Speaker McCormack in accordance with customary congressional practices. He said the real culprit in abusing McCormack's trust had been Voloshen. Prosecutor Seymour scoffed at such arguments, telling the jury that the case had presented the "sorry spectacle" of misuse of the nation's third highest office as a "springboard for the wholesale selling of influence."

The jury deliberated the case for a day and a half, then acquitted Sweig on the conspiracy charge but found him guilty of perjury. Two months later, Sweig stood before U.S. District Court Judge Marvin E. Frankel to hear his sentence imposed. "I am bewildered by all this," he told the judge. "I never had occasion [prior to this case] to be before a grand jury in my life. If I have done wrong, I certainly did not mean to—or to cause harm to anyone." Smith pleaded for clemency, describing his client as "a decent human being [who] has virtually been destroyed" by the indictment and conviction.

Seymour opposed the clemency plea. "We do not have the complete story today," he said. "To that extent, the perjury of the defendant has succeeded significantly in blocking to some extent getting to the true facts."

Judge Frankel then told Sweig: "I am of the view that I would be derelict if I did not impose a substantial prison sentence in this case, and I will." He said he would do so because Sweig's actions presented "corruption of a very profound kind" and he hoped that a stiff sentence would deter other public officials from committing similar crimes. Sweig was ordered to serve two and a half years in prison and to pay a $2,000 fine. Two weeks later, Voloshen was given a suspended sentence in the case—chiefly because of his advanced age and ill health.

The Best Judge Money Can Buy

The Court actions, however, did not end the investigations into Voloshen's activities. It soon developed that Sweig was far from the only public official with whom Voloshen had maintained a suspicious relationship. Among the others was a justice of the New York State Supreme Court, Mitchell D. Schweitzer. The New York Joint Legislative Committee on Crime and a special State Court on the Judiciary launched investigations into Schweitzer's connections with Voloshen.

In testimony before the legislative committee, Judge Schweitzer conceded that he had been a friend of Voloshen for more than twenty years, that he continued seeing Voloshen for several months after the influence-peddler's indictment, that he was "very impressed with" Voloshen's Washington associates, that he accepted cash and other gifts from Voloshen and that he met with lawyers in cases pending before him while Voloshen was also present. Among the cases was one that had figured in the Sweig trial—that of Mafia associate Manuel Bello.

After Sweig and Voloshen had failed to get Bello a parole, Voloshen arranged a meeting at a Manhattan restaurant with Justice Schweitzer and Bello's lawyer, Henry Blumenthal. Following the meeting, Schweitzer ordered a new hearing in the case of the imprisoned gangster. Bello, who was then serving a sentence of fifteen to thirty months, was allowed to withdraw his original plea at the hearing. He then pleaded guilty to an identical charge and Schweitzer resentenced him to a shorter term, which made him eligible for immediate release. Bello walked out of the courtroom a free man.

In another case in which Voloshen was interested, Judge Schweitzer ruled that one of his own previous decisions was "improper"—thus enabling a prisoner to go free ahead of his normal release date. This decision was handed down in the case of Raymond Freda, who had pleaded guilty to unlawful entry, third-degree assault, and carrying a dangerous weapon. Schweitzer originally sentenced Freda to serve a year in prison for the unlawful entry, and ten months each for the assault and the weapons violation. At the time the sentences were imposed, Freda was serving a five-year term in Federal prison. When he finished that sentence, he was turned over to New York authorities to serve the time imposed by Schweitzer. There was testimony before the legislative committee that Voloshen had arranged a dinner meeting attended by himself, Schweitzer, and Freda's lawyer, Stanley Reiben. (In September 1971 Reiben issued a statement denying any recollection of the meeting.) In any event, Reiben filed a motion asking that Schweitzer re-sentence Freda. The judge complied. Ruling that the two ten-month sentences he had imposed had been "improper," he revoked them and allowed Freda to go free after serving only the one-year term for unlawful entry.

The legislative committee also heard testimony on other cases in which Schweitzer's conduct was considered questionable. Schweitzer conceded under questioning that he had accepted a $150 cash "house gift" from Voloshen when he moved into a new home and that Voloshen had given him theater tickets on various occasions and "one or two cases" of liquor every Christmas. In addition, there was testimony that Voloshen had arranged for the operator of a nursery business to give Schweitzer numerous pieces of shrubbery worth between $1,000 and $2,000.

The nursery operator, a Polish immigrant named Teddy Kordus, said he originally went to Voloshen for help in a case in which New York State was condemning his business site on Long Island to make way for a highway. "I wanted legal advice because I was confused," he testified. "I never in my life had been . . . in court." He said Voloshen insisted that, before he would even discuss the condemnation case, he must be paid $2,000 in cash. "I asked him if it could be a check," Kordus testified. "He absolutely demanded cash money—green, they call it. I wanted a receipt, but he wouldn't [give one] and he said there would never be a receipt."

After he had paid the $2,000 in cash, Kordus said, Voloshen told him he would arrange a meeting with Judge Schweitzer. He quoted Voloshen as telling him: "You will meet together . . . and he [Schweitzer] will guide our business the right way." Asked by the committee what Schweitzer was supposed to do, Kordus replied: "Probably influence other judges. Schweitzer was supposed to have contacts in Albany [the state capital]." But when the meeting took place in a Manhattan bar, Kordus said, Schweitzer "was not interested in my case but my nursery business." He testified Schweitzer visited his nursery after the meeting, selected shrubbery for his home and twice sent a truck to haul away between $1,000 and $2,000 worth of shrubs.

Despite paying Voloshen the $2,000 and giving Schweitzer the free shrubbery, Kordus said, he could never get them to provide the promised help on the condemnation case. They kept stalling him, so he ultimately asked Voloshen to repay the $2,000. He said Voloshen told him: "You are nobody. Get out of here." Kordus finally gave up on Voloshen and Schweitzer, retaining a lawyer who had no connection with them. The state later paid him $350,000 for his property, part of which he shared with the new lawyer.

When the legislative committee completed its investigation, it reported: "The relationship between Mr. Voloshen and Justice Schweitzer and other persons referred to in the testimony raises questions as to the propriety of the judge's conduct." The committee, however, had no power to take action against the judge. It forwarded a copy of the transcript of its hearings to judicial officials for possible action.

Partly as a result of the committee hearings, the special State Court on the Judiciary was assigned to investigate Schweitzer's dealings with Voloshen.

Meanwhile, U.S. Senator John McClellan's rackets committee opened its own investigation of Schweitzer. At a committee hearing, an admitted stock manipulator named Michael Raymond testified that he had paid two $25,000 bribes to Schweitzer—one of them for a light sentence in a grand-larceny case and the other for imposition of easy probation conditions. Raymond said the money was paid through an intermediary who was "well connected with organized crime." He testified the intermediary later introduced him to Schweitzer in the judge's chambers and that Schweitzer told him: "Nobody in this court has any intention of hurting you." When he came up for sentencing on charges that could have brought him a maximum of five years in prison, Raymond said, Schweitzer sentenced him to eight months—of which he served only half. In another criminal case in which he was convicted of stock fraud, the witness testified, Schweitzer imposed lenient probation conditions after accepting the second $25,000 payoff.

Senator Charles Percy of Illinois, a member of the rackets committee, asked Raymond: "Would you agree with street talk that Judge Schweitzer is the best judge money can buy?" Raymond replied: "I would agree with you 100 percent. But there's no judge in New York I couldn't reach."

Senator McClellen invited Judge Schweitzer to appear before the committee and give his side of the story. But Schweitzer declined, issuing a prepared statement that said: "After reading the newspaper accounts of the testimony of a long-time criminal identified as Michael Raymond, I can only say that I categorically deny each and every statement he made about indirectly bribing me through an intermediary. Even if there were any point in taking the witness stand to deny these baseless charges, I believe and am advised by my counsel that to do so would be inappropriate at this time in view of the pending proceeding before the New York State Court on the Judiciary."

Raymond later testified in a Massachusetts court that he had also taken part in the bribery of two judges in that state. He claimed that he had arranged to pay $35,000 to the two judges, through an intermediary, to obtain a suspended sentence in a fraud case. He identified the judges as Edward J. Desaulnier, Jr., and Vincent R. Brogna, both of the Massachusetts Superior Court. Raymond said he gave the money to a bail bondsman, who passed the bribe on to the judges. He testified that Judge Desaulnier interceded on his behalf with Judge Brogna, who presided over the fraud case and gave the defendant the suspended sentence. Raymond's testimony was offered at a hearing of the State Supreme Judicial Court, called to investigate the two judges. The bail bondsman pleaded the Fifth Amendment at the hearing. The judicial court disbarred Judge Desaulnier—ruling that he was "unfit to continue either as a judge or as a member of the bar." Although the judicial court had no authority to remove a judge from office, it ordered "as a matter of judicial administration" that Desaulnier not exercise his powers on the bench until further notice. The court entered a separate order of disbarment. Judge Brogna, who presided at the Raymond trial, was censured by the judicial court.

Meanwhile, the inquiry into Justice Schweitzer's activities also continued. Nathan Voloshen died of a heart attack in New York at the age of seventy-three. A month later, on September 24, 1971, formal charges accusing

Schweitzer of extensive misconduct were filed before the New York Court on the Judiciary by the court's counsel, Lawrence Walsh. The court suspended Schweitzer from office, pending the outcome of the hearings. Generally, the accusations made by Walsh paralleled those made against Schweitzer before the Hughes and McClellan committees. "Justice Schweitzer failed to keep his official conduct free from impropriety and the appearance of impropriety and failed to maintain his personal behavior beyond reproach," Walsh charged. "Justice Schweitzer . . . did not administer justice according to law; and he allowed his private interests and those of his friends to interfere with the performance of his official duties." The hearings before the Court on the Judiciary were still pending when Schweitzer decided to retire from the court.

Washington, D.C.—Anything Short of Murder

The furor over the Sweig-Voloshen-Schweitzer affair was still in progress when another scandal involving a congressional aide and a Mafia figure erupted. The new scandal concerned a case in which one of the defendants was Michael Hellerman, who had testified in the Sweig trial that Voloshen had told him: "We can do anything in Washington—anything short of murder."

On November 19, 1970, a Federal grand jury in New York indicted Hellerman and fifteen other men—including three Mafia leaders and three lower-echelon Mob figures—on charges of taking part in a fraudulent scheme to gain control of a Florida investment company and manipulate its stock. The government charged the defendants with using threats and beatings to take over the company and then parlaying the value of its shares up to artificially high selling levels in order to make large profits. Among those indicted, in addition to Hellerman, were Carmine

Tramunti, acting boss of the New York Mafia family formerly headed by the late Thomas "Three Fingers Brown" Luchese; John "Johnny Dio" Dioguardi, a captain in the same family; Vincent Aloi, a captain in the New York family headed by Joseph Colombo; Vincent Gugliaro, a Colombo family associate; Vincent Lombardo, the son-in-law of Meyer Lansky; and James Burke, an accused loanshark with Mob connections. The defendants pleaded not guilty and their case is pending at this writing.

The seventy-two-count indictment charged that Tramunti, Aloi, and Dio conducted meetings to iron out disputes among the sixteen defendants, to rig the market price of the investment company's stock, and to decide on the distribution of profits. It described Hellerman as a prime mover in the plot to violate securities laws and commit extortion. The government said Hellerman enlisted the support of the Mafia figures and got his confederates to beat and threaten those who resisted their takeover of the company, the Imperial Investment Corporation of Miami. Hellerman had previously been restrained from engaging in the securities business in New York State for five years. After that period had expired, he had run into troubles with the Securities and Exchange Commission over issuance of stock in another company he had organized. He had gone to Nathan Voloshen for help in solving those problems.

By the time of Hellerman's indictment in the Imperial Investment case, however, Voloshen had already pleaded guilty in the Sweig case and was hardly in a position to provide further help. U.S. Attorney Whitney North Seymour, Jr., whose office investigated and developed the Imperial Investment case, described it as "a massive security fraud with overtones of extortion and other strong-arm tactics, a complex scheme to reap large profits from the sale of unregistered stock in a corporate shell."

Robert G. Morvillo, the prosecutor in charge of Seymour's fraud unit, said at a news conference the chain of events leading to the indictment began in December 1968 when a businessman named Gerald Devins bought a Miami company that he renamed Imperial Investment Corporation. Devins installed himself as the company's president. A short time later Hellerman and a Miami lawyer arranged with Devins to buy 154,600 shares of the company's stock. Morvillo said Hellerman then enlisted the Mafia figures in the scheme to take over the company. But in August 1969 he said, "the president [Devins] was not being cooperative enough, so they took him into a hotel room until he agreed to go along with their machinations."

The indictment charged that Hellerman, James Burke, and a defendant named Pasquale Fusco flew from New York to Miami, where Burke, Fusco, and Vincent Lombardo (a Miami resident) took Devins into the hotel room and threatened and beat him. Then they took Devins to the company office and forced him to give them all of Imperial Investment's blank stock certificates and company records, the indictment said. It charged that they also obtained an additional 21,500 shares of the company's stock from other investors in the same way.

Morvillo said the defendants then traded among themselves in more than 150,000 unregistered shares of the company's stock, creating the false impression that there was an active market for it. Marvillo said these machinations artificially pushed the stock's selling price from zero to $24 a share. He said Hellerman then sold company stock to the public even though it was not registered with the S.E.C., as required by law. S.E.C. investigators said stockbrokers who traded in the Imperial Investment shares were stuck for $2 million when the stock turned out to be virtually worthless. Employees of three New York brokerage firms were among those indicted on charges of participating in the rigged market.

The initial investigation of the case had been launched by the S.E.C. after it had received reports of questionable transactions involving Imperial Investment stock. When the S.E.C. investigators learned about the alleged beating of Devins, they called the FBI into the case. Meanwhile, the S.E.C. suspended trading in Imperial Investment's stock, which again dropped in value to zero. Prosecutor Morvillo then was assigned the case and a special grand jury was ordered to work on it. Although the investigation took months, it was only in the last few weeks before the indictment was returned that investigators learned of the involvement of the Mafia figures. Among the specific charges contained in the indictment were conspiracy to violate the securities laws, sale of unregistered stock, mail and wire fraud, and travel across state lines to commit extortion.

Ultimately, most of the major defendants in the case were acquitted. But before their trial, the new congressional scandal broke into the open with the indictment of the chief aide to U.S. Senator Hiram L. Fong of Hawaii on charges of trying to fix the Imperial Investment case. Federal officials accused Fong's administrative assistant, Robert T. Carson, of "a brazen attempt to corrupt the administration of criminal justice." Among other things, the indictment charged Carson with telling the second highest official in the Justice Department, Deputy Attorney General Richard G. Kleindienst, that "a $100,000 political contribution would be made if something could be done to stop the prosecution" of the Imperial Investment case.

"The offer was immediately and categorically rejected" by Kleindienst, the indictment said.

The indictment accused Carson of conspiracy, bribery, and perjury. Two New York men were indicted with him —Edward Adams, a fund-raiser for political and charitable organizations, and Joseph Bald, an interior decorator. Bald had been named as a co-conspirator but had not been indicted in the Imperial Investment case. U.S. Attorney Seymour said Carson, Adams, and Bald had been involved in multiple plots to prevent the Imperial Investment indictment, then to halt the prosecution and finally to win lenient sentences for defendants who might be convicted.

Seymour said that an FBI undercover agent had infiltrated "the fix conspiracy" and had attended meetings of the alleged conspirators "in an unusually effective job of investigation." The bribery indictment said the conspiracy began about September 1, 1970—two and a half months before the return of the indictment in the Imperial Investment case. It charged that Bald and his brother-in-law, Harold Blond, agreed to try to fix and quash the Imperial case. (Blond was named as a co-conspirator but was not indicted in the bribery case.) Blond went to see Adams, who purportedly agreed to use his influence in Washington and arranged for Bald to meet Carson at the Senate Office Building on November 16. At that meeting, the indictment charged, Bald offered to pay Carson to help stop the Imperial Investment investigation.

Three days later the indictment was returned in the Imperial case. Five days after the return of the indictment, it was charged, Carson went to see Deputy Attorney General Kleindienst and allegedly offered the $100,000 political contribution to kill the case. (Kleindienst, a veteran Republican political strategist, had served as director of field operations in President Nixon's successful 1968 campaign.)

On November 29, it was charged, Bald and Blond met with Adams at a bar at LaGuardia Airport in New York. The indictment said it was agreed at the meeting that $200,000 would be paid to Adams and Carson in an attempt to halt the Imperial Investment prosecution and to prevent Bald from being prosecuted in other cases that might result from S.E.C. investigations of his activities. On December 1, the indictment charged, Carson met with Adams and Blond in the Senate Office Building and told them "he would not be able to quash the [Imperial] indictment because the case was 'too hot' but that at some future time leniency could be obtained." Carson was accused of accepting $2,500 from Adams during another meeting in the Senate Office Building on December 29 after agreeing to press for leniency for the Imperial Investment defendants and to try to prevent Bald from being prosecuted in other cases.

Carson denied any wrongdoing, but Senator Fong suspended him from his job without pay. The indictment of Carson, as had the indictment of Martin Sweig, shocked official Washington. Carson was one of the best-known aides on Capitol Hill and had carved out successful careers in business and politics in Hawaii before going to Washington.

While serving as Fong's aide for more than nine years, he had twice been elected president of the United States Senate Administrative Assistants Association. Only three months before his indictment, he had been elected president of the United States Senate Staff Club—even though he was a Republican and two-thirds of the club's 1640 members were Democrats. The club's announcement of his election called him "one of the most personable and dynamic persons on Capitol Hill."

Born in 1916 in Butte, Montana, Carson moved to Hawaii in 1934. He later became president of the Honolulu Stock Exchange and served for eight years as chairman of the Hawaiian Republican Party. His career also included stints as a radio and television personality, as executive secretary of Hawaii's Motor Vehicle Licensing Board and as director of the Federal Housing Administration for Hawaii and Guam.

On November 8, 1971, Edward Adams and Joseph Bald pleaded guilty to participating in the bribery plot. When Carson went on trial a week later, they were among the chief witnesses to testify against him. Also testifying was Bald's brother-in-law, Harold Blond.

Blond testified that he had discussed with Adams a year earlier a scheme in which $100,000 was to be paid for the quashing of the stock-fraud indictment. Federal prosecutor Joseph Jaffe asked: "Was there any discussion of what would happen to that $100,000?"

Blond replied: "Yes, that $100,000 Mr. Adams indicated would be going to Senator Fong and individuals in the Justice Department." (No criminal charges were filed against Senator Fong and there was no further explanation of why his name came up. Fong has denied knowing anything about such a scheme.)

There was further testimony that Blond had Adams arrange a meeting among Bald, Hellerman and Carson in Carson's Capitol Hill office. At that meeting, Bald testified, Hellerman offered to pay $1 million to Carson if the stock-fraud indictment could be killed. Carson promised to look into the matter, Bald said.

The FBI undercover agent who infiltrated the alleged

bribery scheme, Paul J. Brana, followed Bald to the stand. He testified that he had seen Carson accept $2,500 as an advance payment to help in the plot. The payment was made, he said, at another meeting in Carson's office—which he attended, posing as an underworld figure, along with Adams. He said Adams placed the $2,500, in an envelope, on Carson's desk. Carson took the money and thanked Adams for it, Brana testified. At that point, Brana said, there was little hope of quashing the original indictment but the plotters wanted to prevent the government from obtaining additional indictments against the stock-fraud defendants. Brana, who wore a concealed tape recorder strapped to his body during the meeting with Carson, said he asked whether "the price for fixing the new indictments was $100,000" and that "Mr. Carson said yes."

A tape recording of the conversation was played for the jury. At one point, Brana was heard telling Carson: "I'd like to get some idea how we're going to work this."

Carson replied: "Ah, ah, the way these things work is that, if something could be done [to prevent the new indictments] somebody will make a suggestion to me that it would be very nice if a contribution could be made."

Blana suggested in the recorded conversation that perhaps, if Carson couldn't quash the original indictment, he might win leniency for an unidentified defendant and also prevent the return of the new indictments. He told Carson: "Supposing that you can handle it, the [new] indictments, the SEC indictments, and there's leniency and maybe the guy does six months, I'd like to know what the arrangements would be for payments or what you would expect."

Carson replied: "It will be all spelled out."

"Okay, very good," the agent replied.

"Don't worry about anything," Adams interjected.

"That's all he says—don't worry about anything," the

agent replied with a laugh. Adams supported the testimony of other witnesses against Carson.

Deputy Attorney General Kleindienst testified that Carson had offered him the $100,000 contribution toward President Nixon's re-election campaign if he would help kill the stock-fraud case. He said Carson had come to his office on November 24, 1970. "After we had exchanged pleasantries, Mr. Carson sat down in a chair in front of my desk and said that he had a friend in New York who was in trouble," Kleindienst testified. "And [Carson said] that if I could help him with respect to his trouble, his friend was a man of substantial means and would be willing to make a substantial contribution of between $50,000 and $100,000 to the re-election campaign of President Nixon. I asked him what kind of trouble this man had. Mr. Carson said he was under indictment for Federal offenses and I said that under no circumstances could I do anything about the matter, even look into it, as a result of the fact that a grand jury had returned an indictment. That was just about all the conversation that existed."

Under cross-examination, Kleindienst said that he talked frequently with Carson about other matters and "worked very closely" with him in raising funds and campaigning for President Nixon. Defense attorney Joseph Brill asked: "It is true, is it not, that on November 20, 1970, you did not regard that in the conversation you had with Mr. Carson that he offered you a bribe?"

"No, I did not," Kleindienst answered.

"If you had regarded that conversation as containing a bribe offer, you would have reported it immediately, would you not?"

"Yes, sir, I would have."

Kleindienst later explained that he first learned Carson

was under investigation when Attorney General Mitchell showed him a memorandum from FBI Director J. Edgar Hoover on December 1, 1970. He said that, after learning of the investigation, he came to the conclusion that Carson's offer of the campaign contribution had been an attempted bribe. Brill asked him if he was "really serious" in giving that account. "Well, I am serious about it, but I have to explain that," Kleindienst replied. He said he had not considered the offer an attempted bribe when he first heard it, but that he came to regard it as a bribe when he learned other details of the investigation of Carson.

Later, Carson took the stand and denied asking for any money or agreeing to try to get any indictments quashed. He conceded meeting with the various persons who testified against him, but said that he had told them repeatedly he did not think anything could be done to kill the indictments. He said he had gone to Kleindienst only to get confirmation that there was nothing that could be done. He admitted taking the $2,500 from Adams, but claimed he considered it a political contribution completely unrelated to the possibility of getting the indictments killed.

On November 20, 1971, a year to the day after Carson's conversation with Kleindienst, the jury found him guilty. He later was given an eighteen-month sentence, which would make him eligible for parole after serving six months. Bald got four months. Carson, continuing to claim he is innocent, has said he will appeal. No matter what the outcome of the appeal, however, it seems clear that the Mob has established various pipelines into Capitol Hill and is seeking to expand them all the time.

President Nixon evidently discerned no conflict between Kleindienst's tough "law and order" stand and his less than eagle-eyed watch over potential corruption. Thus, it can scarcely be expected that major efforts to clean up attempted bribery on Capitol Hill will be forthcoming from the current national administration.

[9]

The Case of Schenley

Who's Who in America describes Louis Burrous Nichols as a corporation executive, former assistant to FBI Director J. Edgar Hoover, former executive vice president of Schenley Industries, Inc., chairman of the Criminal Law Section of the American Bar Association, member of the Masons, the Methodist Church, the Metropolitan Club in New York and the Goose Creek Country Club in Leesburg, Virginia. It also duly records that Nichols entered the FBI in 1934, the same year he was married, and that he named his first child after Hoover—John Edgar Nichols.

What the lengthy biographical sketch fails to note is how Lou Nichols used his inside knowledge of official Washington for activities that have raised eyebrows in the worlds of politics and law enforcement. The story of Nichols's association with questionable private citizens as well as with such public figures as Richard M. Nixon and J. Edgar Hoover is long and complex.

While serving in the FBI as Hoover's aide, Nichols became friendly during the 1950s with then-Vice President Nixon. He also became friendly with Roy M. Cohn, the New York lawyer-entrepreneur, who had formed close ties with Hoover and other top FBI officials while working as chief counsel to the late Senator Joseph McCarthy's Communist-hunting committee. Cohn, in turn, was treated as a virtual son by Lewis S. Rosenstiel, multimillionaire founder and board chairman of the Schenley liquor empire.

When Nichols decided to retire from the FBI in 1957, Cohn helped him land a job with Schenley. Rosenstiel hired Nichols as the company's executive vice president under a ten-year contract calling for a salary of $100,000 a year, plus stock options. In addition, the company bought and furnished a cooperative apartment in Manhattan for Nichols.

Nichols says he checked on Rosenstiel's background before accepting the job and concluded that the liquor magnate had a clean reputation. One can only wonder, however, how thorough this background check was. For, as will be seen, the Rosenstiel story is rife with controversy. An example of such controversy hit public light as part of a series of sensational legal battles between Rosenstiel and his estranged wife, Susan. In a court affidavit, Mrs. Rosenstiel accused her husband of maintaining close ties for years with leading syndicate racketeers. Of course, testimony of an estranged wife may be biased and does not necessarily represent the truth—but Mrs. Rosenstiel's affidavit does give some indication of the kind of controversy her husband generates.

In the affidavit, filed in New York State Supreme Court, Mrs. Rosenstiel charged: "When I refused to bow down to Mr. Rosenstiel's demands for an unjustified divorce, and instead pursued a course of complete vindication in matrimonial litigation in the New York courts, he vowed that he would break me physically and financially. He reminded me of his vast underworld connections and high political influence, a combination which he warned me was unbeatable. During the course of our married life he frequently associated with (and forced me to associate with)

nationally known ex-convicts and racketeers such as
Meyer Lansky; his brother, Jake Lansky; Robert Gould,
an ex-convict convicted of OPA violations; Art Samish, a
former public relations man with Schenley Industries, who
served time in Federal prison; and other gamblers and
racketeers such as Joe Fusco, a former associate of Al Capone; Moe Dalitz, under indictment for tax evasion; and
Sam Tucker, known as the dominant figure controlling
gambling operations in Newport, Kentucky, with other interests in Las Vegas." Rosenstiel denied the charges made
in the affidavit.

Some of the men mentioned by Mrs. Rosenstiel in the
affidavit have highly questionable backgrounds. Meyer
Lansky, whose exploits have already been described elsewhere in this book, needs no further introduction—except
perhaps a reminder that he is fond of boasting: "We [Mob
leaders] are bigger than U.S. Steel." Art Samish, in addition to being a public relations man for Schenley, was one
of the most powerful lobbyists in California. He represented, among others, the California Brewers' Institute,
which gave him control over a $153,000-a-year fund to be
used for "so-called political purposes." Samish often described himself as "the unelected governor of California"
—saying he was "the governor of the legislature and to
hell with the governor of the state." Called before a U.S.
Senate investigating committee to explain the brewers'
fund, he admitted that money from the fund was spread
around among "good, honest, outstanding officials who
subscribed to the temperate use of beer, wine, and spirits."
In addition to these "outstanding" officials, it was disclosed that Samish's associates included such mobsters as
Mickey Cohen, Joe Adonis, and "Dandy Phil" Kastel.
Eventually, Samish was sent to prison for tax evasion but
was released earlier than scheduled—reportedly after the

intervention of a high Federal official. Two other men described by Mrs. Rosenstiel as associates of her husband, Moe Dalitz and Sam Tucker, were originally leaders of the notorious Mayfield Road Gang in Cleveland. After Prohibition era careers as bootleggers, they organized big-time gambling operations and other ventures in Las Vegas and elsewhere.

In 1970 and 1971, testifying in secret sessions of the New York State Joint Legislative Committee on Crime (to be followed eventually by public sessions), Mrs. Rosenstiel repeated and elaborated on the charges she had made against her husband in her court affidavit. The committee, headed by State Senator John Hughes of Syracuse, was investigating ties between organized crime, politics, and legitimate business. Following up on Mrs. Rosenstiel's testimony the committee inquired, among other things, into Rosenstiel's relationship with Lou Nichols.

One possible reason for Schenley's hiring of Nichols was his intimate knowledge of the inner workings of Congress. During his years as aide to J. Edgar Hoover, Nichols had served as the FBI's liaison man and lobbyist on Capitol Hill. He had developed excellent working relations with numerous influential senators and congressmen. Schenley was in the market for a man with just such qualifications at the time Nichols was hired.

Congress was considering the first thorough overhaul of the Federal excise tax law in a quarter-century, and one controversial proposed revision of the law was critically important to Schenley. The company's interest in changing the law stemmed from a serious miscalculation made by Schenley executives seven years earlier. After the outbreak of the Korean War in 1950, the executives gambled that it would be a prolonged war—perhaps even develop into World War III. A lengthy war, they reasoned, would bring about shortages of grain and other ingredients needed to produce liquor; it might cause conversion of distilleries to defense manufacturing. As a result Schenley began turning out millions of gallons more liquor than its normal production. Most of Schenley's major competitors continued producing at their usual rates. Schenley's surplus stocks were placed in bonded warehouses under the supervision of government tax agents. Company officials planned to wait until the war caused a liquor shortage, then remove the stocks from the warehouses and make a huge profit.

But this plan was upset when the war ended in 1953 and the anticipated liquor shortage failed to develop. Schenley was stuck with an enormous stock of liquor for which there was no ready market. That was only part of the company's problem. Under the tax law then in effect, the tax on all liquor in bonded warehouses had to be paid when the liquor reached eight years of age or when it was removed from the warehouses for sale—whichever came first. The tax was $10.50 a gallon.

By the time Lou Nichols joined Schenley, much of the company's huge liquor stock was about to become eight years old. In the absence of a market for all this liquor, the company wouldn't be able to pay the taxes without suffering serious—perhaps disastrous—financial consequences. Some experts said payment of the taxes would have forced Schenley into bankruptcy. The only solution seemed to be to get the law changed. Schenley and a few smaller distillers mounted a high-pressure campaign to persuade Congress to extend the period from eight to twenty years during which liquor could be held in bonded warehouses before the tax became due.

Many of Schenley's competitors, who had not overproduced liquor during the Korean War, also favored extending the collection period to twenty years. But there was a vast difference between the measure they supported and the one backed by Schenley. The competitors wanted the twenty-year provision to affect only liquor placed in bonded warehouses after the law had been changed. Schenley wanted the twenty-year provision made retroactive to include all liquor then in warehouses—including its vast stock of Korean War merchandise. A bitter fight on the issue developed in Congress. Lou Nichols played a leading role in lobbying for the measure supported by Schenley.

The House Subcommittee on Excise Taxes, headed by Congressman Aime J. Forand of Rhode Island, approved an overall revision of the excise tax laws that included the provision supported by Schenley. (The measure became known as the Forand Act.) On the House floor the retroactive nature of the Forand bill was criticized on the ground that it would give Schenley unfair advantages over its competitors. Although Schenley was mentioned by name only rarely in the congressional debates, it was common knowledge that the company stood to become the chief beneficiary of the revised law. Critics of the measure pointed out that, in addition to allowing Schenley to delay its tax payments by as many as twelve years, it would also provide the company with potential sales benefits. By leaving its liquor in the bonded warehouses for several more years before selling it, Schenley would be able to advertise its product as eleven or twelve years old. Other companies, which had not overstocked, would not have liquor that old. Since the buying public tended to equate age with quality in liquor—although some experts said that aging failed to improve the product after a certain number of years—Schenley would have an advantage.

Among the chief critics of the measure in the House was

Congressman Eugene Keogh of New York. "One relatively small segment of the industry is seeking to take competitive advantage over the others because it happens to have accumulated large amounts of spirits which under this proposed law it will be able to retain in bond and, in future years, offer the public those spirits with a greater age," Keogh told the House. "Whether older age makes for better quality is a disputed fact. It has long been the policy of the Congress in amending laws to avoid any retroactive effects which would create competitive advantages. . . . The distilled spirits industry is unique in that it must produce today for an estimated market of four, six, or eight years hence. Each distiller is entitled to know, in planning his operations on the basis of existing laws and regulations at the time of production, that he will not be subjected to the threat of financial disaster by changes of a retroactive nature, which would favor any segment of the industry which, either by design or through circumstances, did not plan its operations in a prudent manner." Despite such arguments, the House approved the retroactive measure sought by Schenley.

The debate in the Senate was even sharper than in the House. Senator Harry Byrd of Virginia, veteran chairman of the Senate Finance Committee, was particularly outspoken in attacking the retroactive legislation. "My objection to this proposed legislation is fundamental," Byrd said. "Its purpose is wrong. In its best light, it is requested to correct an error of judgment. Actually, it will bail out distilleries which gambled on the effects of war and lost. The result will be a stock-market windfall and unfair advantage over competitors."

Byrd pointed out that the value of Schenley stock increased by a total of $33 million on the New York Stock Exchange on the day that the Senate Finance Committee,

over his strenuous objections, approved the proposed legislation. (Schenley stock held by Lewis Rosenstiel alone
rose in value by $6,987,500.) "In my opinion, the result of
this amendment would be a windfall—which would run
into the millions of dollars—for a segment of the liquor industry," Byrd told the Senate.

"That would be the immediate effect of postponing the
collection of the liquor taxes. The fact that postponement
of collecting this tax is regarded as a lucrative windfall is
clearly indicated by the $33 million increase in the price of
stock of one liquor company on the New York Stock Exchange when the Senate Finance Committee reported this
bill with the House provisions unchanged."

Without mentioning any names, Byrd also criticized the
intensive lobbying activities by Lou Nichols and others on
behalf of the measure. He said he had been a member of
the Finance Committee for twenty-five years and had wit-
nessed numerous attempts to change the liquor tax law.
"Frankly, I have never seen the pressure for a change in
this law reach the extremes taken this time," he said.
"When senators search for the reasons, they will find that
certain distillers gambled on the Korean War situation.
That was admitted before our committee. Certain distillers
stocked up with large quantities of liquor, in expectation
that grain and other ingredients would become scarce—
for they thought that a world war would result at that time
and that, in that situation, they would reap a huge profit.
However, the situation which they anticipated did not develop. Therefore, they lost their gamble and now they
want Congress to bail them out." Byrd said he felt so
strongly about the issues involved that, for the first time
since becoming Finance Committee chairman, he would
vote on the Senate floor against a measure approved by his
committee.

Byrd's sentiments were echoed by Senator Frank Lausche of Ohio. "Is there any question that the problem confronting Schenley's has arisen because that company gambled on the war in Korea turning into a long war?" he asked. Lausche said he would never vote to benefit any company that had gambled on World War III. "I have received communications from small distillers who stated that in 1950, because they did not have the money, they could not stock up and that they are now left with liquors that are five or six years old," Lausche said. "And when the time comes to advertise they will have to advertise it as being five or six years old, while Schenley's will be able to advertise its product as being ten, twelve, and perhaps fifteen years old."

Senator Edward Thye of Minnesota introduced an amendment to the Forand bill, seeking to eliminate the proposed twelve-year extension of the liquor tax deadline. Thye said tax experts had reported that the Forand bill provision could lead to deferral of $1.4 billion worth of tax payments in the following two years alone. When another senator disputed Thye's contention that the Forand bill would provide unfair tax benefits, Thye replied by citing the $33 million stock-market increase in the value of Schenley stock. "The stock market must have thought there was an advantage," he said. "Otherwise, the stock of one distilling company would not have skyrocketed in the manner in which it did upon the reporting of the bill by the [finance] committee. I think common sense would dictate that to any of us."

Despite such arguments, Thye's amendment to the Forand bill was defeated by a vote of fifty-one to thirty-nine. Ultimately, in late 1958, the Forand bill—containing the retroactive provision sought by Schenley—was approved by the Senate and signed into law. This writer has learned that State Senator Hughes's committee is still investigating the circumstances of the bill's passage.

The Hoover Foundation

Schenley clearly benefited from passage of the legislation and prospered in the years that followed. Meanwhile, Lou Nichols maintained his close friendships with Richard Nixon, J. Edgar Hoover, and Roy Cohn, among others. After Nixon was defeated for the presidency in 1960 by John F. Kennedy and moved to New York to join a law firm, many of his erstwhile friends lost interest in him and treated him as a has-been. But not Nichols. Frequently, when Nixon returned to New York from his travels throughout the United States and abroad, it was Nichols who met him at the airport with a chauffeured limousine.

As for Hoover, Nichols not only kept in close touch with the FBI director himself, he also brought Lewis Rosenstiel into Hoover's circle of friends. Rosenstiel appeared to become an ardent admirer of Hoover, particularly in his role as a staunch anti-Communist. In 1965, at the suggestion of Nichols, Rosenstiel put up the money to launch a private, tax-free foundation dedicated to honoring Hoover. The J. Edgar Hoover Foundation was established with an original gift of $35,000 worth of Schenley stock from Rosenstiel and a small gift of the company's stock from Nichols. A token contribution of $500 was made by the American Jewish League Against Communism, headed by Roy Cohn. Rosenstiel gave the Hoover Foundation another $6,500 in 1966 and $60,000 in 1967. Then, in 1968, he contributed an additional $1 million worth of Schenley securities. His gifts made him far and away the largest contributor to the foundation.

The foundation, incorporated in the District of Columbia, claims in its charter that its purpose is "to safeguard the heritage and freedom of the United States of America and to promote good citizenship through an appreciation of its form of government and to perpetuate the ideals and purposes to which the Honorable J. Edgar Hoover has dedicated his life." The charter says the foundation also is designed "to combat communism or any other ideology or doctrine which shall be opposed to the principles set forth in the Constitution . . . or the rule of law." Among the activities designated for the foundation to carry out under the charter are "to conduct educational programs; organize study groups; give lectures; establish scholarships and endow [teaching] chairs; circulate magazines and books and pamphlets." In addition, the charter specifies, the J. Edgar Hoover Foundation will work closely with the Freedoms Foundation of Valley Forge, Pennsylvania, a rightwing institution.

Virtually everyone connected with the Hoover Foundation had worked either for the FBI or for Schenley. Lou Nichols became president of the foundation. Two former FBI men, William G. Simon and Donald J. Parsons, became vice presidents and directors. Simon, a former agent in charge of the Los Angeles FBI office, now practices law. Parsons is president of Parsons Paper Company in Washington, D.C. Cartha D. "Deke" DeLoach, who was an assistant director of the FBI at the time the foundation was established, became the organization's secretary. (De Loach retired from the FBI in 1970 to become a vice president of Pepsico Corporation, but retained his position with the foundation.) N. J. L. Pieper, a former FBI man who worked with Nichols at Schenley, was named treasurer of the foundation. Nichols's secretary at Schenley, M. Patricia Corcoran, became assistant treasurer. All officials of the foundation are unsalaried.

Although the foundation is tax-exempt, it is required to

file financial reports with the Internal Revenue Service. The reports, on file in Room 1317 of the Internal Revenue building in Washington, reflect only minor expenditures. Summaries of the reports for the foundation's first four years, the only years on which they are available at this writing, follow:

In 1965: Purchase of one book for the J. Edgar Hoover Library [situated in one room of the Freedoms Foundation building at Valley Forge], $7.20; subscriptions for the Hoover Library, $30; literature donated to a summer institute at the Freedoms Foundation, $227.90; and a contribution to the Freedoms Foundation, $100. In 1966: Books for the Hoover Library, $3,000; compensation for a librarian, $1,500; and a scholarship to attend Freedoms Foundation seminars, $400. In 1967: Compensation for the librarian, $1,000; and donation of a memorial pew to the Freedoms Foundation chapel, $450. In 1968: Contribution to a teacher training institute on crime control and prevention, sponsored by the American Bar Association Fund for Public Education, $5,000; unspecified expenses at the Hoover Library, $2,500; five Freedoms Foundation scholarships for teachers, $2,125; and assistance to three FBI clerical employees in continuing their education at Southeastern University, $1,500.

In view of the kind of controversy generated by Mrs. Rosenstiel's charges, it may be wondered why J. Edgar Hoover would allow his name to be associated with Rosenstiel's. This writer posed the question to the FBI. Tom Bishop, an assistant FBI director who is also involved in the operations of the Hoover Foundation, defended the relationship between the two men. "Do you think we'd take money from questionable sources for the J. Edgar Hoover Foundation?" he asked. "Why, that's ridiculous. We've got people waiting in line to give us money. We have a very tight screening process for contributors. We won't even take money from some rightwingers interested in fighting communism because they're wild John Birch Society types."

Another recipient of Rosenstiel's largesse was Brandeis University, which apparently showed little curiosity when he teamed with former bootlegger Joe Linsey, a Schenley distributor, to contribute the university's "Joseph M. Linsey Sports Center." (Among Brandeis's other contributors was Meyer Lansky, whose donation was solicited by Linsey.) Like Brandeis, the University of Miami evidently had no qualms about taking sizable gifts from Rosenstiel. But there is quite a difference between a university and a foundation dedicated to honoring the director of the FBI. If the FBI didn't know about Rosenstiel's controversial history, then who would? Nonetheless, the Hoover Foundation seemed eager to take Rosenstiel's money.

The Friends of Lou Nichols

Lou Nichols, while serving as president of the Hoover Foundation, was also active on other fronts. He was, for example, chairman of the Criminal Law Section of the American Bar Association—in effect, the legal establishment's chief spokesman on criminal law.

In 1968, Nichols was an ardent supporter of Richard Nixon's presidential candidacy. His close relationship with the Nixon family was indicated at the Republican National Convention in Miami when he entered the Nixon box, kissed Mrs. Pat Nixon on the cheek, and kept her company as she awaited her husband's nomination. During the campaign, Nichols served as a member of Nixon's six-man senior advisory committee. In addition, Nixon assigned him to head a campaign organization designed to protect the Republican ticket against vote fraud. Nichols recruited lawyers and former FBI men in all fifty states for the organization, known as "Operation Integrity." They checked voter registration lists, watched polling places, and took other measures to prevent fraud. Nichols claimed the operation saved the election for Nixon by detecting and preventing vote-thievery in several key states.

That same year, Nichols and Rosenstiel officially retired from Schenley when the company was taken over by the Glen Alden Corporation. They did not, however, divorce themselves from the company. Both kept substantial stock holdings; Rosenstiel's $20 million worth of shares made him Schenley's largest individual stockholder.

Meanwhile, Nichols solidified his ties with the Nixon administration and continued providing advice, particularly on law-enforcement policies. His friends in the administration included not only the President but also Attorney General John Mitchell and Will Wilson, assistant attorney general in charge of the Justice Department's Criminal Division. In addition, he demonstrated that he still had the ear of J. Edgar Hoover.

An example was an incident in April 1969 involving Nichols's friend, Roy Cohn. At the time, Cohn was awaiting trial in Federal court in New York on charges of bribery, conspiracy, and fraud. The charges stemmed from the alleged payment of $23,000 in bribes in connection with New York City's condemnation of the Fifth Avenue Coach Lines, Inc., a bus line controlled by Cohn. In addition to denying all the charges, Cohn claimed the prosecution was part of a personal vendetta against him by Robert

M. Morgenthau, then United States Attorney in New York.

To support his claim, Cohn filed with the court an affidavit from a convict named Milton Pollack, who was serving time for grand larceny and awaiting trial on a charge of possessing stolen securities. Pollack said in the affidavit that members of Morgenthau's staff had offered to help get him a pardon if he would assist them "in inveigling Roy Cohn into some transaction that could result in his prosecution." The affidavit also claimed that Morgenthau's aides had told him about Cohn's personal and financial affairs and had trained him in the operation of electronic eavesdropping equipment, presumably to be used against Cohn.

Morgenthau's assistants filed affidavits denying Pollack's charges. One of them later testified that Pollack's affidavit contained "not a truthful sentence in any of [its] three pages." In addition, Morgenthau asked three agents in the New York FBI office—Donald Jones, Russell Sullivan, and Jack Knox—to submit sworn statements describing their own contacts with Pollack. The agents complied, and their statements also refuted Pollack's charges.

When the FBI men's statements were filed in court, Cohn turned copies of them over to Lou Nichols. Although the agents had presumably been doing their duty in providing the statements—helping the government protect its case—Nichols discovered that they had technically violated standard FBI procedure. They had failed to submit copies of their statements to FBI headquarters in Washington before handing them over to Morgenthau's office. Nichols went to FBI headquarters and demanded that the three agents be censured. He said later that he thought the agents had acted improperly and that headquarters "ought to know about it."

As a result of Nichols's complaint, J. Edgar Hoover personally ordered the agents disciplined and transferred out of New York. On May 2, 1969, each was given a letter of censure and ordered to report to a new post in thirty days. Sullivan was transferred to Louisville, Jones to St. Louis, and Knox to Pittsburgh. When Morgenthau heard about the disciplinary actions, he complained heatedly to John F. Malone, head of the New York FBI office. Malone reported Morgenthau's complaint to Washington. Hoover responded by ordering that, instead of having thirty days to report to their new stations, the agents would instead get only thirty-six hours. The agents complied with his order.

Life magazine, reporting on the incident, commented: "Needless to say, the episode . . . thoroughly shook up some of Morgenthau's witnesses. If Cohn, through Nichols, could bring about the arbitrary transfer of three FBI agents, what chance had an ordinary citizen?" Cohn eventually was acquitted by a jury. And U.S. Attorney Morgenthau, a Democrat who had the most enviable record of any Federal prosecutor in the country but had clashed with the Republican administration over his campaign to expose Mob ties with politics and legitimate business, was ousted by President Nixon.

An Open Contract

In 1970, Senator John Hughes's committee began investigating whether there were any possible connections between such men as Rosenstiel and Nichols and racketeers. Assigned by the committee to do most of the legwork on the investigation was a veteran racketbuster named William Gallinaro, who had grown up with numerous Mafia gunmen in the Coney Island section of Brooklyn and had long conducted a personal crusade against organized crime. Gallinaro, a deputy United States marshal, had previously been loaned by the Justice Department to the Hughes committee as an investigator. A tough cop with a broad network of informers inside the Mob, he had spent seven years specializing in breaking up organized crime. For months, he had pumped the late Mafia songbird Joe Valachi for information about the inner workings of the crime syndicate. As an Italian-American, Gallinaro resented the damage done by the Mafia to the image of those of his heritage; he took it as a personal mission to try to change that image by combatting the Mob.

Gallinaro spent months investigating the activities of Rosenstiel, Nichols, and their associates. He traveled extensively throughout the United States and abroad, checking leads. Simultaneously, this writer was conducting a parallel investigation as part of the research for this book. Arrangements were made with the Hughes committee for Gallinaro and this writer to work cooperatively on certain aspects of the investigation, sharing information and in some cases traveling together to conduct joint interviews.

While this joint effort was under way, word was received that Gallinaro's life was in serious danger. Senator Hughes made a public statement disclosing that organized crime had offered $100,000 "to any hoodlum" who would assassinate Gallinaro. Such an offer is known in the underworld as an "open contract." That is, the money is paid on demand to anyone who can prove he "hit" (murdered) the intended victim.

"I do not intend to permit members of this committee or the staff which assists the committee to become the targets of intimidation by racketeers and thugs," Senator Hughes said. "I think the decision by mobsters to place a price on the head of one of my investigators is unconscionable and

I feel certain that the decision to do so was occasioned by the pressure that our committee is bringing to bear on the Mob. I want to serve notice that such threats will not deter either myself or this committee and will only serve to have the opposite effect."

Hughes did not publicly identify those responsible for the murder plot. But Gallinaro told this writer he had learned that the $100,000 had been put up by persons determined to halt the investigation on which he was working. "We got the information from two different sources," he said. Gallinaro's home and family were immediately put under police guard. Gallinaro himself took extra precautions to keep his movements and activities secret, but continued working on the investigation. Meanwhile, word was received that this writer's life was also in danger because he was the only person besides Gallinaro in possession of certain information important to the investigation.

Several times prior to the threat on Gallinaro's life, Justice Department aides of Attorney General Mitchell—apparently fearing that the investigation might prove embarrassing to the Nixon administration—had tried to get Gallinaro withdrawn from his special assignment with the Hughes committee. Each time Hughes had prevailed upon Mitchell to allow Gallinaro to continue the assignment. After the death threat, renewed efforts were made to get Gallinaro pulled off the committee staff and returned to his duties as a deputy marshal. Hughes and Gallinaro went to Washington, met with Mitchell, and emphasized the importance of the investigation. The Attorney General agreed to extend Gallinaro's assignment, at least temporarily. By prearrangement, this writer met secretly with Gallinaro in Washington to exchange information and discuss the future course of the investigation. Throughout his stay in Washington, Gallinaro kept in his hand a large

Manila envelope. To the unsuspecting, it appeared merely to contain some papers. Actually, it contained a gun—which Gallinaro could fire simply by poking his finger through the Manila to the trigger. If trouble came he didn't want to waste the time of having to reach for a holster.

A short time after Gallinaro's trip to Washington, Mafia leaders in New York met to discuss the threat on his life. They decided that, in view of Senator Hughes's public statement about the plot, any attempt to carry out the murder would bring intolerable heat to the Mob. Word was sent to Mob gunmen that the "open contract" was not to be fulfilled. This writer later was informed that the threat to his own life had also been removed.

The Hughes committee, at that point, was seeking hard evidence to corroborate Mrs. Susan Rosenstiel's charges that her husband consorted with racketeers. In pursuing the investigation, Gallinaro and this writer traveled together to such places as Texas and Mexico. About the time of the trip to Mexico, Gallinaro started getting none too subtle hints from Washington that his investigation was stepping on influential toes.

Justice Department officials then began imposing additional restraints on Gallinaro. He was required, for the first time, to file weekly reports with the department on his activities on behalf of the Hughes committee. Assistant Attorney General Henry Peterson, second in command of the Justice Department Criminal Division, was placed in charge of keeping tabs on Gallinaro. Edward J. McLaughlin, general counsel of the Hughes committee, was obliged to clear with Peterson before sending Gallinaro on certain assignments. In addition, Peterson insisted that a committee lawyer be sent along with Gallinaro on some of his missions. The effect of these restraints, Gallinaro felt, was to inhibit his freedom of action and limit his effectiveness.

Then, in January 1971, the Justice Department suddenly pulled Gallinaro off his special assignment with the Hughes committee. He was given three days' notice to return to his duties at the U.S. Marshal's office in Brooklyn. The only explanation given for yanking him off the committee staff was that the investigative work he had been doing was not benefiting the Marshals' Service or the Justice Department. Moreover, when he returned to the Marshal's office, he was not reassigned to his old job as supervising deputy marshal in charge of organized crime cases. Instead, he was given what he considered the lowliest duty in the office—checking airport passengers and baggage to prevent skyjackings. Gallinaro saw the handwriting on the wall. He resigned from the Marshals' Service and accepted a long-standing offer to become an investigator for U.S. Senator John McClellan's rackets committee.

(Danger continued to stalk Gallinaro during his work with the McClellan committee. Late in 1971 Jack Halfen, the political fixer whose exploits were described in Chapter Seven, again found himself in trouble with the law. He was in jail in San Antonio, Texas, awaiting Federal trial in a complex alleged securities fraud. At the time, the McClellan committee was investigating the Mob's infiltration of the securities world. Gallinaro, who played a leading role in the investigation, arranged through this writer to interview Halfen at the jail. He hoped to persuade Halfen to cooperate in the committee's investigation, in return for which the committee would try to get him immunity from prosecution in the stock-fraud case. Gallinaro arrived in San Antonio on November 15 and spent two days talking with Halfen at the jail. He tape-recorded some of their conversations. On November 16, as he returned to his

hotel room late at night after talking with Halfen, Gallinaro was beaten by mysterious assailants. They stole many
of his confidential papers and recordings, including those
involving Halfen, and destroyed his recording machine.
Gallinaro was hospitalized, but was expected to make a
complete recovery. Halfen was moved from the jail and
placed under heavy guard in a secret location. At this
writing, the beating of Gallinaro remains a mystery.)

Alas for Halfen, he had become embroiled in an alleged
underworld plot to use several hundred million dollars'
worth of stolen securities for investment in legitimate business. He had been called before a Federal grand jury in
Los Angeles and questioned about the plot and his connections with top Mafia bosses, political figures and businessmen. He answered some of the questions, but said he
needed various business records to complete his testimony.
He was excused and ordered to return later. Instead, he
went to British Honduras—where he was eventually arrested on charges of being an "undesirable alien" despite
the fact that he had been hobnobbing with both American
and British Honduran officials during his sojourn there.
He was placed on board an airliner headed for New Orleans. When it arrived, FBI agents were waiting and arrested him.

The charges against him included parole violation, contempt of the Los Angeles grand jury and interstate transportation of fraudulent securities (from Texas to Louisiana). In January 1972 Halfen was convicted of two counts
of interstate transportation of stolen property. He attributed his problems to the fact that he had become involved
with Gallinaro.

This writer's own investigation led to the conclusion
that Halfen's new legal problems did indeed coincide in

time with his agreement to assist in the investigation. It seemed apparent that somebody had put the heat on Halfen immediately after the trip to Mexico. But who?

The writer's conclusions were stated in a letter to U.S. Probation Officer Harold R. Larson and were made a part of the official presentencing report on Halfen submitted to U.S. District Court Judge D. W. Suttle. The letter included the following comments:

"On February 8, Judge Suttle sentenced Halfen to two consecutive five-year sentences. Halfen still faces the Federal charges in Los Angeles. At this writing, he is being kept in a secret "safe house" maintained by the Federal government for prisoners whose lives are considered in danger. Since the assault on Gallinaro, it has been assumed that Halfen may also be a target for violence. The latest convictions and sentences handed down by Judge Suttle are being appealed."

Oddly enough, San Antonio District Attorney Ted Butler—while revealing the failure of Gallinaro to respond to requests that he appear before the grand jury—told the press that Gallinaro had cooperated in the investigation. Several of Butler's aides, however, told this writer that they would not use the term "cooperate." They said Gallinaro did talk to Butler and others in Washington, but had refrained from providing any useful information. At this writing, there is no way of predicting the outcome of the affair—except to say that the FBI is continuing its investigation and that Gallinaro has told various sources he feels it was the FBI that was responsible for the assault. This writer has found no credible evidence to support that contention.

Despite Gallinaro's absence from the Hughes committee, its investigation of the Rosenstiel affair continued. A short time after Gallinaro's departure from the staff, the Hughes committee began public hearings. Senator Hughes said the hearings would examine "the infiltration of organized crime into business, politics, and officialdom."

The Hughes Committee

Among the first witnesses was James P. Kelly, chief investigator for the U.S. House Interstate and Foreign Commerce Committee. Kelly testified that Rosenstiel joined with underworld figures in a "consortium" that bought liquor in Canada during Prohibition and sold it illegally in the United States. He said members of the group, including Rosenstiel, "have continued their relationship through the years and share to some extent [interests] in business ventures." Rosenstiel's associates in the group, Kelly testified, included Meyer Lansky, Joe Linsey, and Joe Fusco, a henchman of Al Capone.

During Prohibition, he said, the consortium bought liquor from Canadian plants operated by Samuel Bronfman, founder of Distillers Corporation-Seagrams Ltd. The liquor was then sold throughout the United States. Kelly testified Linsey was in charge of distribution in New England and Fusco was responsible for the Chicago area. He told how both Rosenstiel and Linsey were arrested on Federal liquor law charges. The case against Rosenstiel was dismissed, but Linsey was convicted. After Prohibition, when Rosenstiel developed Schenley into one of the country's major distilleries, Kelly said Linsey and Fusco set up companies in Boston and Chicago, respectively, to distribute Schenley products.

He testified that Linsey was an associate of New England Mafia boss Raymond Patriarca and other racketeers. Linsey's help was sought by Patriarca, Kelly said, in financing a Mob-controlled Las Vegas casino and in efforts to win paroles for mobsters involved in a $1.5 million Brinks armored-car robbery.

Rosenstiel, vacationing at a home he owns in Miami, issued a statement denying Kelly's charges. "They are utterly ridiculous, absolutely false, and without foundation," he said. He did not reply, however, to a written invitation from the Hughes committee to testify at the hearings. The committee had no authority to subpoena him while he was outside New York State. For months, committee investigators had been trying to keep tabs on Rosenstiel's movements so they could subpoena him—but he had either avoided entering New York or at least kept the investigators from finding him there.

Another witness who did testify before the committee was Mrs. Yolanda Lora, a former secretary to attorney Louis Nizer. Mrs. Susan Rosenstiel had been represented by Nizer in litigation that had prevented her husband from divorcing her. While the litigation was in progress, Mrs. Lora testified, she was employed for three months as a paid companion to Mrs. Rosenstiel—assigned, among other things, to help protect her from harassment by her husband. During that time, Nizer got permission to examine personal effects left by Rosenstiel in a Manhattan town house he had turned over to his estranged wife. Mrs. Lora said she was present when the examination was made and that the effects included papers, documents, and tape recordings containing numerous references to meetings, conversations, and business dealings with such racketeers as Frank Costello and Meyer Lansky. In one tape recording, Mrs. Lora testified, Rosenstiel could be heard discussing a planned meeting with Lansky and Joe Linsey in a Miami Beach hotel. She said Rosenstiel's effects also included a folder full of newspaper clippings about Costello. A ledger found in the town house listed payments by Schenley totaling $40,000 to wheeler-dealer Art Samish while Samish was serving a Federal prison sentence for tax evasion, Mrs. Lora said.

The hearings later turned to Rosenstiel's attempts to dissolve his marriage—attempts that the committee was told involved forgery and payment of more than $160,000 in bribes. This testimony was provided by Jeremiah McKenna, a special counsel to the committee who had conducted an intensive investigation of the Rosenstiels' tangled matrimonial litigation. Two years before marrying Rosenstiel in 1958, McKenna testified, Mrs. Rosenstiel received a Mexican divorce from her previous husband, Felix Kaufman. In 1962 Rosenstiel and his attorney, Benjamin Javits (a brother and then law partner of U.S. Senator Jacob Javits), tried to invalidate Mrs. Rosenstiel's divorce from Kaufman and thus nullify her marriage to Rosenstiel. "If they had succeeded, she would have lost her claims to sizable amounts of property and alimony," McKenna said. These claims were estimated to be in the millions of dollars.

A key element in the plan to invalidate the divorce, McKenna testified, revolved around the creation of a fictitious art dealer called "Sam Goldschmidt." He said Javits filed documents in Mexico purporting to show that Mrs. Rosenstiel's divorce from Kaufman was illegal because she had failed to pay a judgment for paintings that the nonexistent Goldschmidt supposedly claimed she had stolen. Under Mexican law, a person may not obtain a divorce if he has a judgment pending against him. A Mexican court, invoking that law, nullified Mrs. Rosenstiel's divorce. McKenna testified that this ruling had apparently been obtained through the payment of widespread bribes. He said that Javits, acting on Rosenstiel's behalf, had made more than $160,000 worth of payoffs—including $15,000 to a Mexican attorney general, $10,000 to the wife of a Mexican Cabinet member and $68,000 funneled to other officials through two public relations firms. (Javits denied any wrongdoing.)

On the basis of the Mexican court order, Rosenstiel filed suit in New York to annul his marriage and deny his wife any property or alimony rights. McKenna said his investigation of New York court records disclosed that "Rosenstiel's attorney later conceded that Goldschmidt was fictitious and the court concluded [that the signatures] 'Rosenstiel' and 'Goldschmidt' were identical on at least one document." A handwriting expert's testimony in the New York court records charged that one of the "Goldschmidt" signatures had been made by Rosenstiel, McKenna said. Rosenstiel denied the signature was his.

Attorney Nizer proved to a Mexican appeals court that there "was no Goldschmidt, documents had been forged, and bribes given to obtain the lower court order," McKenna testified. The appeals court reversed the lower court's nullification of Mrs. Rosenstiel's divorce from Kaufman. Rosenstiel then stopped using the Mexican proceedings as a basis for his suit in the New York courts, but managed to win an annulment on other technical grounds. The annulment was later reversed by a higher New York court.

Rosenstiel fired Javits as his attorney and denied being a party to the bribery of the Mexican officials. The Appellate Division of the New York State Supreme Court later suspended Javits from law practice for three years, ruling that he had "attempted to perpetrate a fraud upon the courts of Mexico and the United States" in the Rosenstiel affair. Javits called the suspension "unjust, unfair, and improper" and vowed to fight for reinstatement. "It's what happens when you get trapped with a famous name and have to fight as a matter of principle," he said.

In the Hughes committee hearings, a former aide to Rosenstiel was called as a witness. John A. Harrington, who had served twelve years as an FBI agent before becoming Rosenstiel's executive assistant, was questioned about passage of the Forand Act—the legislation that had extended the period for payment of taxes on liquor stored in bonded warehouses. Harrington testified that Rosenstiel, Lou Nichols, and other Schenley officials lobbied extensively for passage of the law. He denied that the legislation was designed solely to benefit Schenley, claiming it helped other distillers as well. But committee counsel McLaughlin, insisting that the Forand Act primarily helped Schenley and "rescued it from bankruptcy," drew from Harrington the admission that the company's chief competitors had opposed the legislation.

Questioned about Rosenstiel's alleged association with racketeers, Harrington denied ever seeing him with Meyer Lansky or Frank Costello. But he did concede seeing Rosenstiel on numerous occasions with Joe Linsey, who the committee emphasized was an associate of Lansky.

Later, Lou Nichols was called before the Hughes committee. He confirmed that he had lobbied vigorously for passage of the Forand Act. He said he had made many contacts with members of Congress while serving as J. Edgar Hoover's assistant and that he had used these contacts in pressing for approval of the legislation. He said he had worked so hard on the lobbying project that he suffered a heart attack, but continued to make telephone calls to Capitol Hill from his hospital room. Nichols estimated at one point that passage of the Forand Act had saved Schenley $40 million to $50 million. He said later, however, that he could not be sure how much money had been saved.

Before joining Schenley, Nichols said, he had used the resources of the FBI to run a background check on Rosenstiel. This check convinced him, he said, that Rosenstiel "shunned organized crime like the plague." He said he was aware of Rosenstiel's indictment on liquor violations charges—involving a purported conspiracy to counterfeit whiskey bottles and labels for illegal sale to the public—but that he gave it "no importance" because the indictment was dismissed. "I used every resource available to me and I found no information, much less creditable evidence, of Mr. Rosenstiel's alignment with the underworld," Nichols said. Under further questioning by McLaughlin, however, he conceded that Rosenstiel had business and social connections with various men described by McLaughlin as having criminal backgrounds.

Nichols acknowledged that former bootlegger Joe Linsey owned a Schenley distributorship in Boston, Whitehall Liquors, and was a close friend of Rosenstiel. He also testified that mobster Michael "Mickey the Wise Guy" Rocco had been employed by Whitehall Liquors. "He was one of Linsey's salesmen," Nichols said. He conceded that Joe Fusco held a Schenley distributorship in Chicago and that Robert Gould, who had served two years in prison for black market violations, held a distributorship in Miami. But he claimed he was unaware that Fusco had been identified in congressional hearings as a former member of the Al Capone gang.

McLaughlin questioned Nichols about whether he had ever asked Rosenstiel if he knew Mafia leader Charles "the Blade" Tourine. "I did and he denied it," Nichols replied. Told by McLaughlin that Tourine had testified in secret sessions that he had met with Rosenstiel on various occasions, Nichols said he believed Rosenstiel.

Under further questioning, Nichols said he was aware that former Chicago Mafia boss Johnny Torrio had once infiltrated a distributing company financed by Schenley in which Rosenstiel's brother-in-law, Herbert Heller, was a partner. But he contended that, when Rosenstiel learned of Torrio's interest in the firm, he ordered Heller to withdraw as a partner. Asked if he was aware that Torrio's share of the business was later bought out by Joe Linsey, Nichols answered: "No, I wasn't."

Nichols testified that Schenley had done business with two New York firms—Alpine Wines and Liquors and Peerless Importers—while they were owned by the late Mafia boss Joseph Magliocco and his brother, Antonio. But he said the firms did not receive Schenley distributors' franchises until Joseph Magliocco was no longer officially affiliated with them.

Several times during his testimony, Nichols clashed heatedly with Senator Hughes. "I think it's high time someone got critical of this committee," Nichols said. "I think there has been an injustice done [to Rosenstiel]." Hughes replied: "The fact that you get excited about it doesn't bother me. We intend to investigate. I have no intention to apologize for the actions of this committee."

Nichols charged that the committee investigation had been sparked by what he called the "vituperation, falsehoods, half-truths, and innuendoes" of Mrs. Rosenstiel. "Her poisonous tongue worked overtime to blacken Mr. Rosenstiel's name," Nichols said. Mrs. Rosenstiel, when informed of Nichols's charges, commented: "They are false and Mr. Nichols knows they are false. Once again, he is doing Lewis Rosenstiel's dirty work. Mr. Nichols is still the same errand boy—a very expensive errand boy—for

Mr. Rosenstiel. Everything he says is absolutely untrue. I will spell out what I think of Mr. Nichols when I testify [in public sessions before the committee]."

Mrs. Rosenstiel, who had previously testified in secret sessions, had been expected to appear at the public hearings shortly after Nichols testified. Other witnesses had been expected to be called immediately thereafter. But, because the New York State Legislature was inundated with an unusually heavy load of important legislation at the time, Senator Hughes recessed the hearings to allow the committee members time for their other duties. Several months have passed and the hearings have not been resumed at this writing, but committee staff members have continued pursuing leads in the investigation. The staff members say the hearings will be resumed and carried to their logical conclusion.

Meanwhile, the committee has been unsuccessful in continued attempts to subpoena Rosenstiel. Through Lou Nichols, Rosenstiel informed the committee that he was too ill to testify. Nevertheless, on various occasions when newsmen tried to reach him, Rosenstiel was described as away on fishing trips. As far as is known, his close friend, J. Edgar Hoover, who has said many times that citizens have an obligation to cooperate with lawfully constituted investigative bodies, has made no effort to persuade Rosenstiel to testify. Nor has the J. Edgar Hoover Foundation shown any inclination to renounce Rosenstiel. The foundation continues, in the words of its charter, "to promote good citizenship" with Rosenstiel's money.

[10]

The Public Face
of the Mafia

"If the black flag of the underworld were to unfurl atop one of the tallest skyscrapers in New York, it would be a fit symbol of how the Mafia has gained control of that building and many other real estate holdings," says a Federal investigator. And real estate management is only one of scores of legitimate businesses infiltrated by the Mob. Indeed, the influence of racketeers on the commercial and financial life of the United States is so pervasive that scarcely any American is left untouched by it.

The cost of this influence to the average citizen is felt in many ways. Since most Mob invasions of legitimate business are designed in one way or another to confound the Internal Revenue Service, billions of dollars in revenue go untaxed—resulting in higher taxes for the typical American. Countless respectable merchants are victimized when the Mafia muscles its way into thriving businesses, milks their assets, and then drives them into bankruptcy. Thousands of working men and women are forced to settle for starvation wages under sweetheart contracts between unions and companies dominated by the Mob. Insurance rates rise because of thefts, frauds, and acts of violence committed by the Mafia to wipe out competition and advance its supposedly legitimate business interests. And consumers suffer when the Mob gains a business monopoly and boosts prices as high as the traffic will bear.

Scams and Bust-outs

Many of the most lucrative Mafia ventures into the business world involve commission of bankruptcy fraud—also known as "scam" and "bust-out." The United States Chamber of Commerce says that at least 200 Mob-inspired bankruptcy frauds are discovered every year, each leaving up to 250 creditors holding the bag. The total debts left in the wake of such "scams" usually run upward of $200,000.

A classic "scam" case, demonstrating how quickly the Mob can take over a legitimate business and milk it dry, involved the Murray Packing Company of the Bronx, New York. Murray was a successful supplier of meat, poultry, and eggs to wholesale markets. It was operated by Joseph Weinberg; his son, Stanley; and David Newman. Although Murray was an established, prosperous firm, it found itself at one point in unexpected need of cash. Bank credit was not immediately available.

The Mob moved to fill the void. A member of the late Vito Genovese's Mafia family, Joseph Pagano, had previously infiltrated the company as a salesman—despite having a long criminal record and having been identified by Joseph Valachi in congressional testimony as one of three men who committed the unsolved murder of a suspected informer. Pagano went to Newman and the elder Weinberg and told them he could get them the money they needed. The source of the funds would be a firm called Jo-Ran Trading Corporation—owned by Peter Castellana, a member of the Carlo Gambino Mafia family, and Carmine Lombardozzi, a captain in the family. Castellana was well known to the operators of the Murray Packing Company.

He headed Pride Wholesale Meat and Poultry Corporation, one of Murray's steady customers, and also operated ten retail supermarkets.

Jo-Ran Trading Corporation agreed to lend Murray Packing Company $8,500 at an interest rate of one percent a week. The loan was made in the form of a check, signed by Lombardozzi. A month later, the mobsters forced the Weinbergs and Newman to sell a one-third interest in Murray Packing to Pagano. They also required that Pagano become president of the firm, so he could "protect the investment." With Pagano in charge, and his signature needed on every check issued by Murray Packing, strange things began happening.

Castellana's Pride Wholesale Meat and Poultry Corporation—which normally bought about $1,000 worth of goods a month from Murray Packing—suddenly launched a massive buying campaign. The first month, its purchases from Murray Packing totaled $241,000. The second month, they totaled $298,000. And, the third month, they skyrocketed to $922,000. All the purchases were made at bargain prices, below Murray Packing's own costs.

Since Castellana had an account at the Commercial Bank of North America, he got Pagano to transfer Murray Packing's account to the same bank. Checks from Pride, made payable to Murray Packing, were taken to the bank and deposited by Pagano. Simultaneously, Pagano presented the bank teller with Murray Packing checks made out to himself for the identical amounts on the Pride checks. The cash was handed over to Pagano. In that way Murray Packing was drained of as much as $125,000 in a single day and $745,000 in an eight-day period.

Murray Packing's creditors throughout the country were left unpaid and the company quickly sank into bankruptcy with a total of $1.3 million in debts. During the bankruptcy proceedings, the mobsters siphoned an additional $112,000 out of the company to defraud the creditors. It took Federal investigators four years to sort out Murray Packing's tangled affairs and bring the conspirators to trial for bankruptcy fraud. The Weinbergs and Newman (who were found to have acquiesced in the fraud) were convicted along with Pagano, Castellana, and Gondolfo Sciandria, an uncle of Castellana who had acted as a messenger in transferring the money.

The system used in the Murray Packing case is known as a "take-over scam." That is, the Mob takes over an established firm and drives it into bankruptcy. Two other types of bankruptcy fraud practiced by the Mafia are called the "three-step scam" and the "same-name scam."

In the "three-step scam," the Mob organizes a new company headed by a front man with no criminal record. A large amount of money is deposited in a bank to establish the company's credit rating. The company usually adopts a high-class name and gets an accountant to issue an impressive balance sheet. It provides prospective suppliers with a list of references, often composed of firms secretly controlled by the Mob. Then, as the first step in the fraud, it places a series of modest orders with suppliers. For the first month or two, all bills are paid quickly in full.

The second step involves placing larger orders, both with the original suppliers and new ones. The new suppliers are paid in full, but the original suppliers are given just enough to satisfy them temporarily. In the third step, the company orders huge amounts of merchandise from virtually all suppliers in the industry. Often, this is done during the suppliers' busy season to limit the chance that an investigation will be made before the goods are shipped. Once the merchandise arrives, it is quickly sold at bargain prices through Mob outlets in other cities or concealed in warehouses. The suppliers are left unpaid. The Mob withdraws its original investment and plunges the company into bankruptcy. Operators of the "scam" simply disappear or explain away the bankruptcy by blaming it on an employee's embezzlement, a fire that destroyed the company's warehouse, or the like.

In the "same-name scam," the Mob sets up a company with a name virtually identical to that of a well-known firm with an excellent credit rating. If the reputable firm is called Ajax Manufacturing Company, for example, the new firm might be named Ajax Manufacturing Sales Company. Sometimes, the Mob even manages to establish its company at an address on the same street as the reputable concern. It may use letterhead stationery similar to that of the established firm. Hoping to be mistaken for the reputable company and to capitalize on its credit rating, the Mob's firm places large orders from suppliers. The fraud, from that point on, works the same way as the "three-step scam"—except that it may proceed at a much faster pace because there is no need to spend time establishing a credit rating.

Selling Soap to the A&P

When the Mafia decides to move in on legitimate business, no company is too big to be immune from its tentacles. The country's largest food retailer, the A&P supermarket chain, learned that lesson. A&P, with 4700 stores and more than 10 million families as customers, offered a tempting plum to the Mob. A prolonged, determined attempt to pluck that plum was made by Jerry Catena, successor to the late Vito Genovese as a Mafia family boss, and Catena's brother, Gene, who served as the family's underboss.

In addition to participating in various rackets, Gene

Catena headed what purported to be a legitimate business called Best Sales Company in Newark, New Jersey. The company negotiated brokerage deals with manufacturers, taking a cut of their profits in return for providing "contacts" that helped promote the manufacturers' products. Through an intermediary, Gene Catena got an introduction to an up-and-coming manufacturer named Nathan Sobol, president of North American Chemical Corporation (NACC). Sobol had converted NACC from a small coin-operated laundry chain into a $3 million-a-year operation that produced and packaged detergent for supermarket chains to sell under their own brand names.

At the time, A&P was making plans to sell a detergent under its brand name—but had not yet chosen a manufacturer. Catena told Sobol he had a way to land A&P's business for NACC. When Sobol asked how he planned to do it, Catena snapped: "That's my business!" Nonetheless, tempted by the prospect that the A&P account would triple his company's volume, Sobol signed a ten-year contract giving Catena a percentage of all NACC sales. If Catena succeeded in getting A&P's business, that account alone would pay the racketeer about $1.5 million during the ten-year period. Moreover, Sobol gave Catena an option to buy 40,000 shares of NACC stock that would increase sharply in value if the company won the A&P account.

Catena, with the help of his brother, enlisted the aid of two labor union officials who regularly bargained with A&P executives on behalf of thousands of employees. The labor leaders were Joseph Pecora, head of Teamster Local 863, a Mafioso who had a long criminal record, and Irving Kaplan, a Mob associate who headed Amalgamated Meatcutters Union Local 464. Between them, Pecora and Kaplan controlled almost 15,000 union members. Pecora previously had led a Teamster strike that had cost A&P an estimated $7 million. Thus, when Pecora and Kaplan recommended strongly that A&P buy its detergent from Sobol's firm, the supermarket executives felt compelled to give their requests serious consideration.

Kaplan, who was shortly to begin negotiations with A&P on a new contract, arranged an appointment for Sobol with the chain's top men. The appointment had been cleared by Kaplan through A&P's labor relations director and one of its division presidents. Eleven other detergent manufacturers were seeking the A&P account, but none had the high-pressure backing Sobol boasted. When Sobol appeared for his appointment at A&P's executive offices at the Graybar Building in Manhattan, he was treated with great deference. The chain's executives listened patiently to his long recitation of his detergent's virtues. Sobol left a sample of the detergent for laboratory testing, and the A&P executives said they would let him know as soon as they had made a decision.

Later, however, A&P repeatedly put off making a choice of detergents. Sobol, assured by Catena that NACC would get the A&P account, increased production. Box upon box of detergent stacked up in Sobol's warehouse while he awaited word on the deal. Kaplan kept putting the heat on the A&P executives—only to be told that laboratory tests were still being made on detergent samples submitted by various manufacturers. The apparent stall infuriated Gene Catena, who reportedly told his brother and Kaplan: "We'll kick A&P's brains out!"

A short time later two tough-looking men entered an A&P store in the Bronx and asked Manager John Mossner to begin stocking a new detergent. Mossner, who was unaware of A&P's plans to market a detergent under its own brand name, said he did not have the authority to comply with their request. He suggested they talk to executives at his division headquarters. Several days later, as he was closing the store, Mossner spotted two men in the parking lot—preparing to toss Molotov cocktails onto the roof. He yelled at them to stop and they ran off, leaving the Molotov cocktails behind. Five hours after that incident, a suspicious fire broke out in a nearby A&P store. It was the third mysterious A&P fire in a period of weeks.

The following month, an assistant manager of an A&P store in Brooklyn was the victim of a Mob-style murder. During the murder investigation, Mossner learned that Federal agents were looking into Mafia control of contracts for garbage removal from various A&P markets. He went to see the agents, and told them about the incident involving the Molotov cocktails. They showed him "mug" pictures of known Mob arsonists. From the pictures, Mossner identified an ex-convict named Albert Maselli as one of the men he had seen with the Molotov cocktails. Maselli, who had previously served seventeen years in prison and was later given a life sentence for murder, was a convicted arsonist. At the time of the investigation, he was working for Nicholas Rattenni—a member of the Catena Mafia family and overlord of the garbage rackets in Westchester County, New York.

A few days after making the identification of Maselli, Mossner was emerging from his car outside his home when he heard someone call his name. As he turned to see who it was, he was shot in the stomach. Despite his wound, he chased his assailant down the street—shouting to passersby to help him. The gunman hopped into a getaway car. Through the car window, Mossner tried to grab him. The gunman shot him once through the chest and twice through the head. Mossner fell dead as the getaway car roared away.

The murder of Mossner, like that of the assistant store manager, went unsolved. Meanwhile, Catena and his allies stepped up their pressure on A&P to decide in favor of Sobol's detergent. Kaplan put the heat on one A&P executive while Pecora concentrated on another. Still, the executives stalled—saying the laboratory tests on the detergent samples had not yet been completed. Actually, the tests had been finished and had given Sobol's detergent the lowest rating of all twelve tested, but the executives had not decided how to handle the problem without antagonizing Kaplan and Pecora.

About that time, another A&P store burned down and investigators found the remains of several Molotov cocktails in the rubble. It was the first definite evidence of arson discovered in any of the store fires. With that evidence in hand, top A&P executives went to officials of the U.S. Justice Department and spelled out their suspicions that the outbreak of violence and arson might be connected with the high-pressure sales campaign on behalf of Sobol's detergent. The Justice Department launched an investigation.

When contract negotiations opened between A&P and Kaplan's Amalgamated Meatcutters Union, Kaplan further increased the pressure by making a series of demands that would have been virtually impossible for management to meet. Company executives decided the time had come to serve notice that they would not be intimidated. They called Sobol in and told him they had decided to reject his detergent. "We don't like your Mafia connections," they said. Sobol angrily threatened to sue them for slander. And Kaplan and Pecora, even more angry, telephoned A&P officials to demand that they apologize to Sobol and withdraw their remarks about the Mafia. The officials refused.

Kaplan then set a strike vote for all members of his union working for A&P in the New York metropolitan area. Shortly before the union's previous contract was scheduled to expire, Federal prosecutors called Jerry Catena before a grand jury in New York. Apparently expecting to be questioned about gambling and other rackets, Catena instead found himself under investigation for suspected extortion in the detergent affair. He repeatedly pleaded the Fifth Amendment. Later, outside the grand jury room, a prosecutor took Catena aside and warned him to take the heat off A&P. Catena claimed that he planned to get out of the detergent business. Meanwhile, Irving Kaplan was informed that he was also under investigation. A few days later, Kaplan substantially reduced his union's demands and agreed on a new contract with A&P.

For a time the wave of trouble that had plagued A&P subsided—but then it erupted anew. A swift-spreading fire destroyed the company's huge warehouse at Elmsford in Westchester County, New York, causing losses totaling almost $19 million. Less than four months later, two separate fires were set in an A&P warehouse in Queens, New York. That warehouse was also destroyed, with a loss of $6 million. Police and fire marshals determined it was a case of "obvious arson."

In their investigation, they discovered that a group of employees, just before leaving work for the night, had stopped to drink coffee and relax for a few minutes in the warehouse lunchroom. One worker who normally was part of this group had been conspicuously absent. He was nineteen-year-old Jimmy Castorina. A foreman went looking for Castorina and found him coming downstairs from the second floor, where the first of the two fires was later discovered. Investigators decided that, if the fires had been set by an A&P employee, Castorina had been the only one alone long enough to be the arsonist.

Under questioning, Castorina denied setting the fires but provided other intriguing information. Chief Assistant Queens District Attorney Fred Ludwig said Castorina told detectives that he lived with his mother and Phil Ingrassia, an A&P employee who awarded and supervised the company's garbage-removal contracts with Nick Rattenni and other Mob figures. Castorina claimed he had heard Ingrassia say the day after the Elmsford fire, that "they" had wanted to burn the warehouse for a long time. He did not identify the "they." But he said he had also heard Ingrassia tell his mother that the A&P warehouse at Garden City, New York, the company's largest remaining distribution center, would be next. Security at the Garden City warehouse was greatly tightened.

When Ingrassia was questioned by investigators he admitted knowing Nick Rattenni and other members of the Catena Mafia family, but denied making the statements about the fires claimed by Castorina. The investigators discovered that two months after the Elmsford fire Ingrassia, whose salary was $9,000 a year, had deposited $5,075 in a newly-established bank account. They also found that during the previous two years his total bank balances had risen from $64 to more than $22,000.

While the investigation continued, three more fires struck A&P buildings—causing more than $700,000 in damages—and four other attempts to set fires were aborted. Eventually, a grand jury indicted Jimmy Castorina on first-degree arson charges in the Queens case. Prosecutors charged publicly that Castorina had set the two fires in the Queens warehouse as part of a Mafia plot against A&P. But a judge later dismissed the case against Castorina, saying the evidence was circumstantial. Other aspects of the campaign of terror waged against the A&P are still under investigation at this writing.

As for North American Chemical Corporation's detergent, after Sobol failed to get the A&P account he did succeed in selling the product to several other supermarket chains—including Grand Union and Bohack Corporation. The detergent, sold in some places under the chains' brand names and in others under its own name, was widely advertised as being safe for the environment and an answer to pollution problems. But in early 1971 the U.S. Food and Drug Administration charged that the product was "extremely dangerous, toxic, and hazardous" to people. The Federal agency ordered seizure of about 2000 cases of the detergent. Fred S. Halverson, an official of the agency, described detergents marketed under all the brand names this way: "They're toxic, corrosive to intact skin, and produce, on contact, a severe eye irritation. They create an open wound on the skin. I've never seen anything like it." North American Chemical officials replied that, if used as directed, the detergent was not hazardous. Eventually, the Food and Drug Administration required that the product carry a label which included a precautionary warning. Simultaneously with the seizure of the detergent, Federal officials disclosed that a Justice Department task force on organized crime was investigating not only North American Chemical Corporation's ties with the Catena Mafia family, but with Raymond Patriarca's New England Mafia family as well.

In October 1971 the U.S. Senate Commerce Committee conducted hearings on the firm's links with the Mob. A&P officials testified about the pressure placed on them to buy the company's product and about the wave of violence and arson that accompanied this pressure. Nathan Sobol testified that he had signed two contracts with Gene Catena. He said the first contract called for Catena's Best Sales Company to act as agent for the distribution of North American Chemical products. When it became apparent that Catena had not been successful in pushing the products, Sobol said, he signed a second contract giving Catena $2,156 a month for thirteen years in order to allow another agent to handle the products. Sobol said he also gave Catena stock options in North American Chemical, let Catena use office space at company headquarters, and gave him use of a credit card. Grand Union officials defended their use of North American Chemical's detergent at the hearings, saying the product was almost as good and cheaply priced as competitive detergents sold by other manufacturers. But the committee entered into the record an affidavit from the director of Grand Union's test kitchen, saying that North American Chemical's detergent contained higher alkalinity than that which the supermarket chain normally accepts.

The Trucking Business

While all this had been going on, another member of the Catena Mafia family had been making deep inroads into the business world—with the help of the Federal government. The Mafioso was John "Gentleman John" Massiello of Yonkers, New York. Through his son, John, Jr., Massiello controlled a Bronx trucking firm, ANR Leasing Corporation. And ANR was the recipient of more than $1 million worth of loans backed by the U.S. Small Business Administration. Some of the loans were made directly by the Small Business Administration to ANR; others were made by the Federal agency to banks and other private corporations that passed the money on to ANR. But all the loans were backed by the government and required applications to be filed with the Small Business Administration by ANR. The name of John Massiello, Jr., appeared on the loan applications as president of ANR. So did the name of the corporation secretary, Thomas McKeever, who had a criminal record dating back to 1940 and had been convicted in 1960 on forty-three counts of racketeering.

At the time the Small Business Administration made its first loan to ANR, amounting to $460,000, John Massiello, Jr., had no criminal record. But a short time later he was arrested following a brawl that resulted in one man's death and the gouging out of another man's eye. The remainder of the loans were made while Massiello was awaiting trial on charges of manslaughter and maiming. Massiello pleaded not guilty and the case is still pending at this writing. His father, the behind-the-scenes power in the trucking firm, had a long criminal record and had been identified by Justice Department officials as an important Mafioso. Yet, the FBI—which was supposed to check the backgrounds of all applicants for Small Business Administration loans—failed to forward any derogatory information on ANR.

Later, the firm defaulted on its original loan and a further investigation disclosed the Mafia's control of the company. Even then, the Small Business Administration neglected to notify a private-lending agency that served as an intermediary in funneling government-backed loans to ANR. As a result, the private agency loaned ANR an additional $60,000.

Congressman Wright Patman's House Banking and Currency Committee launched an investigation in 1970 of the ANR affair. At a committee hearing, Patman made public a memorandum written by Logan B. Hendricks, the Small Business Administration's associate administrator for financial assistance. The memorandum said that the

FBI had "missed the boat" in failing to uncover the Mob backgrounds of the Massiellos and McKeever and that this failure must not be made public. The investigation also disclosed that some of the loans that found their way to ANR had been illegal because the manner in which Small Business Administration funds had been loaned from one private agency to another and then to ANR was specifically prohibited by law.

The Small Business Administration was not the only Federal agency to help ANR. The company also received a contract to lease trucks to the Post Office Department. An investigation revealed that the contract had been awarded after the Massiellos had paid bribes to department officials. The father and son were convicted of bribery in Federal court in 1970. Massiello, Sr., was sentenced to five years in prison and a $15,000 fine; his son got three years and a $5,000 fine. In imposing sentence on the Massiellos, Judge Morris E. Lasker told them: "If we don't have people willing to offer money to people in the government, they can't take it."

Indications were that the words were wasted, at least on the elder Massiello. A short time later, while appealing his conviction in the post office bribery case, he was indicted on charges of bribing an Internal Revenue agent. The indictment accused him of offering the agent $250 a month to keep him posted on the status of a tax investigation pending against him. Several monthly payments were made in accordance with this deal, the indictment said. Massiello was convicted and given an additional two-year sentence and a $5,000 fine. He appealed the case.

Legitimate in Michigan

Of all the Mafia families in the United States, few have made such deep incursions into the world of legitimate business as the family in Detroit, Michigan. With an organizational genius that might well be the envy of their automobile industry neighbors in Detroit, the local Mafiosi have taken control of hundreds of business enterprises—not only in Michigan but also in other states, Canada, and Mexico. In recent years, the Detroit family has been headed by a ruling council consisting of five men—Joseph Zerilli, William "Black Bill" Tocco, Peter Licavoli, John Priziola, and Angelo Meli. Of the five, Zerilli has been the most powerful. All members of the ruling council have gained control of a wide range of purportedly legitimate businesses. Following is a breakdown of some of the businesses in which they are involved. Unless another city is indicated, all are headquartered in Detroit.

Zerilli and his brother-in-law, Tocco, share interests in Lakeshore Coach Lines; T&M Construction Company; Melrose Linen Service; Jarson and Zerilli Produce Company; Hazel Park Racing Association; Detroit Italian Baking Company; Pfeiffer Macomb, distributors; an office building at 16135 Harper, Detroit (in which Licavoli also is a partner); Muller Foods, Jersey City, New Jersey; Deer Valley Citrus Association, Glendale, Arizona; South Branch Ranch, Roscommon, Michigan; a restaurant in Ann Arbor, Michigan; and a grocery store and various pieces of rental property in Detroit.

Licavoli, in addition to his share of the office building at 16135 Harper, has interests in the Chrysler Office Building; Hart Center, Inc.; Lakeshore Underwriters, Inc.; Gold Cup Coffee Company; Fototronics, Inc.; Lakeshore Insurance, Inc.; Apache Nickel Surplus Company; Michigan Mutual Distributing Company; Apache Realty Company; Tucson Printing Company, Tucson, Arizona; the Grace Ranch, Tucson; Casa Catalina Motel, Tucson; and a riding stable and investment property in Tucson.

Meli's investments include the Flint Cold Storage Company, Flint, Michigan; SC & CC Trucking Company; Meltone Music Company; Ace Automatic Music Company, Saginaw, Michigan; a Pure Oil service station in Detroit; Bel-Aire Lodge Motel, Saginaw; various pieces of investment property in Detroit and a 480-acre farm at Marine City, Michigan.

Priziola's interests include the Moravian Acres housing subdivision; the Harper Metro Park subdivision; Balmoral Gardens; the City Barber College; St. Clair Terrace Corporation; the Starlite Motel in Roseville, Michigan; another motel and bar in Roseville; rental property in Detroit; Papa Joe's Restaurant, San Diego, California; the Tropics Bar, San Diego; La Mesa Bowl Corporation, San Diego; and the Cactus Bar, San Diego.

The Detroit family, along with its other operations, has been responsible for its share of bankruptcy frauds. In one such case, seven members of the family—including a son of "Black Bill" Tocco—were indicted by a Federal grand jury in late 1970 on charges growing out of a "scam" involving a Detroit furniture store. The defendants included Giacamo "Jack" Tocco, Dominic T. "Fat Dominic" Corrado, Anthony "Whitey" Besase, Anthony "Tony Long" Cimini, Dominic "Sparky" Corrado, and Peter and Paul Vitale. Eight other men with no known Mob backgrounds were also indicted. The indictment charged that the operators of the Palm Furniture Store had received about $100,000 worth of merchandise by using fraudulently prepared business statements. It accused the operators, in concert with the mobsters, of committing bankruptcy fraud by concealing the store's assets from creditors.

The Mob and the Conglomerates

Even enormous conglomerates find it impossible to fend off infiltration by the Mob. Evidence produced by the

New York State Investigation Commission revealed, for example, that a conglomerate named Twentieth Century Industry, Inc.—which owned drug, plastics, metals, mining, and soft-drink companies—was deeply involved with the Mafia. Martin Goldman, vice president and executive officer of Twentieth Century, testified in secret commission hearings that he had put Aniello Dellacroce, underboss of the Carlo Gambino Mafia family, on the payroll of one of the conglomerate's subsidiaries—the Royal Crown Bottling Corporation of Newark, New Jersey. Goldman admitted meeting with Dellacroce and another mobster named Michael V. Catalano, who has served prison terms for bookmaking and possession of stolen goods, at a lower Manhattan Mafia hangout known as the Ravenite Social Club. When the investigation commission opened public hearings on the Twentieth Century affair, Goldman refused to repeat his secret testimony—pleading the Fifth Amendment. But the earlier testimony was read into the record by Paul D. Kelly, the commission's assistant chief counsel. Kelly commented: "It is odd that so large and detailed a business as Twentieth Century Industry does business in this strange way, with the vice president and executive officer admitting to going on many occasions to the Ravenite Social Club to discuss business, financial matters, and the hiring of employees with a known racket figure like Aniello Dellacroce."

Dellacroce also pleaded the Fifth Amendment when called before the commission. But other witnesses, testifying under grants of immunity from prosecution, provided further details of the Mob's infiltration of Twentieth Century. Among them was Benjamin Goldfinger, former vice president of the Progressive Drug Company, which had been owned by Twentieth Century and had gone into bankruptcy shortly after being sold by the conglomerate.

Goldfinger testified that the drug company had hired a racketeer named Dominick "Nicky" Bando as its chief security officer. Payments to Bando were made secretly, he said. The money was taken out of daily receipts and charged off in company records to "travel and entertainment" expenses. Goldfinger testified that Progressive Drug's general manager, Lorence I. Press, told him that the payments to Bando were made to insure labor peace after a Teamster Union local had replaced an AFL-CIO union as bargaining agent for the company's employees.

Press followed Goldfinger to the witness chair. He testified that he hired Bando on instructions from Martin Goldman, who had described the mobster as "an excellent person" for the chief security officer's job. After drawing an acknowledgment from Press that Bando's job put him in charge of supervising the guarding of warehouses full of pharmaceutical narcotics, commission counsel Kelly read Bando's criminal record into the record—which included two prison sentences for sale of narcotics. The record also included a prison term for assault and conspiracy in the acid blinding of labor columnist Victor Riesel.

Kelly indicated that the Mafia's infiltration of Progressive Drug had driven up its costs and contributed to its bankruptcy. "When this firm was forced into bankruptcy, it left creditors' fees and other costs that are passed on to the consumer," Kelly said.

In Pennsylvania, the State Crime Commission has found that more than 375 major businesses are controlled by the Mob. Angelo Bruno, boss of the Philadelphia Mafia family, owns a shopping center in South Philadelphia; the Penn-Jersey Vending Company; the Garden State Vending Company; Globe Exterminators in Philadelphia; and has interests in a cheese company and extensive real estate holdings in Florida. John S. LaRocca, boss of the Mafia family in the Pittsburgh area, owns the North Star Cement Block Company and has interests in the coin-machine business in Pittsburgh and Gary, Indiana. He is also in the overall and laundry-supply business. Russell Bufalino, boss of the Mafia family in northeastern Pennsylvania, is a partner in the ABS Construction Company of Pittston. He formerly owned the Penn Drape and Curtain Company and City Auto Service in Pittston and was a partner in United Parcel Service in West Pittston. With racketeers James Plumeri and Angelo Sciandra, he owns the Bonnie Stewart Dress Company and Claudia Frocks in New York. An associate of Bufalino, William Medico, is general manager of Medico Industries, Inc., a multimillion-dollar corporation in Luzerne County, Pennsylvania. Peter Maggio, a captain in Angelo Bruno's family, is a partner in Michael's Dairies, Inc., one of the largest dairy companies in Philadelphia.

In Pennsylvania, as elsewhere, businesses controlled by the Mob often have been able to use their political influence to gain government contracts. Medico Industries, Inc., for example, received a $3.9 million contract from the Pentagon to produce 600,000 warheads for rockets to be used in Vietnam. The company also got a contract to produce parts for U.S. Army tanks. Michael's Dairies, Inc., was awarded contracts to provide milk to Dover Air Force Base in Delaware and the Philadelphia Naval Yard. While Russell Bufalino was a partner in United Parcel Service in West Pittston, the firm received a contract to make deliveries for the Federal government. Two companies owned by Nicholas Piccolo, a captain in the Angelo Bruno family, got more than $900,000 worth of contracts from the Philadelphia Naval Yard and the Naval Air Engineering Center.

Turning Cash Into Credit

In Illinois, it is not uncommon for the Mob to join forces with influential political figures in its ventures into the arena of legitimate business. A typical example is a Chicago firm called Frontier Finance Corporation, which has made extensive loans to gamblers and usurers. The president of the company is a retired Chicago police captain, John H. Scherping. The vice president is a syndicate gambler, Frank Buccieri. The secretary-treasurer is a former Cook County deputy sheriff, Michael B. Tenore. Two of the major investors in the firm are Carl A. Schroeder, former Chicago postmaster, and Edward F. Moore, former Cook County Republican chairman and a member of the Chicago Transit Authority.

Much of the money invested in legitimate business by the Mob is first funneled through secret numbered bank accounts in such countries as Switzerland, the Bahamas, Panama, Liechtenstein, Luxembourg, and West Germany. This process is known as "laundering"—that is, making illegal rackets money appear legitimate. Usually, it is accomplished by depositing the money in a secret bank account abroad, then bringing it back to the United States in the form of a make-believe loan. The racketeer pretends he is borrowing the money from a foreign investor, but actually is just juggling his own funds. Besides "laundering" the money, the technique provides the mobster several other benefits. It allows him to hide the original illegal income from the Internal Revenue Service. And, when he prepares his tax return, he deducts the interest on the make-believe loan.

Will Wilson, Assistant Attorney General in charge of the Justice Department's Criminal Division, says the "laundering" process helps the Mob solve the problem of how to use the large supplies of cash it accumulates. "Anyone who has a large quantity of cash would have some difficulty in using it because most large transactions are credit transactions," Wilson points out. "People don't go into a stock brokerage house and buy a hundred thousand dollars' worth of stock and pay in cash generally. And, if they do, it raises questions right off as to where they got it and why they are paying in cash, rather than a check. So it is not easy to do business in the American system in large denominations using cash, and therefore the racketeers' problem is to take cash that they get from the numbers racket or other illegal business and turn it into usable credit. They do that through the process of taking the cash by courier to some foreign bank and then bringing it back in the form of credit."

Robert Morgenthau, former United States Attorney for the Southern District of New York, says his investigators uncovered numerous examples of use of secret foreign accounts by organized crime. "We found many transactions by American hoodlums through banks and brokerage firms in the Bahamas," he says. In addition, it was found that millions of dollars' worth of securities stolen from Wall Street brokerage firms wound up in the hands of Mob figures. The racketeers then sold the stolen securities "through foreign banks both in Nassau and in Switzerland," Morgenthau says.

Secret accounts, he points out, are also instrumental in the Mob's international narcotics smuggling operations. "Our investigations into the importation and sale of heroin revealed that accounts in foreign banks are frequently depositories for the proceeds of heroin transactions. Because those accounts are secret, attempts to uncover persons directing the international dope traffic frequently end up in complete frustration. Generally, money received for the sale of heroin in the United States is either carried to Europe by courier or hand-carried to a local money exchange or bank, where it is forwarded to an account in a Swiss bank. This account is often in the name of a paper (dummy) corporation with an office in Switzerland. From that account, the money is transferred to an account in a European country under the direct control of the initial supplier of the heroin."

Morgenthau recalls one case in which just such a technique was used by a narcotics ring that ultimately smuggled into the United States heroin worth $60 million on the retail market:

The facts in this case revealed that, as part of the payments for smuggling heroin during a three-week period, $950,000 was sent to a Swiss bank account of a Panamanian corporation with offices in Geneva, which was known as the Me Too Corporation. Couriers delivered $800,000 in cash to two money exchange houses in New York City. From there, the money was forwarded to the Secret Swiss account of the Me Too Corporation. While the appearance of unknown persons with large sums of money might have been questioned by the money exchanges, an official of the Swiss bank had previously advised them about the expected delivery of funds. Because of their substantial business connection with the bank, the exchanges accepted these transactions as a professional courtesy. The other $150,000 in currency was deposited in the account of a South American brokerage firm with the First National City Bank in New York City. On the instructions of an authorized signatory of the account, a check for $150,000 was drawn on the First

National City Bank and mailed to the Swiss bank for the account of the Me Too Corporation. Although there was no evidence that the money exchanges or the New York bank or the Swiss bank had any knowledge of the underlying narcotics transactions, the vital part they played in the heroin traffic is unmistakable.

In some cases, Morgenthau says, racketeers are not even content merely to make use of foreign banks' secret accounts; they actually take control of the banks. "A startling development of recent years has been a significant change in the identity and ownership of foreign banks," he points out. "Today, numerous banks in Switzerland and the Bahamas are owned and controlled not only by Americans, but in some cases by American hoodlums closely linked to loansharking, gambling rackets, and other illegal businesses. Such a bank does not need a large working capital to be a useful element of an illegal business. Its function is not to provide funds for the business so much as to provide an unreachable depository for illegal profits."

Congressman Wright Patman, chairman of the House Banking and Currency Committee, has spearheaded a drive to tighten U.S. laws in order to make it more difficult for mobsters and others to conceal their dealings through the use of foreign accounts. Chiefly at Patman's instigation, Congress has recently approved legislation requiring American banks to keep more detailed microfilm records of their transactions, particularly those involving foreign commerce, and requiring all American citizens and corporations to disclose whether they hold secret foreign accounts. Meanwhile, American officials have persuaded the Swiss government to relax its strict banking secrecy laws slightly in order to help track down concealment of Mob money. Despite these steps there are still broad loopholes that allow racketeers ample opportunity for illegal manipulation of money through foreign accounts. As Patman puts it: "Secret foreign bank accounts are the underpinning of organized crime in this country. They are a haven for unreported income. They can be used to buy gold in violation of American law. They can be used to buy stock in our market or in the acquisition of substantial interests in American corporations by unidentified persons under sinister circumstances."

While making use of secret accounts in foreign banks, the Mob has simultaneously moved to gain covert control over domestic banks throughout the United States. In some cases, through front men with clean records, racketeers buy their way into actual ownership of the banks. In other cases, the mobsters achieve control over key bank officials through such tactics as threats and payoffs.

There is virtually no limit to the number of ways in which the Mob can benefit from a bank takeover. Once gangsters get their hooks into a bank, a Federal official says, the bank begins doing "an inordinate amount of business with racket-controlled guys that a legitimate bank wouldn't touch." Suddenly, he says, all the accounts of an area's known racketeers are switched to a single "hoodlums' bank." The bank then makes large loans to mobsters, their relatives and friends—with no questions asked, no collateral, no credit checks. A penciled okay from a top racketeer is all it takes for a loan to be approved.

The bank furnishes excellent credit references on the gangsters' accounts. Often, it allows them to open huge accounts under false names in order to stymie investigators. Bank officials may falsify their records to camouflage Mob transactions. In addition, bank cashiers may deliberately fail to make the required reports to the Treasury Department on abnormally large deposits of currency. Such reports on major cash deposits are used as a "flag" to the Internal Revenue Service—indicating possible sources of illegal income.

Closely tied to Mob infiltration of banks is the underworld's penetration of the securities business, not only on Wall Street but across the country. Leading Mafia figures have been involved in an increasing number of stock-fraud cases in recent years. In some instances, racketeers have bought secret interests in brokerage firms. And, in a great many instances, the Mob has succeeded in planting lower-echelon hoodlums in jobs inside respected securities companies. These hoods have stolen millions of dollars' worth of securities for use by their rackets bosses. Moreover, direct thefts from brokerage houses have been far from the Mob's only means of obtaining stolen securities. Many stocks and bonds have been stolen while in transit—in airport thefts and mail-truck hijackings. Some of the securities have simply been fenced by the Mob and resold to unsuspecting customers. Others have been pledged as collateral on loans obtained from banks. The underworld refers to the process of using stolen securities for collateral as "putting them to sleep." The securities are sometimes left in bank vaults for years. Bankers usually don't discover they have been stolen unless the loans are defaulted and the bank tries to sell the securities.

In June 1971 Senator John McClellan's rackets committee launched a series of public hearings into the Mob's dealings in securities. Attorney General John Mitchell testified that by "conservative estimate" more than $500 million worth of securities had been stolen during 1969 and 1970—much of it by organized crime. The rate of such thefts rose even higher during the first half of 1971, when

$494 million worth of securities were reported stolen. Mitchell said the securities industry's laxity in checking the backgrounds of prospective employees, in developing adequate protective systems and in bookkeeping procedures played into the hands of the underworld. "Many thefts of securities from brokerage firms, banks, and other financial institutions—involving large sums of money—go unreported or unnoticed," he said. Mitchell also testified that the counterfeiting of securities, particularly government securities, had become a major problem. "Counterfeiting of government securities could seriously threaten legitimate transactions in today's financial market," he said.

New York City Police Commissioner Patrick V. Murphy, who followed Mitchell to the witness chair, echoed the Attorney General's criticism of the securities industry's loose procedures. "We encounter considerable reluctance on the part of industry representatives, whether brokerage houses or banks, to concede the disappearance of valuable securities," Murphy said. "As incredible as it may sound, brokers and banks frequently are totally unaware that thousands of dollars' worth of securities have been furtively removed from their vaults." Murphy said that "the most insidious factor" in the recent increase in securities thefts had been the participation of the Mob. "Organized crime has assumed a major role, particularly in the disposition of stolen securities, because it can provide the organizational framework without which thefts of securities would be ineffectual."

Some securities are more attractive targets of thefts than others, Murphy explained. The most popular are U.S. Treasury bills and notes that the bearer can cash simply on presentation. Murphy testified that even some respectable members of the financial community, perhaps unknowingly, were dealing with organized crime in disposing of stolen stocks and bonds. He told of one case in which $925,000 worth of International Business Machines Corporation stock was stolen from a vault of the Toronto Dominion Bank.

"A new, practically unscreeened lower-level employee with an unsavory background was able to walk out of a respected bank with nearly a million dollars in negotiable securities without being challenged," Murphy said. "It took a week for the bank to discover that some securities were missing, and the full extent of the loss was not known until the recipients of the stolen securities began to make overtures about disposing of them. The police were not notified until about ten days after the initial discovery of the loss, and by that time the stolen certificates had been sent out of the city. Some of the certificates came into the hands of unsuspecting businessmen while knowing participants in the criminal scheme directly sought to convert others themselves. But, above all, the central role of upstate New York organized crime figures must be emphasized—for they performed the critical task of distributing the certificates in practical lots to a variety of purchasers with their own schemes for marketing them."

A New York prosecutor specializing in securities theft cases, Assistant Manhattan District Attorney Murray J. Gross, testified that thieves were running rampant on Wall Street. "If I were to describe the situation on Wall Street, I would call it a free-for-all," Gross told the committee. "Everybody is stealing—the messengers, the clerks, even the supervisory personnel." He said certain banks in New York, which he declined to name, were in collusion with organized crime figures in turning stolen securities to the Mob's advantage. Some banks have added stolen securities to their assets in order to improve their financial positions, Gross testified. He said that a number of bank-loan officers have been bribed by racketeers to accept stolen securities as collateral on loans.

Gross sketched profiles of three types of Wall Street thieves for the committee. One was "the heretofore honest employee who steals quite independently of any outside influence," he said. "Be it whim or some vague idea of vast profits, he steals." The second, and most prevalent, type "is the employee who is induced to steal either through fear or the promise of profit by the underworld." Gross said that such an employee or his family might be threatened with harm by the Mob. Often, the threat is coupled with the enticement of profit. "The third type, and perhaps the one potentially the most harmful, is the employee placed in his position by the underworld for criminal purposes." Gross said that such employees could themselves steal, recruit other workers to take the securities, or "finger" a messenger for a robbery.

The prosecutor emphasized the simplicity with which millions of dollars' worth of securities could be stolen. "Most often, the thefts involve simply taking the securities and hiding them on the person," he said. Women put them in their blouses, men under their shirts or in their trousers. In one case, Gross testified, $2.5 million worth of securities were carried out of a brokerage house in an attaché case.

Small fires are sometimes set in brokers' offices to cover up thefts. In other cases, Gross said, the thieves use a stock-switching technique to cover their tracks. Securities stolen from one brokerage house are given to a confederate in a second brokerage house, who steals an identical amount of the same stock. When the first brokerage house discovers its loss, it issues a "stop" order on those shares to prevent them from being traded. But those shares are sitting undetected in the vault of the second brokerage house while the other block of shares is being sold freely on the market.

Gross said that most stolen securities—whether taken by agents of the Mob or by independent amateurs—eventually find their way into the hands of organized crime for conversion into cash. He described a thriving black market in securities, in which leading racketeers "bargain like crazy" over the price of stolen stocks. The going rate is about eighty percent of the market value of the stocks, since that is the amount the securities generally bring as collateral for bank loans.

Gross was followed to the witness chair by Chief U.S. Postal Inspector W. J. Cotter, who testified that at least $71 million worth of securities had been stolen from mail shipments at airports between 1967 and 1970. Next, the committee heard a witness who had been responsible for many such thefts—Robert F. Cudak, a twenty-nine-year-old Federal convict. Cudak, who had agreed to tell the committee about his operations as a master mail thief and his connections with organized crime figures, was led into the hearing room under heavy guard. Two Federal marshals flanked him as he testified. Two other marshals sat directly behind him, facing the spectators' section. Other marshals and Capitol policemen were scattered throughout the hearing room.

Cudak told the committee he had committed nearly 200 thefts at airports, stealing more than $100 million worth of securities and other valuables, during a four-year period. He said he had stolen stocks, bonds, traveler's checks, cash, jewels, furs, and other items from the mails, REA Express shipments, and air-freight cargoes at seventeen airports from September 1966 until his arrest in September 1970.

He was serving a seven-year prison term for mail fraud,

but the McClellan committee was seeking a reduction of the sentence in return for his cooperation. In addition, the committee had guaranteed him immunity from further prosecution for any crimes described in his testimony. Plans were being made to enable Cudak to assume a new identity and a completely new life after his release from prison, to protect him from possible retaliation by the Mob.

Cudak identified for the committee thirty men, many of them Mob figures, who he said had been associated with him in the airport crimes—some as planners of the thefts, others as accomplices, still others as fences. Most of the fences he dealt with were connected with organized crime. Among those he named as Mob fences who helped dispose of his loot were Anthony "Tony Boy" Boiardo, the New Jersey Mafioso; two of Boiardo's associates, Ralph Masciola and Joseph Calarco; Frank Mannarino of Valley Stream, Long Island, operator of a construction business; Leonard Mastrogiacomo of Great Neck, Long Island, operator of a corrugated paper-box company; Cosmos "Gus" Cangiano and his brother, Frank, both Brooklyn racketeers; and Charles "Charlie West" De Lutra, a New York Mafia leader.

Another man described by Cudak as a fence, Joel J. Rostau of Los Angeles, had been found shot to death in the trunk of a rented automobile at New York's John F. Kennedy International Airport. Shortly before his murder, Rostau had been indicted on a charge of theft of securities from a mail shipment at the airport. Two other suspects in related cases had also been found murdered in similar fashion—one at New York's La Guardia Airport and the other at Miami International Airport.

Cudak said he began stealing mail shortly after being hired as a ramp man for Northwest Airlines at Kennedy

Airport. He said the airline employed him, although he had a prior criminal record, without making any security check on him. Northwest's personnel officers took his word for it when he told them he couldn't produce a driver's license or other identification because his wallet had been stolen. Cudak testified he had not intended to steal when he took the airline job, but had decided to do so when he discovered the airport security was extremely lax. After he pulled several thefts, he took on accomplices known as "drop men" who drove to the airport to pick up the stolen goods.

The thefts were so lucrative that Cudak gave up his job after a few months to concentrate on stealing full-time. He said he and his accomplices usually wore airline coveralls as disguises to gain access to restricted sections of airports. Although most of his thefts were committed at airports in the New York area, he said he also pulled jobs as far away as Florida, Los Angeles, and Las Vegas.

On at least twenty occasions, Cudak testified, he found secret government documents among the mail he had stolen. The documents came from the Defense Department, the military services, the FBI, and the Central Intelligence Agency. They included plans for a land-to-air ballistic missile, an FBI report on Cuban agents that contained informants' names and addresses, and an Air Force bag with plans for a ballistic system destined for Elgin Air Force Base in Florida. Cudak said he never tried to sell such material to foreign agents or fences. "I was scared of it," he said. He testified he threw the material into the Atlantic Ocean after a New York fence, Albert De Angelis, warned him to get rid of it. He said De Angelis had learned from a lodge brother who was an FBI agent that one set of documents was particularly "hot."

Without the help of Mob fences, Cudak said, neither he

nor other mail thieves would have been able to operate. They needed the fences to dispose of securities, which made up the major part of their loot. "My share of the loot my partners and I stole in a four-year period came to approximately $1 million," Cudak testified. "I am penniless today. I gambled most of my money away as soon as I received my share from the fences."

One previously unsolved crime about which Cudak testified was a $21.5-million mail theft at Kennedy Airport in 1968. He said the job was pulled by two associates, William D. Ricchiuti and James Schaefer, who asked him to help dispose of the loot through various fences. Ricchiuti and Schaefer, both serving Federal prison sentences for other mail thefts, were called before the committee. Ricchiuti, who had been identified by Cudak as a racketeer with "very good connections with the principal Mob people in New York and New Jersey," pleaded the Fifth Amendment eighty-eight times. But Schaefer agreed to testify in return for a guarantee of immunity from further prosecution. He confirmed that he and Ricchiuti had pulled the huge mail theft, saying they had stolen several bags of mail from a Trans World Airlines plane just before it left Kennedy for Boston. Included in the $21.5 million worth of loot, Schaefer said, were about $2 million in easily negotiable bearer bonds and $70,500 in traveler's checks. While he and Ricchiuti could dispose of the bonds and traveler's checks themselves, they needed the help of Cudak and the fences to get rid of the remainder of the securities they found in the mail bags.

Various other men named by Cudak as his accomplices or fences pleaded the Fifth Amendment before the McClellan committee. But one additional witness, James A. Sanatar of Deer Park, Long Island, admitted working with Cudak and corroborated his testimony. Sanatar testified he had been a "drop man" for Cudak, picking up mail bags stolen at Kennedy Airport. He said he made about $40,000 in three months in that capacity.

Later, a 300-pound underworld character who said he was the grandson of a Mafia don told the committee he had sold about $3 million worth of stolen securities. The witness, Vincent "Big Vinnie" Teresa of Boston, said he grew up in a Mob atmosphere. He was introduced to gangsters as a youngster not only by his grandfather but by his uncle, Dominick "Sandy Mac" Teresa, a long-time bodyguard for former Boston Mob boss Joseph Lombardi. "I knew these people when I was thirteen or fourteen years old," Teresa said. "They treated me like a son." He said he turned to crime at the age of fifteen and later became an independent racketeer—dealing at times with the Mob but never becoming a member.

"There is one big gang that runs organized crime in this country," Teresa said. "We generally call it the Mob. New young people who become members call it the Outfit." Teresa was serving a Federal prison sentence for interstate transportation of stolen securities at the time he testified. Asked whether his Mob friends had done anything to help him or his family when he ran afoul of the law, he replied: "I was dumb. I felt the Outfit was going to take care of me. They never even sent my wife a Christmas card when I went to jail." Then, in one of a series of comments that lent a touch of humor to the hearings, he added: "You can't trust them. They're a shady bunch of characters."

After entering prison, Teresa testified, he was persuaded by FBI agents that he had been sold out by his associates from the Mob. Partly as a result of his disillusionment with them and partly in the hope of getting a reduced sentence, he agreed to cooperate with the government in the prosecution of other underworld figures. He said his testimony helped send about twenty racketeers to prison. His own prison term was cut from twenty years to five. Teresa said Mob bosses responded by issuing "contracts" totaling $500,000 for his murder, but he felt the price on his head was secondary to the possibility that some ambitious triggerman might try to kill him "just for the reputation." Like Robert Cudak, Teresa was kept under heavy guard during his appearance before the committee.

In twenty-eight years of criminal activity, he said, he made about $7 million but never showed more than $50,000 a year in earnings on his tax return. His operations, in addition to dealing in stolen securities, included gambling, credit-card swindles, loansharking, and car-theft rings. He said the rackets involving stolen and counterfeit credit cards were particularly lucrative. "Mostly we used American Express [cards] because they were good anyplace in the world for almost anything you wanted," Teresa testified. He said he and his associates used the cards to rent automobiles, and then sold the cars. He told the committee he gave one car obtained this way, a Cadillac, to the late president of Haiti, Francois Duvalier, in return for a gambling license.

His loansharking activities, Teresa testified, centered around a firm called the Piranha Company—a title "taken from the fish of that name, which is a man-eater." He said reluctant borrowers were persuaded to pay under threats of having their hands held in a fishbowl containing piranha.

Another admitted dealer in stolen securities followed Teresa to the stand. The witness, Edward "The Paper Hanger" Wuensche, was out of prison on probation but was in protective custody. Wuensche testified that he had handled about $50 million worth of stolen or counterfeit securities since the early 1950s. He said his illegal ventures and those of his Mob associates had ranged throughout the United States and into Canada, the Bahamas, Ireland, England, the Netherlands, Switzerland, Israel, and Kuwait.

Wuensche testified that he had obtained loans from "friendly bankers" by placing fraudulent securities with them as collateral. The loans were rarely repaid, he said, and merely served the purpose of converting the stolen or counterfeit securities into cash. He said many bank officials knew the loans were shady, that some had taken bribes and that numerous bank executives across the country served as fronts for organized crime. Among the banks from which he reported receiving fraudulent loans were the Long Island Trust Company, the Devon Bank of Chicago, and the First National Bank of Miami.

He told of making various trips to Europe to place stolen securities in banks, especially in Switzerland. On one such trip, Wuensche said, he and an associate went by way of Canada to Switzerland with $7.5 million worth of stolen securities. "Through a contact in Amsterdam, Holland, with a man named Aronson, I was put in touch with a Zurich bank official by the name of Dr. Schaeffer," he testified. "Schaeffer accepted these securities as collateral for loans which were paid in deutsche marks. These deutsche marks were later changed into Canadian dollars and, on our return to Canada, we purchased American securities with the Canadian dollars. These securities were later sold for American dollars when we returned to the United States."

In 1967 and 1968, Wuensche said, he and his associates put together a $5.5. million package of stolen United States Treasury notes. Through Aronson in Amsterdam, the securities were delivered to persons in Kuwait. "I later learned that these securities somehow or another found their way back to the United States, redeemed by the United States Treasury from the government of Kuwait," he said. In addition, Wuensche testified, persons in Israel "have received stolen securities which were later redeemed by the United States Treasury."

The Long Island Trust Company, he said, made a loan in 1969 to Emanuel Reifler, the father of a Wuensche associate named Lionel Reifler. The loan was for $95,000 and was secured by a stolen $100,000 Federal National Mortgage Association (Fanny Mae) bond, Wuensche testified. "To the best of my knowledge, this loan is not as yet paid off," he told the committee. "If you go to the Long Island Trust Company and inquire about this situation, you should find either the stolen Fanny Mae bond or the records of this loan, which should also show the serial number of the bond. I should point out that Mr. [Emanuel] Reifler is a reputable businessman and that his son, Lionel Reifler, conned him into this transaction."

Wuensche testified that he caused $5.25 million worth of counterfeit bonds—purportedly issued by Washington County, Tennessee—to be placed in the Devon Bank of Chicago through an executive named Dr. Sidney DeLove. "These bonds were printed by the A. & R. Typographers of New York City," he said. "These counterfeit securities should still be in the the Devon Bank or else in the possession of Dr. DeLove. It should be further noted that Dr. DeLove is the president and chairman of the board of the Cook County Federal Savings and Loan Association in Chicago."

(Dr. DeLove was later called before the committee and testified that he had placed the bonds in a safe-keeping account at the Devon Bank on behalf of an Indiana businessman, Thomas H. Redmond. He said he told bank officials that Redmond was the true owner. DeLove claimed he did not know the bonds were counterfeit until after the Devon Bank and the Amalgamated Trust and Savings Bank of Chicago loaned Redmond $600,000 on one of the bogus certificates. The executive vice president of the Devon Bank, Richard Loundy, appeared before the committee and contradicted parts of DeLove's testimony. He denied bank officials had full knowledge in accepting the bonds that DeLove was not the real owner. "We believed we were dealing with Dr. DeLove and that the securities were his," Loundy said. "As far as the Devon bank was concerned, we did not know Dr. DeLove was acting as agent for other owners." He said the bank had loaned money to Redmond because "we were relying to a large extent on the credit and reputation" of DeLove, whose net worth he put in seven figures. At this writing, no prosecutions have resulted from this episode.)

Wuensche, in his testimony, also said he had disposed of part of a $300,000 batch of stolen securities at the First National Bank of Miami—using the loan-collateral gambit. He said that in a number of deals in which he worked with corrupt officials at various banks, the bankers received bribes amounting to five percent of the loans involved. Asked if that were the going rate, he replied: "Not necessarily. Some would extort you for ten percent or more." A committee member, Senator Charles H. Percy of Illinois, questioned whether the corruption among bankers was as sweeping as Wuensche claimed. "If you knew the extent," Wuensche responded, "it would shake you to your boots."

Leading members of the securities industry were also questioned by the committee. Robert W. Haack, president of the New York Stock Exchange, testified that the industry was so swamped with trading that it was literally "out of control" in 1968 and 1969—a period of peak theft activity on Wall Street. He said the stock exchange was so busy keeping 150 to 200 of its member firms under "close surveillance" that it had no time or personnel to devote to the securities-theft problem. But since that period of "near crisis," Haack asserted, the exchange had been actively seeking ways to deal with the problem. One of the stumbling blocks was that the procedures in some brokerage houses were so lax that it was difficult for employees to tell whether securities were stolen, lost, or incorrectly accounted for through poor maintenance of records. While emphasizing that the industry must tighten its own security measures, Haack urged Congress to consider legislation aimed at giving the Federal government a larger role in curbing thefts. He proposed that Congress create a central authority to which all securities thefts and losses would have to be reported; make it a Federal crime to steal securities; give one Federal agency authority to investigate all such thefts; and require the fingerprinting of securities industry personnel to help prevent employment of those with criminal records.

Some of Haack's proposals were echoed in the testimony of Donald T. Regan, board chairman of the brokerage firm of Merrill Lynch, Pierce, Fenner & Smith. In addition, Regan urged that brokerage firms and banks be required by law to make immediate reports to the government on all securities thefts. He asked that the government take action to tighten security in the postal system and the air-freight industry. "Some of the largest securities thefts that we know about have been out of mail sacks and at airports," he said.

By the time of Regan's testimony the committee was well aware of the enormity of the problem posed by securities thefts from the mails and from airports. But understanding the problem and solving it are two quite different propositions. The fact is that at many airports the Mob dominates the handling of cargo. And, with that situation in force, it is almost impossible for law-enforcement authorities to move effectively against thefts.

How the Mob Handles Air Cargo

Rampant Mob rule at Kennedy Airport is typical of the underworld's role at airports across the country. Attorney General Mitchell, in a speech before the American Bankers Association, charged that "the cargo handling at one large eastern airport is monopolized by a combination of a crime-controlled union and a crime-controlled trucking association." Although Mitchell declined to name the airport, it was clear he was talking about Kennedy.

The "crime-controlled union" to which Mitchell referred was Teamster Local 295, whose 3500 members included the cargo handlers, truck drivers, and other airfreight employees at Kennedy. Heading the union, at a salary of $45,000 a year, was an old-fashioned tough guy named Harry Davidoff—a survivor of the Murder Incorporated gang wars of the 1930s. Davidoff, a close associate of Mafia labor racketeer John "Johnny Dio" Dioguardi, had a criminal record that included convictions for extortion conspiracy, gambling and burglary, and arrests on charges of felonious assault with a knife, grand larceny, robbery, extortion, and illegal possession of a gun.

The "crime-controlled trucking association" to which Mitchell referred was the National Association for Air Freight, Inc. (NAAF). The guiding spirit behind the association was Anthony "Hickey" DiLorenzo, a member of Jerry Catena's Mafia family. DiLorenzo's criminal record included convictions for grand larceny, aggravated assault, and interstate transportation of stolen securities. Until his conviction in the securities case, he served as a

$40,000-a-year "consultant" to NAAF. Officially, he gave up the consultancy after being sentenced to a ten-year Federal prison term. But, unofficially, he has continued to act as a behind-the-scenes power in the association while appealing the case.

NAAF was the successor to an organization known as the Metropolitan Import Truckmen's Association (MITA). The New York State Investigation Commission, after investigating the operations of MITA and Teamster Local 295, charged in 1967: "With control of the dominant union and the truckmen's association at Kennedy Airport in the hands of the criminal elements, it could reasonably have been anticipated that the air-freight industry would soon find itself caught between the hammer and the anvil." The commission said "the takeover of MITA [by the Mob] was virtually complete. Persons with criminal records monopolized the payroll." This domination was arranged largely by "Gentleman John" Massiello, the Mafioso whose bribery of postal officials was described earlier in this chapter. Massiello preceded "Hickey" DiLorenzo as a "consultant" to the truckmen's association. He packed the association payroll with Mob "trouble shooters" who had long criminal records. When the State Investigation Commission exposed his role, Massiello withdrew as a consultant to the association but saw that DiLorenzo was installed as his successor. In the intervening years, although the association has changed its call letters from MITA to NAAF, commission Chairman Paul Curran says "the situation has not improved and has probably worsened."

In short, the hammer-and-anvil squeeze has continued to be applied. An example of how the squeeze works was provided in testimony by an executive of Air Cargo, Inc., an organization created by the major airlines to provide ground-support services. "We were told that each of the airlines [at Kennedy Airport] would become a house account of a specific trucking company and that no one else competitively would attempt to take that away from the other company," he said. In other words, the Mob would dictate to the world's largest airlines which trucking companies would haul their cargoes. And, if the airlines tried to buck the system, they faced the threat that Harry Davidoff's Teamster local might close down the airport with a strike.

Two airlines, National and Northwest, did try to buck the system. They started doing business with an independent trucking firm, Direct Airport Service, Inc., which did not belong to NAAF and employed drivers belonging to an independent union. Davidoff warned the airlines to stop using Direct or face a Teamster strike. National and Northwest at first refused to knuckle under, so Davidoff called a work stoppage to bar the delivery of shipments to Direct. Still, the airlines would not back down. Then, in one day, the tires of thirty-eight Direct trucks parked at Kennedy Airport were slashed and ruined. A short time later a Direct truck, riding along the Long Island Expressway, careened out of control when its rear wheels fell off. An investigation disclosed that the wheels' lug nuts had been loosened. Several days after that an identical mishap struck another Direct truck. The airlines eventually got the message and agreed to resume doing business with two trucking companies that belonged to NAAF and employed members of Local 295.

Air-freight companies have also felt the squeeze. One of the nation's largest such firms, Airborne Freight, long declined to join NAAF. But many of its employees were members of Local 295, whose relations with the firm were described by a company executive as "one continual nightmare." The nightmare ended, at least temporarily, when Airborne agreed to hire as a consultant a former Teamster official named Milton Holt, whose criminal record included convictions for perjury and for taking illegal loans from employers while holding union office. Trouble arose again when Airborne acquired a new president who refused to renew Holt's $15,000-a-year contract. He ruled, instead, that Holt would be used intermittently—only when his services became necessary. The necessity arose within a fortnight when Teamsters pulled strikes against Airborne in New York and San Francisco. Holt was called in, and met with Airborne officials and DiLorenzo. The meeting did not concern striking workers' grievances, but rather a new contract for Holt. Airborne agreed to rehire him for the next five years—at a total fee of $190,000. Holt then made one telephone call and put a halt to the twin strikes.

Although DiLorenzo had attended the negotiating session, Airborne was still not a member of NAAF. But several months later, after a series of meetings with Holt, DiLorenzo, and Teamster officials, the company agreed to join the trucking association.

NAAF and the Teamsters Union are now trying to extend the type of control they exercise at Kennedy Airport to the entire national air-freight industry. The union is seeking one master contract with the industry, and is cooperating with NAAF's campaign to recruit additional companies throughout the country. Harold Gibbons, an international vice president of the Teamsters who heads the union's airline division, has met in various cities with DiLorenzo and other NAAF representatives to plan the campaign. Gibbons has sent a letter to Teamster locals in cities where NAAF has member firms, recommending greater recruitment of the companies' employees. "This is an excellent opportunity for your local union to increase its membership and to participate in a master agreement [with NAAF] which should be concluded shortly," the letter said.

The relationship between NAAF and the Teamsters is under investigation by several law-enforcement agencies. Three witnesses who testified before a New York Federal grand jury, including NAAF Executive Board Chairman Frank LaBell, were arrested on perjury charges after denying knowledge of bribery demands purportedly made by Local 295 officials during contract negotiations. The defendants pleaded not guilty; their cases are pending at this writing. Despite the various investigations, the Mob's grip on the air-freight industry seems to be growing tighter all the time.

The Italian-American Civil Rights League

The Mafia's infiltration of legitimate business is closely intertwined with its members' desires to obtain a cloak of respectability. Many Mob leaders have moved in recent years from the inner cities to expensive homes in fashionable suburbs. They want to be accepted as upstanding members of their communities, as members of the local country clubs and churches. They want their children to attend the "right" schools. Legitimate business interests play an indispensable role in gaining the desired acceptance.

Moreover, these interests provide logical avenues for the talents of the college-educated generations of Mafia children and grandchildren. The Carlo Gambino Mafia family, for example, uses the younger generations to help manage its $300 million worth of real-estate investments. In New Orleans, Carlos Marcello's son, Joseph, and son-in-law, Jefferson Hampton, manage Mob-connected hotels.

Often, members of the Mob use supposed "good works" to gain respectability. While serving as a Mafia boss in New York, Frank Costello became vice chairman of a fund-raising drive for the Salvation Army. He tossed a lavish party at the Copacabana night club for the Army's benefit. Twenty judges and many of the city's leading politicians attended the black-tie, $100-a-plate affair, which raised $18,000.

In Buffalo, New York, John Montana was long considered a pillar of the community. He owned the largest taxi company in western New York State, served as a city councilman, belonged to the Elks, the Buffalo Athletic Club, and the Erie Downs Country Club. He even was chosen as "man of the year" by the Buffalo chapter of the National Junior Chamber of Commerce. Then he was unmasked as a leader of the Stefano Magaddino Mafia family—a revelation that jolted Buffalo. As a result of the shock waves, Montana voluntarily took a demotion in the Mob to keep from compromising other Mafiosi.

In recent years, the most visible attempt by the Mob to attain respectability has centered around the activities of a New York family boss, Joseph Colombo. The son of a slain mobster, Colombo turned to crime after a three-year Coast Guard stint that ended with his medical discharge for "psychoneurosis." At first he was a muscleman on New York's waterfront; then an organizer of rigged dice games; later a Mob gunman. Though arrested about a dozen times during his early years in the Mob, he drew only a couple of small fines for gambling convictions.

By 1962, Colombo had become a fast-rising captain in the Mafia family headed by Joseph Magliocco. Then he got his biggest break when Magliocco and another family boss, Joseph "Joe Bananas" Bonanno, decided to order the murder of three rival bosses—Carlo Gambino, Thomas "Three Fingers Brown" Lucchese, and Stefano Magaddino. Bonanno and Magliocco gave the "contract" for the murders to Colombo. But, instead of carrying out the assignment, Colombo tipped off Gambino. The murders were averted. Bonanno was forced to surrender his family's leadership. And, when Magliocco died a short time later of natural causes, Colombo was named to replace him both as family boss and as a member of the Mafia's national commission. At the age of forty, he was the youngest family boss in the country.

For more than seven years Colombo led the life of a typical Mafia boss. His Mob family indulged in the usual rackets—numbers and sports gambling, loansharking, hijacking, fencing stolen goods, and the like. He controlled about twenty ostensibly legitimate businesses, including a funeral home and a florist shop. But he claimed that he was a simple $18,000-a-year real-estate salesman, and he had a real-estate license to support the claim. In 1966, he was jailed for thirty days for refusal to tell a grand jury what he knew about Mob infiltration of legitimate business. Other than that he was relatively free from harassment by law-enforcement authorities until 1970.

Then began a series of intensive investigations by Federal agents, local police and district attorneys. Colombo was indicted on an assortment of charges—including masterminding a $10 million-a-year gambling syndicate, conspiring to pull a $750,000 jewel theft, contempt of court, and committing perjury by concealing his criminal record when applying for his real-estate license. Colombo and his associates were kept under frequent surveillance by the FBI. Their friends and relatives were questioned constantly. But the final straw, Colombo said, was the FBI's arrest of his son, Joseph, Jr., on charges of conspiracy to melt silver coins into more valuable ingots.

Claiming the arrest of his son proved that he and other Italian-Americans were being harassed because of their heritage, Colombo began leading a group of pickets in nightly demonstrations outside the FBI's Manhattan office during the spring of 1970. As many as 4500 persons a night joined the picketing. They carried signs with such slogans as: "FBI Is Anti-Italian"; "All Americans of Italian Descent Only Want a Fair Shake"; "President Nixon—Why Only Italian-Americans Involved in Organized Crime [Drive]?"; and "FBI, Think Twice. We Can Question Your Children and Picket Your Homes."

From this bizarre picketing came the formation of an organization called the Italian-American Civil Rights League, which was to become extraordinarily powerful in a very short time. Colombo later said the league was organized spontaneously on the street outside the FBI office. "Right there we formed the Italian-American Civil Rights League, right on 69th Street and Third Avenue, right out in the open under God's eyes, under the stars."

While Colombo and some of his rackets associates played major roles in the league, it was clear that the organization also included many law-abiding citizens of Italian descent. Within a year, the league claimed a membership of more than 45,000. One of its chief aims was to try to purge the word "Mafia" from the American vocabulary—claiming that no such criminal syndicate existed. "Mafia, what's the Mafia?" Joe Colombo said. "There is not a Mafia. Am I head of a family? Yes. My wife and four sons and a daughter. That's my family."

Just two months after the formation of the league, it drew close to 50,000 persons to an Italian-American Unity

Day rally in New York's Columbus Circle. The rally sought to foster ethnic pride, to salute the accomplishments of Italian-Americans and to accuse law-enforcement agencies of persecuting some members of the Italo-American community. Some of New York's leading political figures—including Congressmen Allard Lowenstein, Richard Ottinger, Adam Clayton Powell, and Mario Biaggi and City Controller Mario Procaccino—shared the speakers' platform with Colombo. The lustiest applause was reserved for Colombo, who told the throng: "This day belongs to you—to you the people. You are organized, united, and nobody can take you apart anymore." Thousands of spectators responded with a symbol of unity, jabbing their index fingers skyward and chanting: "One . . . one . . . one!"

Organizers of the rally distributed copies of a pamphlet called "The Mafia Is a Myth." Congressman Biaggi told the crowd that there were 22 million Italian-Americans in the country and that only about 5000 were reported to be members of organized crime. "That's better than the 99 and 44/100ths purity of Ivory Soap," he said. He urged the spectators not to "use a wide black brush on the FBI—and let not the FBI or any other law-enforcement agency use the same brush on us."

One prominent New York politician of Italian descent, State Senator John Marchi, boycotted the rally and criticized other office-holders who attended. "You can forgive the people who come in good faith, but any public official who shows up is incredibly naïve or has lost his perspective and sense of values," Marchi said. There were not many officials willing to follow his lead; the league had quickly become a formidable force. Throughout New York, many stores and restaurants in Italian neighborhoods stayed closed in honor of Unity Day. Work in the

Port of New York practically shut down for the day as only ten percent of the longshoremen reported to their jobs. Some merchants complained that they had been pressured by league organizers into closing for the day, but no formal charges were filed with the police.

In the aftermath of the rally, the league swiftly broadened its scope and its activities. Within a matter of months, it claimed to have twenty-five chapters in the New York metropolitan area—plus other chapters in Buffalo, Albany, Newark, New Haven, Hartford, Providence, Boston, Miami, Detroit, Chicago, St. Louis, Las Vegas, Los Angeles, San Francisco, and a handful of other cities.

League officials in various cities represented a mixed bag—some identified with the Mob, others considered highly respectable. Joe Pepitone, first baseman for the Chicago Cubs, became a league organizer in that city. In Providence, Richard Callei—an associate of New England Mafia boss Raymond Patriarca—was named chapter president by acclamation on Colombo's recommendation. In Rochester, a mobster named Frank Valenti became a charter member of the local chapter. Another member of the same chapter is Joseph Farbo, chairman of a draft board, former vice mayor of the city and past president of the Rochester Board of Education. In Miami, the chapter is headed by an attorney; in New Haven, by a life insurance executive; in Newark, by a court officer.

Among the league's activities were various good works —including a summer camp for underprivileged children, drug-education programs, fund-raising for hospitals and such other causes as Pakistani refugee relief, blood donations, and organization of youth recreation programs. But the main focus remained on improving the image of Italian-Americans and destroying the notion that organized crime was primarily attributable to that one ethnic group.

The campaign achieved many of its public-relations aims. Attorney General John Mitchell, who had frequently used the terms "Mafia" and "Cosa Nostra" in speeches and testimony before congressional committees, ordered the words banned in future statements by the Justice Department and its subordinate agencies such as the FBI. Mitchell said he issued the order, with the blessing of the White House, because "a good many Americans of Italian descent are offended" by such terms. Various state and local officials, under pressure from the Italian-American Civil Rights League, followed Mitchell's lead.

Next, bowing to similar pressure, producers of the American Broadcasting Company television series, "The FBI," agreed to delete references to the Mafia and Cosa Nostra from future scripts. Warming to its work, the league protested to Miles Laboratories that its celebrated Alka Seltzer commercial—containing the line "datsa somma spicy meatball"—was offensive to Italian-Americans. The commercial was removed from the air.

Perhaps the league's most highly publicized venture into the field of censorship concerned the motion-picture version of the novel, *The Godfather*. The book had been nothing if not a Mafia story. The words "Mafia" and "Cosa Nostra" had been sprinkled liberally through its pages. Yet, the league wanted the words omitted from the movie and insisted on other assurances that the film would not be "anti-Italian." After a series of meetings with league officials, including Colombo's son, Anthony, movie producer Al Ruddy announced that the film script for *The Godfather* would be revised to eliminate all references to the Mafia or Cosa Nostra. In addition, Ruddy agreed to turn over to the league all proceeds from the premiere performance of the picture. Some of Colombo's underworld associates served as unofficial technical advisers on the film—thus presenting the ludicrous spectacle of providing advice on subjects about which they kept telling the police they knew nothing. To put it as simply as the circumstances allowed, the Mafiosi were telling the movie people what the Mafia was really like—while refusing to call it the Mafia and insisting that the organization actually didn't exist.

All of this provoked waves of criticism from various quarters. *The New York Times* commented: "It is one thing . . . to oppose irrational smears but quite another to deny that some illegal associations or rings are led or dominated by members of certain ethnic or nationality groups. This is why the efforts of the Italian-American Civil Rights League in fighting not the Mafia but all references to its existence are so deplorably misguided. The latest chapter in that incredible campaign to make the Mafia disappear by expunging the term from the American language is the league's success in persuading Al Ruddy, producer of the motion picture *The Godfather,* to censor the forbidden word. . . . The league could render its most effective service if it were to join with Americans of all nationalities and races in opposing the Mafia, instead of trying to render it invisible by making it unmentionable."

Other editorials were more sarcastic: "If there is a Madison Avenue in the sky, the press agents, flacks, and drumbeaters of yesteryear are applauding the notable contemporary accomplishments of Joseph Colombo. Unlike his peers in publicity, this man did not make something from nothing. He performed the even more difficult feat of making nothing out of a very real and very menacing something. That something is an American crime syndicate, known to Colombo and its other members as the Cosa Nostra, which had its roots in the Sicilian crime syndicate called the Mafia."

State Senator Marchi, who became one of the league's most persistent critics, wrote an angry letter to Ruddy that said: "Apparently, you are a ready market for the league's preposterous theory that we can exorcise devils by reading them out of the English language. Yes, Mr. Ruddy, there just might be a Mafia and if you have been reached I have only the feeling that the Italian-American as well as the larger community has been had. . . . Your action amounts to a monstrous insult to millions upon millions of loyal Americans of Italian extraction who must deeply resent this assault on the right of free expression at their expense. Thanks for nothing."

Joe Colombo seemed to thrive on the publicity—good and bad. People wanted his autograph, wanted him to pose for pictures, to pat their babies' heads. He obliged with relish. Walter Cronkite and Dick Cavett, among others, interviewed him on television. Frank Sinatra came to New York to appear at a fund-raising benefit sponsored by the league at Madison Square Garden's Felt Forum. More than 1400 persons turned out for a $125-a-plate testimonial dinner for Colombo at a Long Island catering emporium. A fourteen-carat-gold plaque presented to him by the league at the dinner called him "the guiding spirit of Italian-American unity" and claimed he had "restored dignity, pride, and recognition to every Italian." A second plaque was presented by a New York weekly newspaper, *The Triboro Post.* It named Colombo as "man of the year."

Not all was going swimmingly well for Colombo. Although his son, Joseph, Jr., had been acquitted in the silver-melting case after the key government witness had recanted his earlier testimony and claimed he had falsely accused the defendant, the elder Colombo's own legal problems could not be disposed of so easily. In the perjury case resulting from Colombo's purported concealment of his criminal record in applying for a real-estate license, he was found guilty and sentenced to twelve to thirty months in prison. While appealing that case, he was faced with a series of other criminal charges.

Meanwhile, Colombo was in trouble with some of his fellow Mafia bosses. These men, older and more traditional than Colombo, clung to the Mob philosophy that Mafiosi should try to maintain anonymity. Colombo's image-building campaign, they felt, drew unwanted attention to the syndicate. As one Federal agent put it: "Every time Joe Colombo's face appears on the front page of a newspaper or on the evening news, a lot of the old guys in the Mafia hit the ceiling."

When Colombo and the Italian-American Civil Rights League announced plans for a second annual Unity Day rally, to take place on June 28, 1971, the other Mafia bosses were far from enthralled. Carlo Gambino ordered members of his Mob family to stay away from the rally. Gambino's men and members of an insurgent faction within Colombo's Mafia family, headed by the notorious brothers Joseph and Albert Gallo, pressured New York merchants to defy Colombo by keeping their shops open on Unity Day. Signs advertising the rally were seized and burned by the anti-Colombo forces. Longshoremen, who had strongly supported the first rally, decided to boycott the second.

Nonetheless, Colombo pressed on with his plans. Seventeen days before the rally, Gambino sent word to Colombo that it would be wise to call off the event. Colombo refused. A week later, he was roughed up by a group of hoods. Still, he would not back down.

On Unity Day, Colombo showed up in Columbus Circle about an hour before the rally was to begin. The area was festooned with streamers of red, white, and green—the colors of the Italian flag. As the crowd gathered, vendors hawked buttons bearing such slogans as "Kiss Me, I'm Italian" and pennants reading "Italian Power!" Colombo walked slowly through the throng—smiling, making jokes, and shaking hands.

A Negro named Jerome A. Johnson, holding a movie camera and wearing a press badge issued by the Italian-American Civil Rights League, asked Colombo to stop and pose for pictures. Colombo halted, and those around him spread out to make room for the "photographer." Suddenly, Johnson whipped out an automatic pistol and fired three shots into Colombo—one lodging four inches inside his brain, the others hitting his neck and jaw. Seconds later, another fusillade of shots rang out—killing Johnson.

Colombo, critically wounded, was rushed to a hospital in a coma. He survived, but his chances for anything resembling a full recovery were considered remote. Police launched a widespread investigation to try to determine why Johnson had shot Colombo and who had killed Johnson. No police bullets had been fired during the incident, so the investigation of Johnson's slaying centered on two theories—either that he had been shot by a Colombo bodyguard or that there had been an elaborate underworld plot in which Johnson had been hired to rub out Colombo and had, in turn, been murdered by a second "hit" man to silence him. Although various witnesses told of seeing Colombo shot, none came forward with information on who had killed Johnson. Within hours after the slaying, Carlo Gambino and the Gallo brothers were picked up for questioning but apparently provided the police with no valuable information. Gambino claimed that he and Colombo "were the best of friends" and that he was "grief-stricken" over the shooting.

Investigation of Johnson's background disclosed him to be an enigmatic character. He had run up a police record of seven arrests in New York, New Jersey, and California on such charges as robbery, burglary, rape, and possession of drugs. But he seemed to have serious ambitions to become a professional photographer. He also had an abiding interest in astrology, talking about the subject constantly and referring to himself as "the Pisces man." Friends and relatives said he had told them several months before the shooting that he was working as a photographer for the Italian-American Civil Rights League, but officials of the organization denied ever hearing of him until his death. There was no explanation of how he had obtained the league's press badge. Nor was there any explanation on another point. About three months before the shooting, Johnson gave one of his relatives a telephone number where he could be reached. After the shooting, it was discovered that the number had recently been changed. The new listing was the number of the Manhattan office of the Italian-American Civil Rights League.

Police discovered several possible links between Johnson and the Mob. His last known address was the Christopher Hotel in Greenwich Village. The hotel is managed by Michael Umbers, who the police said has ties with organized crime and was an "associate" of Johnson's. Umbers, however, denied the Mob connections and said he knew Johnson only casually. Among the items found in Johnson's belongings after his death were several blank checks bearing the name of a company that specialized in publishing pornographic books. The company is partly owned by a mobster named Joseph Brocchini. An attorney for the firm claimed that a quantity of company checks had previously been stolen and he assumed that some of these had fallen into Johnson's possession.

On July 2, 1971, Deputy New York City Police Commissioner Robert Daley called a press conference and announced that both shootings were part of an underworld plot—"a struggle for pre-eminence among certain segments of the Italian-American community." Daley said "rivals of Colombo in the Italian underworld community" had hired Johnson to kill Colombo and then ordered another gunman to kill Johnson. He said the police had determined there were "two 'hit' men—Johnson and the man who 'hit' Johnson." Reporting that the plot was extremely detailed and "approved only days before" the shooting, Daley said those involved had been identified and would eventually be arrested. But he could not say when the arrests would take place or provide any information about the conspirators. The shooting of Colombo was intended to be followed by attacks on other Mob figures, Daley said. He speculated that the police discovery of the plot might have prevented further bloodshed.

At this writing, there have been no arrests and no additional outbreaks of Mob warfare. But, assuming that Daley's account was accurate, the attack on Colombo showed clearly that the Mob hasn't changed. Despite its ventures into legitimate business, its attempts at image-building, its search for respectability, it is still the same old Mafia.

[11]

The Mob Is
Everybody's Business

"Law enforcement's way of fighting organized crime has been primitive compared to organized crime's way of operating. Law enforcement must use methods at least as efficient as organized crime's. The public and law enforcement must make a full-scale commitment to destroy the power of organized crime groups."

Those were the words of the President's Commission on Law Enforcement in summarizing the ineffectiveness of attempts to combat the Mob. Since the commission report was issued, some advances have been made by Federal, state, and local governments in their techniques for neutralizing the Mafia. But the net results have been minimal. For the Mob is growing more sophisticated all the time and developing a new countermeasure for every crime-fighting measure adopted by the law-enforcement establishment. Because the underworld operates with greater efficiency than the cumbersome machinery of government, the Mob constantly remains several steps ahead of the law. This gap is particularly wide in such fields as attempts to curb racketeers' corruption of public officials and infiltration of legitimate business. It is in these fields that recent anti-Mob programs have experienced their greatest failures. Moreover, the type of "full-scale commitment" to destroy organized crime prescribed by the commission—

313

which is particularly essential in rooting out corruption and Mafia infiltration of business—continues to be conspicuously absent.

This is not to say, however, that there has been any shortage of rhetoric on the subject of organized crime. President Nixon declared in a congressional message seeking new anti-Mob legislation:

> Today, organized crime has deeply penetrated broad segments of American life. In our great cities it is operating prosperous criminal cartels. In our suburban areas and smaller cities, it is expanding its corrosive influence. Its economic base is principally derived from its virtual monopoly of illegal gambling, the numbers racket, and the importation of narcotics. To a large degree, it underwrites the loansharking business in the United States and actively participates in fraudulent bankruptcies. . . . It quietly continues to infiltrate and corrupt organized labor. It is increasing its enormous holdings and influence in the world of legitimate business. To achieve his end, the organized criminal relies on physical terror and psychological intimidation, on economic retaliation, and political bribery, on citizen indifference and governmental acquiescence. He corrupts our governing institutions and subverts our democratic processes. For him, the moral and legal subversion of our society is a lifelong and lucrative profession. . . . [Past government programs] have not substantially impeded the growth and power of organized criminal syndicates. Not a single one of the twenty-four Cosa Nostra families has been destroyed. They are more firmly entrenched and more secure than ever before. . . . As a matter of national "public policy," I must warn our citizens that

the threat of organized crime cannot be ignored or tolerated any longer. It will not be eliminated by loud voices and good intentions. It will be eliminated by carefully conceived, well-funded, and well-executed action plans.

Attorney General Mitchell, on the other hand, said organized crime could never be eliminated. "What we hope to do is convict enough of its members so that its organizational structure breaks down," he explained. He foresaw the possibility that such a disruption would neutralize the Mob to the point "where it is no longer a substantial influence in American life."

What came of the Nixon-Mitchell legislative package was a loudly trumpeted measure known as the Organized Crime Act of 1970. There are grave doubts, however, that the law will come anywhere close to living up to its billing.

One section of the new law makes it a Federal crime to use income obtained from organized crime to acquire or establish a business engaged in interstate commerce. On paper this might appear to be a useful step toward curbing Mob infiltration of legitimate business. But many legal experts believe the prohibition will be virtually impossible to enforce. As one authority told this writer: "All money is green. How the hell do you go about proving that certain money invested in a business came from organized crime? Even if you can prove that a racketeer made the investment, which is usually very hard in itself, that doesn't necessarily mean the money can be traced to a specific illegal activity. It could have come from anywhere." Moreover, if the money can somehow be traced to a criminal operation, that operation itself would seem to be a more logical target of investigators and prosecutors than the secondhand use of the cash. Failing that, already existing income-tax laws would appear more practical to enforce than the new measure.

Another section of the bill empowers Federal judges to impose additional sentences as long as twenty-five years on certain racketeers convicted of crimes that carry lesser penalties. A judge could consider any information, written or oral, concerning the "background, character and conduct" of a defendant in deciding whether he should be given the extra punishment. This information would not be subject to proof under the usual rules of evidence. To be given the additional sentence, the racketeer must be found by the judge to be a "dangerous special offender"— defined in the law as someone who has two previous felony convictions, whose criminal offense was part of a pattern of criminal conduct or whose crime was part of a conspiracy to engage in a pattern of criminal conduct. There is considerable doubt among some lawyers whether this section of the law is constitutional and will ultimately be upheld by the Supreme Court. Various witnesses questioned the wisdom of the provision during congressional hearings considering passage of the measure. Former New York City Police Commissioner Vincent Broderick, representing the New York County Lawyers' Association, testified that the provision would have the effect "of punishing status rather than activities." In other words, a man would be punished because he was considered a racketeer —not because of specific criminal offenses. Besides being subject to challenge on constitutional grounds, this section of the law had another drawback. Although billed as a major weapon against organized crime, it failed to confront the central problem. As Attorney General Mitchell and other Justice Department officials conceded in their congressional testimony, the mere imprisonment of individual Mafia leaders does not break up the organization.

Substitute leaders simply take their places, and the Mob continues doing business as usual. What is needed is a weapon that strikes at the organizational structure of the Mafia itself and cuts into its sources of wealth. (Proposals to accomplish these ends will be discussed later in this chapter.)

A third section of the Organized Crime Act of 1970 promises to be more useful than the first two provisions. This section gives Federal agents and prosecutors jurisdiction over large-scale gambling rings even where it cannot be proved that the operations cross state lines. Subject to prosecution are any gambling operations involving five or more persons who have been in business thirty days and handled bets totaling $2,000 a day.

Under previous law, Federal agents could make gambling arrests only if they could prove that some sort of interstate activity was involved. For example, members of the ring would have to travel across state lines or make interstate telephone calls. To get around these provisions, some shrewd mobsters—protected from local and state prosecution by payoffs—carefully avoided leaving any trace of interstate activity. Now, their immunity to Federal prosecution is gone. Perhaps even more important, the new law makes it a Federal crime for a law-enforcement officer or public official to protect a gambling operation. Under this provision, sixteen policemen were arrested in Detroit on charges of taking payoffs from a major gambling ring. In New York, the FBI launched an investigation into charges by the operator of a $6 million-a-year policy racket that he had made payoffs to thirty-two policemen. Similar investigations are under way at this writing in other cities. Thus far, there have been no arrests of important political figures under the new law. Of course, the measure does not cover official protection of any Mob activities besides gambling. But even so, if enforced zealously against top politicians as well as policemen, it could serve as an effective tool against corruption.

A fourth provision of the new law enables special Federal grand juries to issue reports—as distinguished from indictments—on officials' acts of misconduct involving organized crime. In the past, Federal grand juries were obliged to remain silent if there were insufficient evidence to support an indictment. Now, if a grand jury discovers official misconduct but does not have enough evidence to indict, it can file a public report with the Federal court in which it serves. While the report will have no legal effect, it may serve as a catalyst for reform.

Besides the new law, the administration has said that one of its chief tools for fighting the Mob is a series of organized crime strike forces established in key cities across the country. The strike forces are made up of specially trained lawyers and investigators from various Federal agencies—including the Justice Department, Internal Revenue Service, Secret Service, Bureau of Narcotics and Dangerous Drugs, Bureau of Customs and Labor Department. Initiated during the administration of President Johnson, the strike force program has been expanded by the Nixon administration. At this writing, there are seventeen strike forces at work—two in New York and one each in Baltimore, Boston, Buffalo, Chicago, Cleveland, Detroit, Kansas City, Los Angeles, Miami, Newark, New Orleans, Philadelphia, Pittsburgh, St. Louis, and San Francisco. Plans call for eventual creation of three more anti-Mob units of this kind.

The theory behind the strike forces is that the representatives of the various agencies—each with their own expertise, sources of information, and extensive files on diverse areas of organized crime—can pool their resources for concentrated attacks on major Mob figures. Members of the strike forces are put on detached duty by their agencies to work exclusively on the assigned projects. They are under the supervision of the Justice Department's Organized Crime and Racketeering Section. Except for one case, the members are drawn solely from the ranks of Federal employees. The exception is one of the two strike forces in New York, which also includes representatives of state and local law-enforcement agencies.

While the concept of the strike forces seems sound and they have achieved some notable successes, they can hardly provide the panacea for organized crime that government spokesmen have occasionally claimed. As Attorney General Mitchell conceded in testimony before a congressional committee: "Because, currently, we do not have the manpower to make an across-the-board attack on organized crime in all American cities, strike forces can only be deployed in cities where the problem is most acute."

In addition to this shortcoming, the strike forces have other problems. Frequently, rivalry and distrust among members drawn from different agencies leads to a frustrating lack of cooperation. Law-enforcement agencies traditionally have shown great reluctance to open their files to outsiders, to share information and especially to risk exposing the identities of their informers. The strike force concept relies on members' willingness to cast aside such parochial interests on behalf of the team approach. But the theory, while fine in principle, has not worked out ideally in practice. FBI agents, long noted for a go-it-alone policy, have been particularly unenthusiastic about operating within the strike force framework. And other investigators' hesitancy to confide fully in their colleagues from different agencies has been heightened by a scandal that erupted within one strike force. Only a few months after joining the New York strike force made up of Federal, state, and local investigators, a New York State Police lieutenant was arrested and accused of being an infiltrator from an organized gambling operation. Arrested with the lieutenant were three other state troopers charged with being members of a betting syndicate controlled by Mafioso Nicholas Rattenni.

The strike forces have also been hampered by bureaucratic conflicts within the Justice Department. Although the strike forces are under the supervision of the department's Organized Crime and Racketeering Section, they operate within the jurisdictions of various United States Attorneys. Some U.S. Attorneys consider the presence of the strike forces in their cities as a usurpation of their power. They resent the implication that they are incapable of handling organized crime cases themselves. And they hate to lose the publicity that arrests, indictments, and prosecutions in such cases usually produce.

Attorney General Mitchell has issued a set of guidelines intended to reduce friction between the strike forces and the U.S. Attorneys. They provide that the strike forces will investigate and develop all organized crime cases in their areas, but must keep the U.S. Attorneys advised of their activities. The U.S. Attorneys must have a hand in drawing up all indictments, must sign them and have the right to take jurisdictional disputes to Washington for settlement. Despite the guidelines, however, clashes continue to arise—hamstringing the anti-Mob forces.

All in all, the Federal program for combatting organized crime can be summarized as ambitious but inadequate—characterized more by show than by substance. And state and local programs are generally less ambitious and far less adequate. From time to time, state and local governments announce with great fanfare new approaches to fighting the Mob. But more often than not, despite the initial publicity, these projects produce few significant long-term results.

A typical example occurred recently in New York State. During 1970, the state established a new Task Force on Organized Crime that was widely heralded as a major attack on Mob operations. Governor Nelson A. Rockefeller appointed a deputy state attorney general, Robert Fischer, to head the task force. Fischer was quickly dubbed the state's "super-cop," and the public was led to believe that he would soon bring results. Instead, a year passed without any visible action by the task force. Finally, in late August 1971, Fischer directed simultaneous raids—conducted mostly by officers borrowed from the state police and New York City Police Department—that resulted in the arrest of forty accused bookmakers and loansharks in ten counties spread from Long Island to Albany. Of the forty, not one was considered a major Mob figure; only two were known to be members of Mafia families. As one law-enforcement expert commented after the raids: "If all they can come up with after more than a year is forty bookies, that's not much to crow about."

Apologists for the task force said the new agency had never been granted all the investigative powers it needed to be effective. The New York Legislature, it was said, refused to give the task force the authority to review state tax returns, to send its own representatives before local grand juries or to initiate its own requests to courts for permission to use electronic eavesdropping devices. But these shortcomings weren't discussed when state officials originally made extravagant claims about the important role the task force was expected to play in fighting the Mob. Besides, investigative agencies virtually always feel they should have greater powers, so the contention that the task force had been short-changed sounded fairly typical. State Senator John Hughes, chairman of the Joint Legislative Committee on Crime, feels creation of the task force was an inadequate, half-way measure. He favors establishment of a powerful State Department of Criminal Justice along the lines of the U.S. Justice Department—a step that has thus far been rejected by the Legislature. "I think the task force falls far short of what we need," Hughes says. "We need some overall supervision of all these police agencies and district attorneys. Right now, we are fighting organized crime with a very divided army."

Such failings afflict anti-Mob programs throughout the country. What can be done at the Federal, state, and local levels to weld a truly effective machinery for combatting organized crime? More specifically, what can be done to halt the Mob's corruption of public officials and infiltration of legitimate business?

The first step is for those in authority to recognize that the present system is inadequate at all levels of government and must be drastically overhauled. As the President's Commission on Law Enforcement put it: "Investigation and prosecution of organized criminal groups in the Twentieth Century has seldom proceeded on a continuous, institutionalized basis. Public interest and demands for action have reached high levels sporadically; but . . . spurts of concentrated law enforcement activity have been followed by decreasing interest and application of resources."

At the Federal level, high priority should be given to creation of an independent agency assigned to root out corruption throughout the government. As previously pointed out, a number of states and cities have established investigation commissions with such authority—but there is no comparable agency in the Federal government. Various Federal departments and bureaus maintain corps of inspectors to conduct internal checks on their personnel. But these inspectors often concentrate chiefly on investigating employees' efficiency, rather than on exposing possible corruption. Moreover, even when corruption is uncovered, experience has shown that men assigned to investigate members of their own agencies may tend to be less than zealous. Frequently, the emphasis is on saving the agency from embarrassment—even if it means whitewashing official misconduct.

A recent case illustrating the need for a Federal investigation commission involved accusations that Will Wilson, who was Assistant U.S. Attorney General in charge of the Justice Department's Criminal Division, had been involved in a Texas banking and political scandal. Wilson was a former Texas Attorney General and former justice of the Texas Supreme Court. After leaving state office, he operated a private law practice in Texas for several years before becoming the Federal government's chief criminal prosecutor. Among his main law clients was a Houston wheeler-dealer named Frank W. Sharp, who had built a $100-million banking and insurance empire.

In 1970, after Wilson had taken office in Washington, Sharp's empire collapsed—leaving unwary investors holding the bag for millions of dollars. The Securities and Exchange Commission, after investigating the affair, accused Sharp and various associates of entering into a vast scheme to "systematically loot" a bank and several insurance companies that he controlled. The investigation disclosed that numerous Texas political figures, including Governor Preston Smith and Lieutenant Governor Ben Barnes, had been involved in one way or another with

Sharp's operations. Sharp and his companies had benefited from special banking bills pushed through the Texas Legislature.

An investigation by a state grand jury resulted in the indictment of the speaker of the Texas House of Representatives, Gus F. Mutscher, Jr., on charges of accepting a bribe and conspiring to accept a bribe in connection with passage of two banking bills. Also indicted were State Representative Thomas C. Shannon and an aide to Mutscher, Stirman Rush McGinty, both charged with conspiring to bribe, and John Osorio, former president of an insurance company controlled by Sharp, charged with false swearing to an insurance report. All the defendants pleaded not guilty and are awaiting trial at this writing.

When the Justice Department launched its own investigation of the affair, Will Wilson officially disqualified himself from taking part because of his association with Sharp. Whether he played any informal, behind-the-scenes role is unknown. But, with or without Wilson's participation, the Justice Department's handling of the case can best be described as strange. In the face of what the S.E.C. called a multimillion-dollar fraud, the department filed only two relatively minor charges against Sharp—accusing him of making one false entry in his bank's records and of one count of selling unregistered securities. Sharp quickly pleaded guilty and was let off with a mere $5,000 fine and five years' probation.

In addition, the department granted Sharp immunity from further prosecution—saying he had agreed to cooperate in the investigation. Usually, such immunity is given to lesser figures in an investigation in the hope of convicting more important offenders. In this case, Sharp seemed to be the major offender. Congressman Henry Gonzalez of Texas, among others, charged that the grant of immunity was part of a Justice Department attempt to whitewash the affair and cover up Wilson's part in it. Wilson replied that he had played no part in the immunity decision—that it had been made by Deputy Attorney General Richard Kleindienst. That did not, of course, rule out the possibility that Kleindienst had been involved in a whitewash scheme.

The furor resulting from the affair has brought forth disclosures that Wilson's connection with Sharp went far beyond the normal client-lawyer relationship. In an affidavit, Sharp said Wilson had shown him how to get around Texas banking regulations. In addition, it was revealed that Wilson had received $297,000 worth of loans from Sharp; that one unsecured $30,000 loan had been made after Wilson had been appointed to his Justice Department post and while Sharp was under investigation by the S.E.C.; that Wilson's wealth had tripled, to $1.3 million, while he represented Sharp; and that Wilson had used his brokerage account to buy stock in the name of a Federal bank examiner who was supposed to be checking the accuracy of Sharp's books.

Thus far, in addition to the charges filed against Sharp, the only tangible results of the Justice Department investigation have been Federal indictments against four banking examiners, three former officials of Sharp's bank and a Houston real estate man. One of those indicted was Ted Bristol, the banking examiner for whom Will Wilson acknowledged buying stock. Bristol and the three other indicted examiners were charged with accepting illegal loans from Sharp's bank. The other four defendants were charged with misapplying bank funds and making false bank entries. The eight defendants were not considered major figures in the case. All pleaded not guilty and have not yet been tried at this writing.

Despite the disclosures concerning Wilson's role in the Sharp affair, his activities apparently were not subjected to any official scrutiny. Both the Justice Department and the White House repeatedly asserted that he had done nothing wrong. But, under continuing criticism from other sources, Wilson ultimately resigned his Justice Department job on October 15, 1971, saying he wanted to spare the Nixon administration embarrassment. In a resignation letter to the President, Wilson insisted that his connections with Sharp had been entirely innocent and proper. "Political enemies of the past, misplaced confidence and forces whose faces I do not recognize have assailed my character," he wrote. He told the President that recent events, "through no fault of mine, created difficulties and embarrassment which your administration should not be taxed with." Attorney General Mitchell, in accepting the resignation "with regret," praised Wilson for bringing "experience, skill, and dedication" to the fight against organized crime. There was no indication what course the investigation of the Sharp affair would take from that point.

If a Federal investigation commission existed, it could have been expected to conduct a searching inquiry into a case such as Wilson's, to recommend whether he had deserved to remain in office and to determine whether any attempt had been made at a whitewash. A commission of this sort, to be effective, obviously must be divorced as much as possible from partisan political considerations. One way to move toward this end would be to provide by law that the membership of the commission must be bipartisan. The President could appoint half the members, with the opposition party leaders in the House and Senate appointing the other half. The law could stipulate that no more than half the members could be from one party. Trained investigators and lawyers, with experience in combatting the Mob and political corruption, should be hired for the commission staff. To insulate them from political pressure, the staff members should be given Civil Service status.

Another step that can be taken at the Federal level against the Mob is to start applying the anti-trust laws to organized crime. Both the Sherman and Clayton Anti-Trust Acts forbid "every contract, combination or conspiracy in restraint of trade." Legal experts generally agree that many Mafia activities, particularly those in which Mob-controlled companies have gained local or regional monopolies over the delivery of certain goods or services, involve violations of the anti-trust laws. There has been much discussion recently about using such laws in organized crime cases, since they would enable the government to attack the Mob's all-important economic base. Under the anti-trust measures, the government could file suit against Mob enterprises—seeking triple damages, injunctions, heavy fines, and even forfeiture of property.

President Nixon said in describing this approach:

The arrest, conviction, and imprisonment of a Mafia lieutenant can curtail operations, but does not put the syndicate out of business. As long as the property of organized crime remains, new leaders will step forward to take the place of those we jail. However, if we can levy fines on their real-estate corporations, if we can seek treble damages against their trucking firms and banks, if we can seize the liquor in their warehouses, I think we can strike a critical blow at the organized crime conspiracy.

Despite such talk there has been virtually no follow-up action by the government in this field. Strict enforcement of the anti-trust laws against the Mob, combined with criminal prosecutions for other violations, would make possible a double-barreled attack on organized crime. There is no reason for further delay in adopting this strategy.

In Congress, serious consideration should be given to creation of a permanent Senate-House committee on organized crime. At present, a variety of committees in both houses conduct investigations of the Mob. The best known is Senator John McClellan's Rackets Committee. Others include Senator Warren Magnuson's Commerce Committee, Congressman Wright Patman's Banking and Currency Committee, and Congressman Claude Pepper's Select Committee on Crime. The work of the committees often overlaps, creating jurisdictional conflicts that delay and sometimes prevent passage of necessary legislation. A permanent committee on organized crime, drawing its members from both houses, would centralize the jurisdiction and could be expected to speed the legislative process. It would also provide a more effective vehicle than the present disparate committees for focusing public attention on the menace posed by the Mob.

Perhaps the most important step that can be taken at the Federal level to curb organized crime's control over politics and government is to overhaul drastically the laws covering political campaign expenditures. Because of the weakness of current laws, the Mob is able to put politicians in its pocket by secretly financing their campaigns. The laws forbid anyone to make a contribution larger than $5,000 to a campaign for Federal office and prohibit a campaign committee from collecting or spending more than $3 million in any one year. But broad loopholes allow these regulations to be circumvented or ignored. An unlimited number of dummy campaign committees may be established for a single candidate, each of which may collect or spend up to $3 million a year. And an individual may likewise make as many $5,000 contributions to various campaign committees as he chooses—even though all of them support the same candidate. Nobody has ever been prosecuted on charges of violating the provisions limiting contributions.

Other weaknesses in the laws permit candidates and campaign committees to cover up many of their sources of funds by providing only sketchy financial reports. Occasionally, information surfaces on the Mob's financing of political campaigns—as, for example, the revelation that underworld figure John "Jake the Barber" Factor had contributed $102,500 to the Democratic Party in 1968. But, in the great majority of cases, racketeers are able to keep their contributions secret.

Mob-controlled companies, among others, also regularly circumvent a law that prohibits campaign contributions by corporations. While refraining from making direct cash contributions, such companies use subterfuges to provide indirect financial aid to candidates of their choice. They may give their employees cash bonuses, with the understanding that part of the money will be contributed to certain campaigns and that the remainder will be used to pay the increased income taxes generated by the bonuses. They may continue to pay employees' salaries while the employees are "on loan" to work in political campaigns. They may provide candidates with free services, such as printing of campaign literature, and allow campaign workers to use company credit cards. They may retain lawyers for nonexistent legal work, with the agreement that most of the fees will be donated to specified campaigns.

In revising the laws, Congress should set reasonable, enforceable limitations on campaign contributions and expenditures. It should eliminate loopholes such as those that permit contributions to multifarious dummy committees. It should establish realistic rules requiring accurate reporting of contributions and expenses, with stiff penalties for violators. But new laws alone will not suffice. Federal officials must adopt a genuine determination to enforce them. The tacit understanding in effect for years—that virtually anything goes in financing a campaign and that the laws can be ignored with impunity—has helped the Mob immeasurably in its seizure of political power. Unless strict laws are passed and enforced, all efforts to reduce organized crime's political clout are doomed.

Improved programs at the Federal level to combat the Mob must be accompanied by parallel programs at the state and local levels. Every state and every major city should have an investigation commission empowered to investigate organized crime and political corruption. Such commissions should be given permanent status, adequate finances, and investigative staffs, subpoena powers, and authority to initiate contempt actions against balky witnesses. They should issue regular reports, exposing official misconduct and pointing out necessary reforms.

The attorney general's office in every state should have a special force of lawyers and investigators assigned exclusively to organized crime. In addition to conducting statewide investigations of the Mob, they should be available to help local district attorneys handle rackets cases. They should concentrate on major Mob figures—not the kind of lower-echelon bookies arrested in the initial raids by New York State's Task Force on Organized Crime. Where there is evidence that local police or public officials have been corrupted, the attorney general's men should have authority to investigate and prosecute them.

There should also be an intelligence unit on organized

crime within the police department of every major city. The day is long gone when an ordinary patrolman or detective, even if totally incorruptible, can cope with the Mob. If a police department is to be effective in combatting racketeers, it needs a special unit of sophisticated, highly trained men assigned to work solely on organized crime cases.

Since Mafia operations frequently cross state borders, provisions should be made for greater cooperation by law-enforcement authorities from various states. A constructive first step in this direction has been taken by six Middle-Atlantic states—New York, New Jersey, Pennsylvania, Maryland, Delaware, and West Virginia. They have formed a group designed to attack organized crime on a regional basis. In addition to sharing intelligence information on the Mob and conducting joint investigations, members of the group are considering the feasibility of exchanging undercover agents. Once an undercover man has worked for a while in a certain area, he usually gets "burned out"—that is, his identity becomes known to the local underworld. He then is generally withdrawn from undercover work and given another kind of assignment. By shifting such an agent to a new undercover role in another state where he is unknown, the six-state group hopes to make use of his expertise for a much longer period than is now possible. Other states throughout the country should follow the lead of the Middle Atlantic states in adopting a regional approach to the problem of coping with organized crime.

In some cases, grand juries trying to investigate the Mob and political corruption have been hamstrung by the obstructionist tactics of crooked prosecutors. State laws should be changed, where necessary, to permit grand juries to ask state officials for appointment of special prosecutors to replace recalcitrant district attorneys in such investigations.

Government action alone cannot wipe out the Mob or eliminate its corruption of American politics. Honest officials and law-enforcement officers must have the unwavering support of the citizenry if they are to move effectively against organized crime. Experience has shown that the Mob is strongest where the public is most indifferent to corruption.

What can the average citizen do? He can refrain from giving a bookie or numbers runner the bets that provide the Mafia with its greatest wealth and make possible widespread bribery. He can refuse to borrow money at usurious interest rates from Mob loansharks. If he is a businessman, he can refuse to deal with companies controlled by organized crime. If he is a union member, he can fight to prevent racketeers from gaining control of his local. If he has information about Mob operations or corruption, he can offer his testimony to honest officials. Perhaps most important, he can get actively involved in politics and battle to keep it clean.

In this era of wheeler-dealers, angle-players and quick-buck artists, such suggestions may strike some as naïve. They are not. It will take a resurgence of old-fashioned morality and public indignation to break the Mob's grip on American society and political life. The people must make forcefully clear that they will not abide corrupt government. They must exhibit a genuine determination to take the risks, spend the money, and make the sacrifices necessary to obliterate the scourge of Mob rule from the national scene.

To date, that sort of determination has not been apparent. As the President's Commission on Law Enforcement put it: "The extraordinary thing about organized crime is that America has tolerated it for so long." It would be not only extraordinary, but catastrophic, if America continued to tolerate it any longer.

Acknowledgments

A book such as this, as previously discussed, depends in great measure on information from sources who must remain anonymous. To those underworld figures, government officials, politicians, law-enforcement officers, judges, lawyers, private investigators, businessmen, and others who were good enough to take time to talk with me, I want to express my sincere appreciation. The biggest favor I can do many of them is to keep their identities secret.

I am indebted to Miss Elizabeth Otis, Mrs. Phyllis Grann, Ken and Eleanor Rawson, Dan Catlin, Mary Jane Shields, and John Walton for faith, patience, and counsel.

As always, thanks are due to my wife, Jeanne, and daughters, Pamela and Patricia, for standing up to the rigors of life with a writer.

Michael Dorman

g